Utopian Ambition
Constitution of the
2100
Atlantian Republic

Celebrating the 500th Anniversary
of Sir Thomas More's
Utopia

Utopian Ambition
Constitution of the 2100 Atlantian Republic

Written & Edited by
Tiago Lameiras

Utopian Ambition: Constitution of the 2100 Atlantian Republic
– Edited by Tiago Lameiras.
Includes a table of contents and footnotes.
Printing and finishing by CreateSpace Independent Publishing Platform.

ISBN10: 1534835296
ISBN13: 978-1534835290

Typeset in Sabon Roman
by Linotype

To my very own Principessa,
with all my heart in loving madness

"Death does not come with old age,
it comes with oblivion".

— Gabriel García Márquez

"Peace can only come as
a natural consequence of
universal enlightenment".

— Nikola Tesla

Table of Contents

Introduction

Dear Reader,

Welcome and thank you for purchasing this book. If you are, however, just having a look at the free preview so you may make up your mind about whether to buy my work or not, you are welcome all the same and I hope you feel inspired toward an in-depth read.

I should take the time of this introduction to provide you with a word of caution with respect to this tale. The contents ahead are obviously original, albeit the generality of the several ideas portrayed herein have been exploited ever since the beginning of Literature. You and I both know the first known oeuvres to have set the canons of Western literary authorship are the two Homeric poems, *Iliad* and *Odyssey*, thought to be dated from around the 8th century BC. About five hundred years later, in 360 BC, one of the most famous myths in all History of Humanity came to be by the hands of Greek philosopher Plato[1], via the

---

[1] Who was born between 428 and 423 BC and died in either 348 or 347 BC, aged about 80-years-old.

Timaeus and *Critias*[2] dialogues, and that is the myth of *Atlantis*, Greek for "Atlas's[3] island".

The location to this ancient city-state has been turned into a quest by multiple researchers over the course of time, and though technology has evolved to an insurmountable extent to this day, no evidence of the nation's actual existence was ever found. The most common explanation to the inclusion of Atlantis in Plato's dialogues is the allegory of the failed Athenian invasion of Sicily in 415 – 413 BC, though the story had a reverse purpose, one that showed how powerful Athens could be as an ideal sovereign State, repelling any possible invasion from potential foes, namely the Atlantians, who, because of their loss, fall foul of the Olympians and end forever submerged in the middle of the Atlantic, "beyond the Pillars of Heracles[4]".

Mythology is an undeniably enriched source of creativity, not only with respect to Literature, but also for the justifying of certain events that might occur under natural circumstances, though Humanity has always attributed common catastrophes such as droughts, floods, earthquakes, hurricanes, thunderstorms, tornadoes, tsunamis, etc. to divine, supernatural entities. I wish to stress the plural form of the last sentence's final word because it is a worldwide renowned fact not every religion is monotheistic. That is not even close to how the presence of metaphysical beings was firstly demonstrated and reflected on multiple works of art, spanning from architecture to painting and sculpture (including

---

[2] The latter of which was left unfinished.

[3] The Titan of endurance and Astronomy, sentenced to holding the sky (usually depicted with an orb on his back representing the entirety of planet Earth) after the mythological episode of Titanomachy, the war fought between Titans and Olympians, the latter of which eventually became the rulers of Mount Olympus and consequently of Man. The Atlantic Ocean is also named after Atlas.

[4] The Rock of Gibraltar, southern Spain (under British domain) and Ceuta, North Africa (under Spanish administration).

high and bas-relief). To every aspect conditioning the life of humans, there was a god that backed it, and most of them were associated not only to one thing alone, but rather multiple. Picture, if you will, a form of Government made of deities. To each secretary of state or minister, one department or ministry, respectively, subsequently divided into several organizations. What of the role of the President or Prime Minister? Given to the most powerful god among all others, the Commander-in-Chief, the Chief of Staff, the Chairman of the Board.

It was mythology, precisely, that Plato recurred to in order to justify the total annihilation of the Atlantian people and their radio-centric city. May we recall the temporal location of Atlantis takes place circa 9,000 years before Plato's own lifetime, which would make it about 9428 BC, assuming the first possible year of his birth is accurate. In 9428 BC, there was no such thing as a modern-like *Homo Sapiens*, as the first wise man (as we know him today) rose only in about 8000 BC. Of course, a time setting in a work of fiction can rarely be trusted, otherwise it would not be fiction and people would not read that kind of book for fear of believing it was all true. I mean, just take a look at those interpreting the Good Book the way they most feel appropriate, according to their principles of ethics and moral. Not one single passage says you should condemn the LGBT *community* for their nature, but I guess the Sodom and Gomorrah episode was more than enough to make a few bad decisions, including not only recent History, but contemporaneity itself[5].

But, you know what? I am being prejudiced myself, which was deliberate, hence the italic above, and I will tell you why. Though

---

[5] Reference to the «Sodomite Suppression Act», a California ballot initiative proposed by Orange County attorney Matt McLaughlin, which stated that any person behaving homosexually in public should be either shot in the head or taken down by "any other convenient method", which is, of course, utterly repulsive.

it may not be our intention, whenever we utter the words «LGBT, Black, Latino, Asian, etc. *community*», we are being prejudiced. You are probably thinking I am taking this somewhat too far, but just bear with me: we never enounce the words «White/Caucasian, Straight/Heterosexual, Baptist/Catholic/Protestant *community*», because we do not take these individuals as a *minority*, a *subculture*, a *group*. We always assume human nature as being originally white, straight (which is another prejudice alone, meaning the only way you ever get to *fit* society in a *straightly* fashion is via heterosexuality) and god-believing. God-Almighty is the ultimate King of the «Children of Israel», the Jewish, and yet they lost him to the Christians, whichever the denomination, claimed as their own and none other's.

However, it has been archaeologically and scientifically proven a long time ago Man has his origins in South-Southeast Africa. So, when you think about it, everyone or everything who showed for the first time in some place other than Europe, the renowned civilized continent, was then claimed as rightfully belonging to Europeans. If you are an American-born citizen, though Caucasian, researching your family tree a few generations back will most assuredly take you all the way to your immigrant relatives, the Founding Fathers of the country you are (and should be) proud of.

Is it acceptable, in the American case, that the former Confederate States still fly the Confederate flag on Government flagpoles? You know what the American Civil War was all about for the South. They wanted to withhold the rights of African-Americans and keep them as slaves. Their riches depended on slave work. Does this still make any sense in a Democratic State of Law? The President himself is African-American and, yet, his authority as Commander-in-Chief still is questioned because of his birth certificate after nearly eight years in office. The 2008 Presidential Election was the final proof we needed that anyone, re-gardless, of color, disability, ethnicity, faith, gender or political choices has the constitutional right to run for office and bring, not only the United States, but this very planet into its rightful, civilizational era.

Europeans did build a civilization. The Greeks at first, then the Romans, and after the fall of the Empire to the West, the entire continent began to be populated by several Dark Age king-doms, most of which defined the current national borders of pre-sent-day countries. The ideal of unity quickly came to an end and the Barbarians were not so much so anymore. New customs, new forms of Government, new languages (though several are Latin-descendant), new mythologies, new art forms and even new clothing, that was what the new European subjects could expect from their kings. An imperial nation overthrown, a lot of other aspects intact, just like the fall of Greece to Rome herself.

Nonetheless, this whole process was not made real so lightly. Like I said before, Modern Man had his origins in South-South-east Africa, populating afterward Europe, Asia, Oceania and the Americas. This last event was possible because, over 12,000 years ago, there was a land connection[6] between modern-day Siberia and Alaska, now submerged as early as of 11,000 BP[7], due to the several cyclical climate ages of the planet. When there is an ice age, sea levels drop, because there is more frozen water increasing the size of icecaps. Every time temperatures rise, which is not only a human-blaming event, sea levels rise, as there is more liquid water in the oceans, to put it quite simply.

---

[6] Known as Beringia or Bering land bridge. Scientists believe this migratory movement began in about 12,000 BC with early humans, either in a single voyage or multiple at the same time. These migrants shared the same genetic code as any Native-American, who are their descendants.

[7] Before Present, an age scale or timeline used in Geology to determine geological periods.

Because of multiculturalism, a consequence of the geographical proximity and physical connections between Europe, Africa and Asia, Ancient Romans had a lot of work to do as far as uniformity is concerned, i.e. in order to spread Rome's customs and idiom. Anything against Roman principles was ruled barbaric, and therefore had to come to an end. The only way Man has ever put an end to anything threatening his domain is suppression, namely highly coercive or, in order to make sure it did not happen again, fatal. If you are a caveman whose very life is at stake because a grizzly bear is looking to have you over for dinner (and not in a polite kind of way, as a guest, of course), and if you have already discovered the power of fire[8], which is a crucial aspect to consider with respect to human evolution[9], then you have to defend yourself. Even if rationality is still not one of your strongpoints, you can always count on basic survival instinct to keep you alive. No species in this world, apart from those who have no other choice and whose natural defense mechanism is death itself[10], accept death so lightly. That is the meaning of «living being». It is alive and it was meant to stay that way.

The correlation between this and maintaining an authoritative empire is, even though your very survival is not at stake but, however, someone else acts different from you, praises other gods, likes a different kind of food, wears a different kind of clothing, speaks a different kind of language (which may sound apparently unintelligible), you are afraid it might attract a great

---

[8] Further reading: ADLER, Jerry, 06-2013, *Smithosonian.com*, «Why Fire Makes Us Human: Cooking may be more than just a part of your daily routine, it may be what made your brain as powerful as it is», (http://www.smithsonianmag.com/science-nature/why-fire-makes-us-human-72989884/?no-ist), accessed 04-01-2016.

[9] Ibid.

[10] Further reading: DARWIN, Charles, 1859, *On the Origin of Species, The Illustrated Edition*, ed. David Quammen, New York City: Sterling Signature, 2011.

deal of popularity and, consequently, disregard for the rules you imposed and that everyone should follow, according to you, because you know what is best for the people, as their supreme leader and god among men. I mean, let us face it, we are building an expanding empire and yet we allow others to act different from the norm? Dissecting this last word, «norm», what can you see? Norm... -al. A norm, a rule, a regulation, whichever you might want to call it, is meant to *normalize* your behavior by making it *regular*, common, so it does not look or sound strange to the rest of society.

Like I previously stated in another piece of work[11], I do not concur with Anarchy. The *absentia* of rules does not make a free State civilized and ready for social interaction. If you want to be a free citizen and have the right to say whatever you feel like or do what you please, you must know you cannot do either of that light-headed and without *respect* for your fellow citizens, whether countrymen or foreigners. This is naturally just an introduction to the many things I want to talk about throughout this book, so I am not going to make an entire exposition here, though I wish to stress as of now that only a Participatory Democracy is a self-sufficient enough political doctrine that can include all citizens belonging to the same society, regardless of any differences right-wing extremists may come up with.

Perhaps you may think it is too harsh of me to make a statement such as this, but being prejudiced toward other people on the grounds of skin color, ethnicity or sexual orientation (just to name the two most common, still preventing civilization from total fruition in many so-called first world countries) is an unquestionably neo-Nazi attitude to take. And those with the power to shape minds (no, not the school teachers), but rather the media, are the ones who most condone this kind of behavior,

---

[11] LAMEIRAS, Tiago, 2016, *Actor Being: A Role in Mankind*, North Charleston, SC: CreateSpace Independent Publishing Platform.

siding with the most convenient members of Politics, those funding the networks themselves in all means of broadcast, whether televised, in print or online.

And there it is. As you can see, there is a certain kind of Politics which, instead of becoming a form of Government, is rather a way of making business and attracting the masses via propaganda, claiming people are getting the contents they want to see and listen to. Indeed, you install cable in your home so you can have a wide selection of TV channels to choose from and yet, you are flooded with plain ideological garbage standing up for your right to carry a gun and shoot indiscriminately at anyone you do not care much for. And this kind of people actually gather public endorsement when they say something like «I could "shoot somebody and I wouldn't lose voters"»[12]. It is not the people making this sort of statement who are ill. They are absolutely certain of what they are saying, because they know there are others who are incredibly willing to believe in them, therefore condoning such words, which is a lot different from *condemning*.

I decided I should divide my work into three different parts: first of all, there has to be a National Consolidation. This means that, as long as we keep turning our backs on each other and ignoring the fact we are all worthy of a dignified life as a dominant species, progress will never become achievable. Our home needs to become tidy, before we move on to the next stage, whether it is our planet's futurization or the ability to create both an affordable and a profitable way of touring space.

Second, when everyone is able to live a life worthy of human conditions, unlike any other animal in the wilderness, there will come the time for Transhumanism to prevail. Of course, we all

---

[12] DIAMOND, Jeremy, 01-24-2016, *CNN.com*, «[Donald] Trump: I could "shoot somebody and I wouldn't lose voters"», (http://edition.cnn.com/2016/01/23/politics/donald-trump-shoot-somebody-support/index.html), accessed 04-01-2016.

know not everyone is willing to accept a biological transcendence toward the bionic, and you know the Church is still powerful enough to present credible evidence (though only to those of faith) that it was God who made us and that we are a consequence of Creationism, instead of anthropological evolutionism[13]. What most people do not realize is that we have been transhumanizing our bodies for decades. Still skeptical about it? When people have to, yet unfortunately, require the aid of a pacemaker to prevent arrhythmia of the heart and have their blood circulation flow correctly, they already are bionic. The myocardium is supposed to beat on its own at a regular pace, but if it cannot perform the task on its own, small electric pulses making it beat properly via the device in question are the best alternative to this day. So, if we are able to admit such changes to our body, one out of plenty others Science has come up with in the last decades to extend our average life expectancy, I am pretty sure there will be other changes we are willing to grasp as well, regardless of any opposition. It has to be like so, if a Democratic State of Law really is laic[14].

Third, and though both planet Earth and our Sun have only reached half of their entire life span[15], the most renowned space agency in the world, NASA[16], is already looking into outer space via its orbiting telescopes for the so-called exoplanets, similar to Earth in their atmospheric and geological composition. Once a way of traveling, at first, inside our own Solar System, between planets, and into outer space, later, has been produced, terraforming missions will take place, so as to adapt these exoplanets to human survival. However, if there really are planets, such

---

[13] Or Darwinism.

[14] Autonomous from the Church's influence.

[15] Depending on the Sun's very existence, which is now at 4.6 billion-years-old, the Earth was formed approximately 0.06 billion years later, making it about 4.54 billion-years-old.

[16] Acronym for National Aeronautics and Space Administration.

as Kepler-452b[17], similar to Earth in natural constitution, with a viable star providing them energy like the Sun in the Solar System[18], it is not so surprising that we may be looking at the home to someone else. Whether we will find humans or not depends entirely on the planets' history. Remember, it was only due to the Cretaceous-Paleogene mass-extinction geological episode that dinosaurs' domain on Earth came to an end, giving mammals a chance to rise. That is why there might be dinosaurs in exoplanets like the one I mentioned above, though we still do not have strong enough visibility devices orbiting Earth that can take such a detailed peek similar to those of our present-day satellites. Should we be unable to produce an artificial star with at least the same power as of that of the Sun, moving away and saying goodbye to Earth is both a cosmological and natural consequence. That is why I will be favoring a worldwide citizenship for each and every one of us.

Finally, so we may move on to the actual matters at hand, I would like to let you know that, even though I am going to talk to you about matters such as Economy, Politics, Science, Technology and even Transhumanism, I promise you I will not be too specific, not because I do not realize what I am writing about (otherwise, what would the point of writing a book be?), but rather because I want to make this about Literature. This does not mean, however, theory cannot be turned into reality. It means that, whatever it is you theorize today, may well become practical enough to be a part of your day-to-day life tomorrow.

All you need to do is dream, reflect upon it, and make it work. It is in our own hands to turn something supposedly impossible to possible and, better than that, doable.

— April 2016
Lisbon, Portugal

---

[17] Discovered July 23rd, 2015, by NASA's «Kepler» mission.
[18] A G2-type star.

Part I
National Consolidation

1
We Are One

«All human beings are born free and equal in dignity and rights. They are endowed with reason and conscience and should act towards one another in a spirit of brotherhood».

— Article 1
Universal Declaration of Human Rights[19]

If you take a look at the footnote below regarding the quote above, you will see the Declaration containing this article as its first, guaranteed principle toward the protection of Humanity was approved in 1948, three years after the end of World War II, one of the most vicious conflicts to ever take place on our planet, part of the lives of many people still living to this day, whose testimony was and still is of severe importance to understanding

---

[19] United Nations General Assembly, 12-10-1948, *UN.org*, «General Assembly Resolution 217 A», Paris, (http://www.un.org/en/universal-declaration-human-rights/), accessed 04-04-2016.

what happened during the Nazi regime of Adolf Hitler[20].

Obviously, it would be legitimate to ask a question such as, "and what kind of conflict is not vicious?". Indeed, I agree at one hundred percent. All kinds of conflict are ridiculously time-wasting, physically-ageing and mentally-disruptive. Beating death is presently uncertain, so we should do our best to seize the day[21], instead of just jeopardizing our very youth with unsolvable issues.

Psychology may question my previous statement, claiming that, sometimes, it is good for you to have a slight argument with, let us say, your better-half, so it may liven your relationship up, but I sincerely do not think you have to go around fighting, just to make amends with each other and figure out you cannot live without each other's presence. Keeping it cool right from the start can be actually productive toward that same path.

But let us not be cast astray from the reason why I mentioned the Universal Declaration of Human Rights in the first place by my own discourse. Until we do not set our differences to the side, which are not even that much differentiating, and please excuse my being redundant, as far as our immediate circle is concerned, there can be no progress toward the future, at all. In order to evolve, there has to be, at least as of a first instance, a small group of people willing to make changes to their way of living, who are also intelligent enough to attract other people's attention and bring them to the cause. This obviously already does take place, especially when you have politicians campaigning for an election, whether presidential, governmental, etc., for example, but there is a clear difference between what you tell people so you may

---

[20] 1889-1945. Chancellor of Germany from 1933 to 1934, accumulating this office with the Presidency after the death of President Paul von Hindenburg (1847-1934), becoming *Führer* (Leader) of Nazi Germany until his own death by suicide.

[21] English translation to the Latin expression «*carpe diem*».

grow on them and what is the undeniable truth that you consider your voters should know about, so they may deem you worthy of their trust, because, if you only attract them through what you think they want to hear and then stab them in the back after they have elected you for any sort of local or national government, you might as well expect a *coup d'état*[22]. There you have one of the reasons why mentioned Hitler earlier. Sure, the people were well aware of what he was all about. *Mein Kampf*[23] was made available in 1925 in German and in English in 1933, when he rose to power. Jewish hatred was clear enough and, when he moved to Vienna, Austria to pursue a career in Art, he knew what society thought of Jewish-controlled Government and media, together with their opinion on Bolshevism, which was not pretty, whatsoever. Though inhuman, Hitler was a formidably able statesman. Even though he claimed the German people had chosen the National-Socialist party and thus had to face the consequences of a destroyed country[24], they only did so because of his eloquence.

At the time of my typing on this page, in the United States, there is a Presidential election going on, like I said in the introduction to this title. Many have already compared Donald J. Trump and his followers to the rise of Neo-Nazism, making their rallies look like Nuremberg, Germany in 1935. People claim the right to carry personal handguns, just in case somebody decides to disturb the mood, thus declaring a hunting season open for the unfaithful, left-wing supporters or homosexuals, killing them indiscriminately at close-range. I have to become really personal

---

[22] French for «blow of State».

[23] *My Struggle*, in English, Hitler's autobiography and manifesto of the Nazi ideology, divided into two parts, respectively.

[24] Cf. *Downfall* (original title *Der Untergang*), based on the books by Joachim Fest and Traudl Junge & Melissa Müller, *Inside Hitler's Bunker* and *Until the Final Hour*, respectively, starring Bruno Ganz and Alexandra Maria Lara, directed by Oliver Hirschbiegel, Constantin Film, 2004.

about this and tell you such an attitude, in a country where the United Nations were born and have their headquarters located, the same organization that wrote, discussed, voted and approved the document I began this chapter with, is incredibly and unmistakably repulsive. I am aware of what the Constitution of the United States reads:

> «A well-regulated Militia, being necessary to the security of a free state, the right of the people to keep and bear Arms, shall not be infringed».

> — Second Amendment of the Bill of Rights
> Constitution of the United States of America[25]

Take a look at the footnote I added. This amendment, informally renowned as the constitutional right to «keep and bear arms», has been active *ever since* the latter part of the *18th century*, just *fifteen years* after the Declaration of Independence from Great Britain, on July 4th, 1776. It was *240* years ago and still, Congress refuses to make a constitutional update to prevent the indiscriminate murder of dozens, if not hundreds of people every single year in a country that just *had* to set the example to other so-claimed democratic countries, and by «democratic» I do not mean to point out my partisanship preferences, at all, as I cannot even vote, not being an American citizen, but rather to make my political doctrine choice clear enough.

Access to weaponry, which is pretty much the same as access to warfare, *cannot* continue to be a right of the common citizen. Only authorities should be allowed to carry guns and still, they should be thoroughly examined in order to come clear with respect to sleeping or invisible mental illnesses, together with the

---

[25] Officially adopted on December 15th, 1791.

civilian willing to carry a gun for his own protection. This paragraph has not even been entirely utopic thus far. One of the most important ways for us to become peaceful toward each other, starting right in our neighborhood, and not just in the US alone, because the subtitle to this book is not even «Constitution of the 2100 American Republic», but *all over the world*, is to put the gun down, from the start, hand it over to the police and have them all dismantled. A society that is gun-violence or any other sort of violence-free is the strongest point we have toward our very own survival as part of the human race. Why should we be worried about a possible alien invasion from another galaxy or hidden Martians, if we already are too busy destroying ourselves? Furthermore, let us just learn how to live with each other, first, then we can consider exosphere-related matters. Money can be made from far more cleansed projects, instead of counting on gun lobbyists – just a small hint some Governments should heed, nothing personal.

The following Americans, President John F. Kennedy[26], civil rights activist and attorney Martin Luther King, Jr.[27] or politician

---

[26] 1917-1963. The Democrat President was shot while in a presidential motorcade in Dallas, Texas, allegedly by Lee Harvey Oswald (1939-1963), who kept denying the accusation while in police custody, saying he was just a patsy. Oswald was shot and killed himself when being transferred to county jail by Dallas nightclub owner Jack Ruby (1911-1967), live on television and amid several police officers at the scene. Though the motives of Oswald or any other killer present at the scene were never truly discovered, the fact the President endorsed (albeit limitedly, due to Congress) Equal Rights for African-Americans, a Soviet conspiracy or a Cuban conspiracy are the main reasons behind the assassination. Other theories, such as deception by the US Government itself in order to inaugurate Vice-President Lyndon B. Johnson (1908-1973) as Commander-in-Chief and revert President Kennedy's decision of withdrawing from Vietnam, has also been made public and taken to court by New Orleans, LA District Attorney Jim Garrison (1921-1992), who was portrayed by Kevin Costner in Oliver Stone's 1991 film *JFK*.

[27] 1929-1968. After thirteen years fighting for the Civil Rights Movement, of which he was the main advocate, Dr. King, as he is also known, the 1964 Nobel Peace Prize laureate, was shot during a speech at the Lorraine Motel in

Harvey Milk[28] were three key people to the withstanding of civil and human rights in general. My guess is hitmen do not seem to realize that the more they try silencing an icon, all the more their respective message will spread throughout the masses. One of the speeches from our lifetime we know best is this, of which I quote an excerpt focusing on the last part:

«Let us not wallow in the valley of despair, I say to you today, my friends.

And so, even though we face the difficulties of today and tomorrow, I still have a dream. It is a dream deeply rooted in the American dream.

I have a dream that one day this nation will rise up and live out the true meaning of its creed: "We hold these truths to be self-evident, that all men are created equal"[29].

I have a dream that one day, on the red hills of Georgia, the sons of former slaves and the sons of former slave owners will be able to sit down together at the table of brotherhood.

I have a dream that one day, even the state of Mississippi, a state sweltering with the heat of injustice, sweltering with the heat of oppression, will be transformed into an oasis of freedom and justice.

I have a dream that my four little children will one day live in

---

Memphis, Tennessee, dying on the operation table at St. Joseph's Hospital. The murderer was identified as James Earl Ray (1928-1998). The motel is now the National Civil Rights Museum, displaying a wreath on the balcony where King was shot. Following the assassination, Civil Rights riots spread across the entire nation.

[28] 1930-1978. The first openly American homosexual to be elected for public office in the State of California. He was killed together with San Francisco mayor George Moscone by Dan White, another city supervisor. He would commit suicide seven years later, after leaving prison on parole to Los Angeles and trying to rebuild his life in San Francisco with his wife and children.

[29] A phrase by Thomas Jefferson (1743-1826), third President of the US, included in the United States Declaration of Independence, stylized to its final form by Benjamin Franklin (1706-1790), another Founding Father of America.

a nation where they will not be judged by the color of their skin, but by the content of their character.

I have a *dream* today!

I have a dream that one day, down in Alabama, with its vicious racists, with its governor[30] having his lips dripping with the words of "interposition" and "nullification" – one day, right there, in Alabama, little black boys and black girls will be able to join hands with little white boys and white girls as sisters and brothers.

I have a *dream* today!

I have a dream that one day every valley shall be exalted, and every hill and mountain shall be made low, the rough places will be made plain, and the crooked places will be made straight; "and the glory of the Lord shall be revealed and all flesh shall see it together"[31]»[32].

Dr. King did not live to witness his "dream" come true and, though it eventually did become legally real, it has not grown into the minds of a lot of people. The sad part is those people are very influential themselves and just keep dragging other sheep to their personal flock.

When we claim "that all men [and women] are created equal", who is it we really want to become equal to any regular citizen of any country in the world like you and I? Africans, Arabs, Asians, Gypsies, Hindis, Natives, etc. wish to be treated like Caucasians. Homosexuals, bisexuals and the transgender want to share the rights heterosexuals have, be it lawfully or religiously. Adventists, Anglicans, Baptists, Buddhists, Calvinists, the Jewish,

---

[30] George Corley Wallace, Jr. (1919-1998), 45th Governor of the State of Alabama, who stood up for the maintenance of racial segregation in his state, denying African-Americans the same rights as Caucasian individuals.

[31] Isaiah 40:5.

[32] KING, JR., Martin Luther, 08-28-1963, «I Have a Dream Speech», Washington, D.C., (http://www.americanrhetoric.com/speeches/mlkihavea-dream.htm), accessed 04-05-2016.

Lutherans, Muslims, the Orthodox, Presbyterians, Protestants, Shaivists, Shaktists, Smartists, Taoists, Vishnuists, etc. demand to be *tolerated* exactly as Roman Catholics. Did you notice the italic? The Roman Catholic Church has often stated "outside the Church there is no salvation"[33]. Such a statement, coming from an incredibly popular religious leader, perhaps only matched to by the incumbent[34], is undeniably segregating on its own. Every time either a religious or political organization/regime appears to open up from either an autocratic[35], plutocratic[36] or plain totalitarian[37] doctrine, History says there has been a spring, meaning the former regime is peacefully blooming toward Democracy. Such an event took place, for instance, in 2010, in Tunisia, which became known as the Arab Spring. It happened also long ago in Portugal, when there was an apparent transition from Salazar's New State to Marcello Caetano's, in 1968.

You would think the current Pope, Head of both the Vatican microstate and the Roman Catholic Apostolic Church, could endorse some modernization on behalf of his institution, which he has, such as dialogue between faiths, either by welcoming other religious leaders to St. Peter's Basilica or by visiting them in their own countries; disposal of clergymen's riches, when they are supposed to have taken a vow of poverty; ethnic, racial and social

---

[33] In the original Latin, *Extra Ecclesiam nulla salus*, promulgated in 1992 by Pope John Paul II (1920-2005, born Karol Józef Wojtyła in Krakow, Poland), via the Catechism of the Catholic Church, also known as CCC.

[34] Pope Francis (1936), born Jorge Mario Bergoglio in Buenos Aires, Argentina.

[35] A form of supreme government entrusted to one person alone without requiring any consultation from either legal bodies or the people being governed by said individual.

[36] Another form of government in which wealth is the sole decisive factor for people to be included in a ruling political body.

[37] A political system that sees no boundaries or restrictions whatsoever in the ways the State deals with its citizens, prying into any private or social matter as it pleases. Stalin or Hitler are just a couple of examples for totalitarian statesmen.

equality. At first, when Pope Francis took on his papacy, he did seem to empathize with gay marriage and even the Big Bang theory[38], though the latter is attributed to a "Creator". It would really not make sense for a man of the Church to refuse such a possibility, turning his back on creationism, but preaching equality and still refusing to recognize a homosexual couple[39], either childless or with coadopted children as a family, based on the Holy Scriptures, is simply senseless.

In the Dark Ages[40], early European kingdoms depended on the Vatican's avail to become recognized as sovereign, independent nations. Making decisions against the papacy was an excuse for puppet kings to go to war on behalf of the faith, which was the main reason for the Anglo-Spanish War[41] to take place. As I keep writing over and over again in multiple posts I make public, either online or in paper, Christendom took care of delaying scientific progress in about 1,000 years, recurring to suppressing organizations such as the Holy Inquisition[42].

Even though the Church *virtually* has no political interference in present-day European national sovereignty, the fact is that its

---

[38] The predominant explanation for the origin of the Universe as we know it, through a massive explosion (hence the expression designating it), having occurred approximately 13.8 billion years ago and still expanding to this day, producing uncountable billions of galaxies, stars, planets and other cosmological bodies.

[39] BISHOP, Mac William, 10-25-2015, *NBC News*, «Monsignor Krzysztof Charamsa: The Church Needs to Wake Up», (http://www.nbcnews.com/news/world/monsignor-krzysztof-charamsa-church-needs-wake-n449896), accessed 04-06-2016.

[40] Early European Middle Ages (5th to 10th centuries AD).

[41] An undeclared feud (1585-1604) between Spain (and Spanish-ruled Portugal) and England, under the rule of Philip II (I of Portugal) and Elizabeth I, "the heretic queen", respectively, resulting in *status quo ante bellum*, Latin for how it all was before the war, loosely translated, meaning there were no victories or losses with respect to either geopolitical territorial or economic possessions, which was confirmed through the signing of the Treaty of London (1604).

[42] Having begun in 12th century France.

views are still shadowing the way people think, though the Papal States are slowly losing their predominance to the Law of Man[43], instead of Mosaic[44]. However, and unfortunately, many other political decisions such as presidential promulgations of civil rights and equality bills become delayed due to clerical influence[45], though anthropological and sociological concerns are claimed. One of those is something like "when a child is developing amid either a gay or lesbian couple, instead of a *regular* family, it is very likely said child will grow up to become either gay or lesbian themselves". You can most assuredly tell such an argument is so ridiculous it should not even bear our time. Still, I wish for you to understand my point of view entirely, and that is why I feel like showing you how amusing this is to me. Amusing, not funny, not at all.

Homosexuality is *not* a disease, an illness, a hormonal imbalance, an influence or a preference. It is a person's own *nature*. You are either born gay or not, and if you are, there is nothing you can do about it, or even should. Changing a person's nature over religious brainwashing, therefore contaminating social mentality, is not something any person at all should be prepared to tolerate. Bearing this premise in mind, how is it there are still half a dozen people in the entire planet still demanding control over countries' sovereignty?

We have already talked about making comparisons between living people and dead dictators, some of which we do not even

---

[43] McDONALD, Henry, 05-23-2015, *The Guardian*, «Ireland becomes first country to legalise gay marriage by popular vote», (http://www.theguardian.com/world/2015/may/23/gay-marriage-ireland-yes-vote), accessed 04-06-2016.

[44] In short, the Ten Commandments Yahweh passed unto the «Children of Israel» through Moses, inscribed in two stone tablets.

[45] KHALIP, Andrei, 02-10-2016, *Reuters*, «Portugal parliament overturns veto on adoption by gay couples», (http://uk.reuters.com/article/uk-rights-portugal-adoption-idUKKCN0VJ1Z0), accessed 04-06-2016.

know about, due to the lack of documentation (available) during the Middle Ages. I placed the word «available» in brackets because the Vatican Archives are obviously not available to the regular citizen. If you are an undergraduate student (a Bachelor or prior to that academic degree), you do not have clearance. And if you are a graduate or postgraduate, your personal data, such as your name, address and Higher Education affiliation has to be made clear, if you want to be successful in your application for a free pass into the Archives. Even then, not all areas are accessible.

Some may find such an endeavor rather extreme, like I said earlier, comparing inhuman Mankind murderers to present-day mentalities. But I assure you it is not. And this is the moment when I have no other choice but to introduce you to eugenics. Quite simply put, this term applies to the improving of a specimen's genetic quality, being the final purpose the achievement of purity within the population of a certain species. You and I both probably became aware of this policy when reading about Nazism. Indeed, either murder or forced sterilization of people contributing to population with negative eugenics was a part of Nazi policy toward non-Aryans (or handicapped Aryans), which ended in the annihilation of more than eleven million people, *excluding* concentration camp murders[46].

If you are acquainted to Nostradamus'[47] prophecies[48] (I am not

---

[46] Approximately six million, most of which Jews, making it a total of seventeen million people dead at the hands of Hitler, probably one of the most hypocritical people to have ever walked this earth, as his origins were Jewish, he had no traces of Aryanism and was not even German-born, in the first place, but Austrian, hence justifying the Pan-Germanism movement and the *Anschluss*, Austria's total annexation to Germany, forming one, single Greater Germany.

[47] Michel de Nostredame (1503-1566), French apothecary and plague healer, said to be gifted with clairvoyance.

[48] *Les Propheties*, French for *The Prophecies*, a prophetical book authored by Nostradamus, whose first known edition dates back to 1555.

claiming I either support or deny them), you know of the «Antichrist». A great deal of reputed studies claim the French witch-doctor foresaw the rise of either two or three different men, born in different places and different eras, as the three «Antichrists» that would bring Humanity to total destruction. The first was Napoleon Bonaparte[49], after which came Adolf Hitler[50]. There has been speculation regarding the foreseeing of the third «Antichrist», who was supposed to rise in the beginning of World War III. So far, there has not been any conflict after 1945 designated as such, but those interpreting Nostradamus' predictions say the conflict began September 11th, 2001[51]. Hereon, individualities

---

[49] 1769-1821. He was the most prominent figure of the French Revolution (1789-1799), putting an end to French monarchy by liberalizing society via three values still entrusted in present-day France, shown in the country's flag – freedom/liberty (blue), equality (white) and fraternity (red). His empowerment, however, ended up transforming an early form of the French Republic into an Empire, conquering most of Continental Europe and thus declaring an embargo against trade with England. Portugal was one of the countries disrespecting the decree due to a military alliance with the English Crown and because of that was invaded by three different French generals (Jean-Andoche Junot [1771-1813], Jean-de-Dieu Soult [1769-1851] and André Massena [1758-1817]). Napoleon capitulated at the Battle of Waterloo, Belgium, in 1815, at the hands of the English Empire.

[50] Vide note 19.

[51] On the morning of Tuesday, September 11th, 2001, a series of four co-ordinated terrorist attacks took place in the United States, on behalf of terrorist group Al-Qaeda, of which the most damaging were the ones destroying the twin towers of the World Trade Center in Manhattan, New York (the heart of American financial hegemony), killing nearly 3,000 people in total, hijackers included. Of a total four hijacked planes by nineteen Al-Qaeda-related terrorists, two (American Airlines Flight 11 and United Airlines Flight 175) were thrusted into the towers, one for each, in a suicide attack. The third (American Airlines Flight 77) was used to hit the Pentagon (the heart of American military). The fourth plane (United Airlines Flight 93), originally bound to Washington, D.C., was brought down after its passengers heroically overcame the terrorists, claiming all lives. All these buildings are symbolical, but the symbols do not just lay there. The date chosen also has its relevance. If you write the numbers down, you get 911, which is the national emergency number, three digits that were dialed thousands of times that day.

like Osama bin Laden[52] or George W. Bush[53] were pointed out by the prophet's supporters as the final embodiment in the predictions.

Eugenics based on different creeds, and not just in a religious way, are still alive in a far extremer way. Even though homosexuals cannot biologically reproduce, there is always the possibility of either adopting or having one of the individuals in the couple become the biological parent, by ceding either sperm or an egg and combining them with the required opposite, which is something accessible to anyone, via reproductive cell banks. These fertility treatments, however, are not accessible to all as far as family budgets are concerned. When you do not have the possibility of naturally having a baby, the alternatives can be compared to a migraine, not just because of the money required to pay for them, but also because of the immense bureaucracy, unjustifiable in modern societies. *In vitro*[54] fertilization is regarded by some «opinionated» minds as a form of eugenics, because there is artificial meddling with either sperm or egg quality, most of the time based on their donors. Regardless of family constitution, either homosexual couples, single fathers or mothers, a donor's background is always checked for any sorts of vices or genetic malformation. Personally, I do not call this eugenics, because no one in the artificial fertilization process, whichever the method, is preventing anyone from being born, shaping the genetic quality of the general population with only the best specimens. Indeed, eugenics only become real when people are castrated by order of

---

[52] 1957-2011. Head of Al-Qaeda, he was the one behind the 9-11 terrorist attacks. He was killed by US Navy Seal Robert O'Neill (1976) in Abbottabad, Pakistan, already under the Obama Administration.

[53] Born 1946. He was the 43rd President of the United States, living through 9-11 and initiating US invasions in Iraq and Afghanistan.

[54] Latin for «in glass», where an egg fertilization takes place before being implanted into a woman's womb.

the State, may it be via a vasectomy, in men, or chemical poisoning of the genitalia[55], sterilizing them for good.

Any sovereign State opposing gay marriage or gay adoption by a same-sex couple is being eugenic, claiming the child's welfare is at stake, forcibly placing homosexuals in the abnormality section of society, as common outcasts. The truth is, however, when there are so many children waiting to become adopted by a caring, loving family, having lived in an institution ever since they can remember, something insurmountably wrong must have taken place amid an opposite-sex family, and this is surely not a woman's fault. No women can ever become pregnant on self-account[56], and you know how the saying goes, "it takes two to dance" or "it takes two to tango".

Most of the time, heterosexual couples become *accidentally* expectant. The only remaining alternatives they have is to either have an abortion or send their baby away for adoption. Whichever the result, both men and women suffer during either process (or most of them involved in such a situation, rather), only it is a lot worse for women, of course, as it is not just an emotional issue they have to face. There are many physical concerns related to both abortion and giving birth which can kill the mother, the child or both. Having a baby has always been a risk for a woman,

---

[55] Nazi human experimentation was used to develop sterilization methods under the Law for the Prevention of Genetically Defective Progeny, passed in 1933, which was supposed to diminish the number of individuals carrying hereditary illnesses or deformities. During the war (1939-1945), new methods were used to save up time and resources, having been tested with prisoners. The first stage comprehended poisoning through iodine and silver nitrate injections, though there were side effects deriving from it, such as severe abdominal pain, vaginal hemorrhage and cervical cancer. Radiation was then introduced, unknown to civilians, who were asked to complete forms, taking a maximum of two to three minutes, while being sterilized. Many of them often got radiation burns.

[56] Unless, of course, we witness an extremely rare event known as Parthenogenesis, which is the natural ability of asexual reproduction, possible among humans.

and I am positive real mothers have just as much always been willing to take that risk, as motherhood undeniably becomes rewarding to any mother delivering a child to the world, never forgetting, most naturally, the father.

However, not everything is an accident in this world. Many moms and dads actually do wish to become acquainted to parenthood, but, unfortunately, social welfare does not allow it. Indeed, it has come to this, to an extent in which experiencing the likes of becoming a parent has got to mandatorily be kept for later, after both or just one parent has solidified a good enough career that can provide the child or children with dignifying healthcare, and this means being able to either pay an insurance company and/or social security, focused solely on tax-deductible 401Ks and so forth. When, though, this natural course of life is not accessible to these couples, because they know, they are *certain* that, if their economic and financial powers are at capacity, their children cannot stay with them, because full support cannot be provided. This is when Social Services come in and take your children away from you, if suspected you cannot raise them in a financially healthy environment, whatever these words put together mean. So, let us get this straight: both father and mother want to build a family together by having children, but their minimum wage is below the minimum acceptable for an industrialized society and cannot thusly provide for their babies, unless they starve, of course, which will diminish both their physical and psychological strength, required to keep a nine-to-five job, during which time productivity does not reach its full potential. Social Services then claim the children and institutionalize them, either in State or Church-run facilities. They are made available for adoption (I know putting it this way sounds like I am talking about your everyday market product, but that is really *not* what I intend to say). A homosexual couple who is either gay or lesbian (and I should probably stress «gay» can be used for both genders)

43

and is self-sufficient enough to have a child at their care is denied the possibility, because it goes against the *Church's* picture of a family, due to their *immorality*. My suggestion is, henceforth, we consider how Church-run orphanages and adoption centers are *really* taken care of[57] (please make sure you read the footnote I have provided matching this statement).

It actually worries me that the regular citizen has to work hard their entire life for the sake of a nice pension being spared to their savings account. Are we protecting banks, the State's needs for warfare or just both, granted the last person to worry about is the taxpayer? I do not agree with the fact that you have to work tremendously hard to put bread on the table (or just some bread-crumbs, for that matter), aging rapidly, not only because of blood-oxygenation of the cells, but also because of the wearing out of both your mental and physical capacities abilities. When you get to old age and leave the *active sector* of the population, meaning you no longer have labor capacities to offer the State's economy, you have to be taken care of, as your health grows de-bilitating. You do not have to necessarily become housed at a nursery home, but you will most likely have to take medication to prevent your body from being all the more worn out. The pharmaceutical industry is pretty much the same as an oil refin-ery business in the middle of the ocean, highly profitable and un-touchable, no matter how much Greenpeace[58] protests against its

---

[57] Cf. *Spotlight*, starring Mark Ruffalo, Michael Keaton, Rachel McAd-ams, Liev Schreiber, John Slattery and Stanley Tucci, directed by Tom McCar-thy, Open Road Films, 2015, portraying the homonymous investigative jour-nalism team working on one of the largest pedophile scandals involving the Catholic Church ever, for *The Boston Globe*, in 2001, having released the story in the beginning of 2002, after covering the September 11th events in New York City.

[58] Non-governmental environmental organization, founded in 1971, Van-couver, Canada.

tycoons. As long as people age and increase the likelihood of becoming sick at the most fragile stage of their life, medication is as essential as textiles for us to wear on the street and conceal our body since we are given birth.

Strong health is not just a work-related factor, it also has to do with personal habits, but one of the most common habits most people experience across most of their lifespan is indeed labor, if they are lucky enough to find it, in nowadays' social terms.

Likewise, the drainage of people's personal budget is not the pharmaceutical companies' fault alone. There is a far more devious corporation behind this social problem: the insurance companies. No one has to be a genius, in order to understand how an insurance policy works. You, as the insured person or holder of insured property, pay an annual instalment to the insurance company, whether for your car, which is mandatory, naturally, your home, life or health in general. Basically, if you want protection, you have to pay for it, regardless of the State's welfare.

People in Ancient Egypt and further eras, up to the Renaissance, the latest, had death in the center of their life. As soon as the country had a new ruler, i.e. the Pharaoh, in the Egyptian case, they would immediately begin construction of their tomb, so it would be ready in time for their interment. Across the Dark and Middle Ages, death was also literally at the center of day-to-day life, with common grave cemeteries in the middle of town, streets reeking of filth and sewage and social dwelling amid plague-infected mice and rats. Daily bathing was something that lost relevance from Antiquity onward, with people favoring a yearly bath only, which used to be in May. That is why it is fabled people got married in June, so as to avoid bodily odor becoming too much unbearable. Brides, inclusively, began carrying their bridal bouquets with fresh flowers to help conceal said odor.

From the 1500s on, but not necessarily across the whole of Europe, of course, a change of mind began to take effect and the dead, instead of having their burial in churches, a place where everyone gathered, were entombed in the outskirts of town, for the sake of public health. Said change of mind continues to be effective nowadays, and not only are people focused on their life, but also on their way of living and its very indefinite extension, which is something we will explore in detail further ahead, in Part II.

In short, you and I, together with 6,999,999,998 other human beings, have had the right to live a long, healthy life, ever since we became real. Defining when a human being becomes real, however, is a matter of legal interpretation and I shall not, therefore, question the abortion laws of every country in the world. Though immortality is not an issue I intend to discuss right away, for the sake of book material planning coherence, the truth is we now live longer than ever before, but not all fatal threats have been cleared out of our path.

According to the World Health Organization[59], the top ten causes of death in 2012[60] were, beginning with the deadliest: ischemic heart disease[61], stroke, COPD[62], lower respiratory infections[63], trachea bronchus and other lung cancers, HIV/AIDS[64],

---

[59] Founded in 1948 and headquartered in Geneva, Switzerland, it is a specialized agency coordinating public health worldwide. It is a part of the United Nations.

[60] *WHO.int*, «The top 10 causes of death», (http://www.who.int/media-centre/factsheets/fs310/en/), accessed 04-12-2016.

[61] Mainly known as coronary heart disease, a cardiovascular illness, which can be caused by factors such as diabetes, high blood pressure, high cholesterol or smoking.

[62] The abbreviation for chronic obstructive pulmonary disease, featuring lack of airflow, mainly caused by smoking, though air pollution and genetics are also key factors.

[63] Associated with pneumonia, it can also mean acute bronchitis. It is mostly parasitical and therefore requires antibiotic treatment.

[64] The Human Immunodeficiency Virus/Acquired Immune Deficiency Syndrome is basically the long-term destruction of the human immune system through viral infection, slowly disabling an individual from their natural defenses against all sorts of diseases, making them as vulnerable as a newborn

diarrheal diseases, diabetes mellitus[65], road injuries and hypertensive heart disease.

Among these ten main death causes worldwide, many types of cancer can surely be found. Not all tumors are, of course, malign. There is a chance that, with preventive tracing, benign cancer cells may be found and treatment can be provided without recurring to rather strong methods, such as radiotherapy, which is the use of radiation to eliminate cancer cells. Chemotherapy is a complementary form of treatment via medication.

Cancer can show just about anywhere, even where people least expect it to be. If neither radiation nor chemicals can treat it, a surgical intervention might be able to remove the tumor. However, not all areas of the body are operable and, usually, "only a miracle can save you". Even the most skeptical of doctors use that expression.

Species are always evolving, humans included. You can tell from Darwin's *On the Origin of Species*, right in the first chapter, of a total fourteen, there is «Variation Under Domestication»[66], as far as animals domesticated by us are concerned. As a dominant species, due to the intellect we have developed, we are organized and communicate with each other, therefore building civilizations, in the beginning of Humanity, then moving toward smaller groups we call «societies», geopolitically dividing territories into sovereign nations. Unsatisfied with the total portion of said territories, some societies feel the need to expand and thus engage in *casus belli*[67] over the conquest of land, expropriating

---

baby. Primary causes are unprotected sex, contaminated blood transfusions and needles, transmission from mother to fetus during pregnancy or, if not at this stage, when breastfeeding.

[65] Diabetes occurs either when the pancreas does not produce enough insulin or cells across the entire body do not respond to the amount produced in an appropriate manner.

[66] Vide note 10.

[67] Latin phrase for «occurrence of war», both singular and plural.

and killing its native citizens, which is what European expansion in the Age of Discovery[68] is all about. Craving independence, the newly ex-colonials would then take genocide into their own hands.

Instead of utilizing our progressive abilities toward the improvement of our life, we improve our warfare, which is really not a no-brainer, but I felt the need to stress it once more. War is what finances the system, a lot more than Education, or so some think. There is always enough money for us to keep killing each other. And I will not say I do not appreciate the sacrifice war heroes and veterans have done for their respective countries, risking their life in order to maintain peace, but I would definitely prefer there were no veterans at all. Spending billions yearly on defense mechanisms is just bad drainage of resources. But thus is human nature and changing it toward the common goal of living sustainably, together, is unfortunately too much of a hippy-like fantasy.

You have to pay for your very existence. Who is it we owe money to, in the end? The people who get to decide whether you will live a little longer, or just die without even trying to save you, not just because of the lack of medical evidence there might be a chance for you, but especially because, instead of continuing to be a quiet paymaster, you claim your right for coverage, turning you into a burden, at the eyes of the insurance companies. It is basically the same as saying something like, "you are nearly dead, so, there is no point in trying, at all".

This is the way we develop. Through two philosophically simple processes known as trial and error, together with cause and effect. We need to learn and adapt properly, before we can ever accept change to come anywhere near us. Allow me to explain in detail. Let us go back about one hundred years, to April 10th,

---

[68] Though imprecise, this era spans between the 15th and 18th centuries.

1912. Surely this date reminds you of something rather important and historically changing, the maiden voyage of the RMS[69] Titanic, the largest manmade object to have ever existed in its time, "the ship of dreams", one "God himself could not sink". Back then, Plutocracy was, as it is now, really, at its peak. Only those with money had enough power to save themselves in a moment of crisis, which is exactly what would happen, should we need to escape Earth and avoid the end of Mankind, but let us not drift away too far, not for now, at least.

Basically, you are worthy of any comfort you desire, as long as you pay for it. If you cannot, the minimum dignity required to respect a human being will apply, but only at the lowest of levels. On the ocean liner in question, there were three different classes, each of them deciding their respective passengers' fate. In first class, there was a total of 324 lives. In second class, 285. In third class, 708 souls[70], making it a total of 1,317 passengers. Over 900 other people were also aboard and part of the staff[71].

Not only did wealth determine who slept where, so did social insertion, and I do not mean it the way we all are used to thinking of it. Let us take a look at the numbers. Paying for a berth in first class, which was basic accommodation, though luxurious enough, meant spending around $150, which in today's money would be something like $1,725. If, however, a berth was not enough and therefore a parlor suite was required, total payment would be $4,350, the equivalent to $50,000 in today's cash. Accommodation in second class was $60, which is to say $690 at

---

[69] Royal Mail Ship. Vessels carrying this prefix in their designation are under contract to the UK Royal Mail. Its usage began as early as 1840.

[70] *Encyclopedia Titanica*, «Titanic Passenger List – The Maiden Voyage», (http://www.encyclopedia-titanica.org/titanic-passenger-list), accessed 04-16-2016.

[71] *History of the Titanic*, «The Crew of the RMS Titanic», (http://www.historyofthetitanic.org/the-crew-of-the-rms-titanic.html), accessed 04-16-2016.

present. As for third class, also pejoratively designated «steerage», ticket prices would go up to $40, or $460, currently speaking. This is the section of the ship where European immigrants traveled with as little as a suitcase and the clothes they wore on their body, in search for a better life, willing to live the American dream.

Though this event took place not only in 1912, but very much across the end of the 19th century to the end of the 1960s, to say the latest, when a so-called «immigration boom» took place, considering both World Wars had already happened and a Cold War was being carried away, in a self-proclaimed civilized continent such as Europe, we still see Arab refugees being treated like scum within the European Union today, whose earliest predecessor was the European Coal and Steel Community, created especially for the unification of continental European countries after the end of World War II, which revealed sordid, unimaginable secrets, regarding the extinction of Humanity itself. The fact they travel under inhuman conditions is not just an origin problem, it is a sheltering issue as well, allowing traffickers to continuously risk hundreds of lives on miniscule crafts adrift in the Mediterranean Sea, stealing from said lives all they have, just to end rounded up in a concentration field with barbwire around them, preventing them from getting away, so as to deliver them back into the middle of the conflict, only this time, without any possessions at all. That is not what Europe is supposed to be made of. Paris and Brussels, the heart of the continent and headquarters to the Union, were attacked in 2015 and 2016, respectively. People say they fear sheltering refugees. The truth is all terrorists involved, recruited by *Daesh*, were born and raised European. Much of the world's evil was generated where peace was supposed to prevail, and yet, Europe calls itself the «old continent», where «Western civilization set its cradle». You would believe it to be unthinkable having a reproduction of the Roman Empire's vices in the 20th century, at exactly the same location. The so-called «Games», played at the Colosseum, in Rome, together with other places, such as Patricians' private villas, were turned back into reality by the hands of Nazism, nearly two thousand years later. Setting the difference between one human being and another is what enables one person alone to command the mob into agreeing to their words, which they believe are exactly what they want to hear. All men and women are democratically elected by the citizens empowered to do so. It is what comes of these elections afterward that reveals what human nature really is about.

When Titanic struck the iceberg in the North Atlantic Ocean, at 11h40 pm of April 14th, local time, her designer, Thomas Andrews[72], who had also boarded the ship on her maiden voyage, was sure there was nothing that could be done to prevent disaster, for the ship was set to founder. Captain Edward John Smith[73] then ordered evacuation of the vessel immediately, and this is where the point I am trying to make comes alive, which I believe you have already guessed. In 1912, there were two key factors that decided the fate of many lives, in case of a tragedy at sea: the «women and children first» principle and the Board of Trade's regulations.

As much as it may sound gentlemanly enough to bring women and children to safety as quickly as possible, placing "every man for himself" is deliberate assassination. So is placing women and

---

[72] 1873-1912. He was the managing director for the Harland and Wolff shipyard, in Belfast, capital city of present-day Northern Ireland, part of the United Kingdom of Great Britain, and naval architect for the Titanic, the sister ship of White Star Line's Olympic. Together, these ships formed the company's duo competing against rival Cunard Line's own Lusitania and Mauretania.

[73] 1850-1912. Captain Smith had been a commanding officer within White Star Line for twenty-five years. Regardless of his experience at sea and numerous successful transatlantic voyages, his last maritime campaign before retiring was ill-fated right from the start, putting an end to both his career and life.

children first from the first and second classes, moving to «steerage» after most lifeboats have been dispatched, carrying between ten to twenty people, fearing they might buckle. You probably remember English actor Jonny Phillips from James Cameron's[74] 1997 blockbuster feature film *Titanic*[75], who portrayed Second Officer Charles Lightoller[76], saying that to Andrews, played in the movie by Victor Garber, who replied the boats had been "tested in Belfast with the weight of seventy men".

Failure to help a victim in risk of death is a negligent homicide. Of course, that is the law today. Back then, men dying under these circumstances was an event directly involved with the Board of Trade's requirements. Any vessel of either ten thousand gross register tons[77] or more was required to carry sixteen lifeboats, which were enough for 960 people, out of a total 2,200, approximately, which is to say forty-three percent. Total GRT for Titanic was 46,328.

Though Andrews originally planned having enough lifeboats for everyone aboard, J. Bruce Ismay[78] overruled him, claiming

---

[74] B. 1954. Canadian film director, producer, screenwriter, engineer and sea explorer. He is best known, not only for *Titanic*, but also other major productions such as the *Terminator* saga (1984 – Present), of which he directed the first two instalments, featuring Arnold Schwarzenegger, and *Avatar* (2009 – Present).

[75] Starring Leonardo DiCaprio, Kate Winslet, Billy Zane, Bill Paxton and Gloria Stuart, written and directed by James Cameron, 20th Century Fox and Paramount Pictures, 1997.

[76] 1874-1952. He was the most senior of officers to have survived the Titanic disaster and the one who applied the «women and children first» principle to its utmost. Though there was bravery enough in Lightoller's actions, as he stayed on board to the very end, a lot of men were prevented from being rescued, having the lifeboats lowered half full when there were no women or children to fill the remaining seats.

[77] Or GRT. Each of them is equivalent to one hundred cubic feet.

[78] 1862-1937. He was the chairman and managing director of White Star Line. The fact that he fled the Titanic while there were women and children still aboard, jumping into one of the last lifeboats available, tarnished his reputation for the rest of his life.

there were too many, cluttering necessary deck space for the passengers' strolls. Everyone was made to believe, perhaps Andrews himself, the ship really was unsinkable and even if it was not, it would take an extraordinary amount of time before it went down, providing enough time for all people on board to be rescued.

The paragraph above is the first stage of the trial and error process. Picture, if you will, a theatrical *hybris*, which is Greek for defying your own fate and an essential constituent of ancient tragedies. This is one of our main conditions as human beings. We have to try, see where something will lead us, without even questioning all possibilities or hypotheses. If nothing wrong has ever happened before, what is there to fear? That is what said tragedies meant to explain to the audience at The Great Dionysia, the largest theater festival to be displayed in Athens: *what if* something like this (the situation portrayed in the plot) took place in reality? What would you do to prevent it? How would you react? What would you learn from it and would you try to enlighten everyone else who seemed unconvinced to you? Lives have to be claimed before the living can attribute any importance to fatal events. Pretty much that slangy way of thinking we usually say out loud, which is "if it ain't broke, don't fix it", in detriment of "better to be safe, than sorry".

Indeed, with all our technology and life-prolonging tools, our consideration for fellow humans is utterly down below. Sometimes, even, we value the life of our housebroken animal companions a lot more than other people. You could ask me, of course, as I am very open to discussion and conversation in general, if animal lives do not matter to me at all. Well, obviously, they do. There are many people around the world cherishing their pets in detriment of other people. You might be one of them. I will have you know I do not blame you at all. You can often count on animal loyalty a great deal better than people's. It is not in their nature to double-cross you on behalf of their interest or gain, which are none, aside from your protection and wellbeing. A dog, for instance, will psychologically adapt to your behavior. If you are sad and depressed, your animal friend will become so as well. If you become nervous or stressed out, so will they. If you are happy, so will they. Precisely, you may have noticed I chose «they» for a pronoun, instead of «it», mirroring the feeling animal lovers nurture for their pets.

The truth is, after two hours and forty minutes at the surface, the Titanic sank in the North Atlantic, claiming the lives of over 1,500 people. About 700 were saved and, on the following days, around 300 floating corpses were recovered. This is the second and final stage of the trial and error process, which is a misleading designation, as far as I am concerned, and I will tell you why: «tri-» is a prefix determining a number. Not in «trial», as it is part of the vocable's root and etymology, but in other words, such as «trinity», for example. That number is obviously three. «Trial» and «error» are two stages. Which is the third? «Solution», which can be subdivided in two other phases, «learning» and «applying», but I figure it is somewhat complex to place such ramifications on a textbook chart. I will add, however, this third and actually final stage should yield to «prevention».

About ninety years later, we know what happened and we have even already talked about it[79]. Safety during flights was also incredibly improved, but doubling the number of lives lost at sea in 1912 was the ultimate sacrifice for changes to apply. Who would have thought carrying short-length knives or any other sort of blades into the cabin of a plane would produce such threatening results? Or disregarding cockpit security, for that matter?

Unfortunately, that is not all. It does not take third-parties to

---

[79] Vide note 19.

create a disaster. *What if* the fatal events taking place are nothing more than an inside job? Remember what happened on March 24th, 2015? Germanwings[80] flight 9525 co-pilot, Andreas Lubitz[81], deliberately thrusted the Airbus A320-211-type aircraft into the French Alps, killing 150 people, himself included, when making the connection between Barcelona, Spain and Düsseldorf, Germany.

I mentioned below, in the footnote referring to Lubitz, that his suicidal actions were eventually disputed. Indeed, when someone traverses an illness such as a severe depression, it is rather natural there might be certain instincts the victim experiences that lead them to a self-harming kind of behavior. People who have never experienced such a thing may claim a suicide-propitious person is rather egotistical (or selfish) because said person does not care about the people who are a part of his or her life. But let me ask you this: if you could not withstand your own existence, would you care about what others might feel if you were gone? Surprisingly enough, I think you would. And, instead of taking the pressure away, thinking about it would only leave you a great deal more anxious and without any structure at all that could be strong enough to prevent you taking your own life, making you fantasize about your own funeral and the attention you would get from people mourning your passing, with a flower wreath placed on your casket, in the center of the circle.

However, when your suicidal intentions involve claiming

---

[80] A subsidiary company of German flight operator Lufthansa, the largest in Europe.

[81] 1987-2015, aged 27. Lubitz suffered from severe depression, for which he had previously put his pilot training on halt in 2009, having informed the company at the time. His suicidal actions were disputed when investigations to the accident were concluded in May, after discovery and analysis of both black boxes, the flight data recorder (FDR, which registers a flight's parameters several times per second) and the cockpit voice recorder (CVR, which tapes conversations between pilots, so as to ease investigations in case of an aviation accident).

other lives, it is not suicide, anymore. It is homicide, assassination, murder. No matter how much you are suffering, planning on taking your own life is one thing, either considered as a crime on itself or not, depending on national law; bringing others down with you is just not the same. In Lubitz's case, dragging 149 other lives with his own was a homicidal plan.

The world refers to September 11th, 2001 as a day of suicidal terrorist attacks. You and I both know it was plain murder, justified, from the terrorists' perspective, naturally, by the *jihad*, the holy war. They considered themselves martyrs, as they died for the faith, killing, in addition to themselves, the infidels. Lubitz, on the other hand, and according to official investigations, had another sort of purpose: to be remembered worldwide for something he had done. The only problem, of course, is, while he made his wish come true, he is not remembered as a victim, but rather as a criminal, taking away with his own the lives of one hundred and a half innocent people who had nothing to do with his personal demons.

What was there to learn, from this? A great deal. In the US, because of September 11th, no one in the cockpit ever stayed alone. All domestic flights and those inbound had to begin complying with this new rule: there must be at least two people in the cockpit when one of the pilots has to leave, even if for a short bathroom break, which is what happened during the flight Lubitz was in charge of, after allowing Captain Patrick Sondenheimer to leave for said break and locking him out, disabling the door code panel from the inside. Then again, if a flight attendant is asked to stay in the cockpit while one of the pilots is away, will they know enough about aircraft piloting to understand whether the one staying is doing something threatening to the flight's safety? That is another mystery of trial and error. Try first, fail second, and hope no more lives have to be claimed because of an apparently minor detail. Either way, since nothing of these proportions had ever happened in Europe, the American regulation was disregarded for intracontinental flights.

As human beings, we have the right to our multiple freedoms, may it be of speech, thought, etc., and no State should ever try to control its citizens for its own empowerment. However, as long as we do not make an effort to filter out of our nature the homicidal need to jeopardize the life of other fellow citizens, regardless of their nationality, ethnicity, faith, whichever, especially for personal endeavors and reasons, united progress is exactly that, utopic, which increases the need for law enforcement and, sometimes, justifies the democratic election of future dictators, who then oppress us, claiming it is what is best for us all, until the inevitable *coup d'état*, leading us to live an unending life cycle of both trial and error, though no learning is grasped from said errors.

That is what cause and effect are for. There is a trial. That trial generates a cause. That cause produces an effect. That effect makes you conclude you erred. What of learning from it, then? Here you find the missing piece to finish the puzzle once and for all.

2

Governmental Concerns

In this chapter, I plan to tell you how I envision the perfect form of Government. It is an understandably laughable statement. You and I both know there is no such thing as perfection. It is nothing more than an ideal, an ambition. So is Utopia, but that is not what is stopping me from typing my thoughts on how I would like to make it real, hence the existence of this book. Therefore, I ask you, and you ask me, how could Government ever become perfect and how is it possible to transform a sheer desire such as Utopia into something palpable?

Theory (or the process of theorization) is indeed a treacherous path to pursue. Putting in words what you feel is right for you and the rest of the people you love the most or those you might not even be acquainted to and never imagined you would meet is always ideological. A form of Government is supposed (*theoretically* speaking, n.b.[82]) to defend the principles of a sovereign State and its citizens' rights, notwithstanding making sure their duties are also executed, so as to maintain social order and prevent the generation of chaos.

---

[82] *Nota bene*, Latin for «take good note».

In my previous work[83], I explained the origins of Justice and its application in the first Western civilizations to walk on this earth, namely the Egyptians (though considered to be Near-Eastern, but mainly since the country was submitted to Arab rule) and the Hellenes[84], afterward, who also assumed control of Egypt before the ascension of the Roman Empire, for which reason I shall not repeat myself. Nonetheless, the need to rethink the purpose for Justice does arise.

What do we need a penal system for? The immediate reply from anyone you ask this last question to is always something like, "to put criminals behind bars", adding, perhaps, "so they are kept away from the people they might kill in the future". This is true. Those who hurt other people need to be locked away, but certainly not forever, and that is the apparently moralistic part of my statement, though there is some purpose to it, as we will now find out.

Not all countries in the world share the same thoughts on law enforcement or incarceration brutality. Not all the countries in the world share the same thoughts on human rights, come to that. Such a disregard remains still active, not only because of the political or religious influence a country may live under, but also as a means to justify, if not avenge the inevitable death of those who were murdered in another senseless killing, either individual or at a massive extent. Basically, the doctrine is, "if you think you have the right to kill, then you have a duty to die".

Any life lost is irrecoverable, at least for the time being. And even then, someday in the future, the ability to keep people alive, whichever the vessel to which their mind is downloaded, will obviously not become an excuse to kill anyone, especially if the concept of death ceases to exist (which would be the ultimate ironic

---

[83] Vide note 11.
[84] Greeks.

peak)[85]. Nonetheless, the death penalty only becomes alive after it has been authorized by the ultimate form of Government in a certain jurisdiction, like the Governor of a state, in the case of Federal Republics. Disposing of other fellow humans like a used tissue is something that publicly made sense and was even endorsed by the crowd until as late as the second half of the 20th century, and I am well aware I am being optimistic. Let us just say I am trying, all the same, to set some boundaries as far as a timely context is concerned. It is not something, however, we should accept in 21st century societies trying to set the example in other areas of the world, as said example will only live enough to be disrespected.

Authorities cannot claim the life of a criminal in memory of their victim. Sure, if you are a relative of the person murdered, even if you are not naturally aggressive, the first thought that might come to your mind is actually to kill the perpetrator, again, to avenge the victim. They are not coming back to life because of that. It made sense in Antiquity. In fact, popular justice was the way, back then, of dealing with something as personal as the homicide of someone a person was related to. Even today, when an individual is being prosecuted in a court of law for a crime, usually horrendous and unimaginable to most people, the mob finds themselves perfectly capable of lynching said individual in the middle of the street, regardless of being escorted by the police.

I believe in second chances. I honestly do. Placing someone in jail for life means both society and the State itself have given up on them. A person who is convicted and sentenced to either half of their life in prison or the day of their last breath has got to sooner or later embrace a moment of epiphany, which means they start thinking about what they did that brought them inside

---

[85] Further reading: SARAMAGO, José, 2005, *Death with Interruptions* (*As Intermitências da Morte*, in Portuguese), trans. Margaret Jull Costa, San Diego, CA: Mariner Books, 2009.

and reflect upon a possible path toward the light. Prison pastors, preachers, priests, rabbis, reverends, etc. step forward with a holy-kind of scripture and try talking some sense into the inmates by quoting book, chapter and verse.

I admit that religion is supposed to reconnect people among themselves and then, as one, single group of brethren, to a god, a divinity. However, that is not necessarily the case of always. Embracing a religion by the book, literally, habitually results in hatred for those who are deemed unfit to belong to the same cause. I mentioned a few lines above those incarcerated are approached to by a representative of a doctrine for which a «guidebook» has been written, either thousands of years ago or in contemporaneity, by a self-proclaimed clairvoyant, prophet or visionary, whichever you might want to call them.

We have to remember that in either of those cases, the founders of a religious doctrine are men believing in certain fundamentals, considering some of them worthy of a sacrament and others plain blasphemy and sacrilege. Agreement is something that is not always possible to find amid people, even when they belong to the same group, faction, institution, party, sect, etc. A determined number of precepts will most of the time be accepted, whereas others shall see debating and disputing, probably facing changes before the approval of a majority. We have to remember another factor regarding this topic: even though the final approval of a measure or principle is the responsibility of the higher number, it will not always be the best. You would think that, if a large number of people feel right about something, then one or two others will really not make a difference, because they are wrong. No, definitely not. To put it quite simply, majorities do have the required strength to make the change and either condone or condemn any kind of policy or regulation, but if an individual is onto something, even if unrecognized as or not taken for an expert, said majority should always give them a go by taking a listen. Sometimes, a single mind is able to question what an entire group of other minds did not or could not see, mostly due to lack of the required enlightenment. "Great minds think alike". Indeed, but let us not forget about giving a deserving shot to a possibly greater mind. You can live to be a hundred-years-old and fail to see what was right in front of you, under your nose, for having believed so fervidly there was no other possible answer to the problem.

This is the kind of perspective a self-righteous inmate can face during their time. But none of it will matter if the chance for parole is cast into oblivion, and all because death is inevitable, either from living in jail to old age or forced euthanizing. A dog mauls someone alive, veterinarians «put it to sleep», which is a euphemism for «they kill it». A human being does the same to another and is not treated for psychopathy. Treatment is too expensive. So is keeping them alive. What do we do? We kill them, straightforward approach. Because the usage of an electric chair or hanging by the neck became unpopular in the meantime, possibly due to their graphic brutality and display, as far as the international community is concerned, lethal injections are administered to those sentenced to death. This kind of injection is usually a combination of three different drugs, each of them producing a separate effect: sodium thiopental, to render unconsciousness and, therefore, avoid agony and suffering; pancuronium bromide, to paralyze all muscles and induce respiratory arrest; and, finally, potassium chloride, to put a halt to the heart. Preceding death row, the convicted may often choose their «last supper», before Government betrays them, so they feel satisfied and happier as they walk down the green mile, on their way to the public display of their killing, making it "eye for an eye".

At some time in your life, you, who had been so rational up

until then, always thinking twice before performing a certain action, may all of a sudden snap, and do something crazy, usually out of despair or lack of internal structure to deal with the problem you have in front of you. If a person has an entire family to feed, they are unemployed (though actively looking to find a job) and the State does not provide for them a sufficient amount of money each month to dignify their lives, we all know how it is going to end: petty theft. And by this I am talking stealing a loaf of bread, for example. In some countries, theft is punishable by severing the dominant hand, so the perpetrator does not feel like trying it again. In some other, by death. In those, however, who consider themselves to be civilized and part of the so-called first world, an insurmountable amount of money, within the hundreds of dollars, euros, etc., is spent on a lawsuit over, sometimes, an expense of a few pennies or cents. At least, there is no corporal or capital punishment, indeed. Nonetheless, corporations selling perishable goods at an inflated price, backstabbing the original producer and seller, would do better if they just gave that loaf of bread away to the starving family, instead of taking them to court and paying a lawyer their thousands of dollars-worth of honoraria. Such a way of thinking does not even make any sense. Or better yet, give the man or woman responsible for said petty theft a job, and pay them a decent salary by the end of the month. That way, they can honestly provide for their family.

Justice is either made by Man or a deity, which means it is ultimately imagined by Man in the voice of an imaginary entity. In the case of the latter, those laws are interpreted, obviously, by Man, as he most pleases. In the end, the legislator has every right to put a certain bill into their own words, recurring to «God's» authority over «His» little lambs to apparently stand up for human rights and yet discriminate those "different" from the rest of society, *legally* going around their own law-making. I know, it is utterly absurd.

Then, of course, there is the question of taking someone else's life over petty theft so they do not get caught. People gifted with strong self-righteousness cannot stand the guilt of having killed a person for their own survival or their relatives', in which case, self-defense does not apply. A sorry excuse of a felony then turns into a serious crime. It was not premeditated, though, and should it be properly proven as such, the penal system has a duty of placing felons back in society, especially if they are willing to turn themselves in peacefully, without resisting arrest and assuming all guilt before a judge, a jury or both.

It is far more concerning when we are talking teenagers. Their mind is still in development. Even when someone reaches the age of majority, variable in different countries or federal states of one, same nation, it only means they are lawfully responsible for their actions, but it does not always mean they knew what they were doing. So these teens are placed in *correctional* facilities. Please take a note of the italic. That word means the Government (remember, of any country, without any specification) is taking care of *correcting* people and delivering them back in the world. It is the way they are *corrected*[86] that concerns me, together with the stigma associated to them afterward, unless said Government can find a suitable way of taking advantage of the individuals in question[87] for its own purposes. And even if it cannot, the individuals' intelligence is seized all the same, shaping it accordingly, which will eventually lead us to the eternal debate regarding free will and mind control.

Vaccination is not the cause for governmental control. No one is taking GPS shots in the place of substances that are supposed

---

[86] Cf. *A Clockwork Orange*, based on the homonymous title by Anthony Burgess, starring Malcolm McDowell, written, produced and directed by Stanley Kubrick, Warner Bros., 1971.

[87] Cf. *Good Will Hunting*, starring Robin Williams, Matt Damon, Minnie Driver, Ben Affleck and Stellan Skarsgård, directed by Gus Van Sant, Miramax Films, 1997.

to eradicate diseases and improve public health, that is ridiculous and not even worth talking about. It is the way society is politically shaped that defines what the regular citizen is supposed to think, unless they have both a strong enough mind and spirit to resist and filtrate uniformity.

Plurality is supposed to be one of the core values of Democracy, but it is not always so. A Government does not just simply feed on taxpayer money to survive. There are other multiple sources of income, namely corporatism (or corporativism), helping a political structure withstand moments of crisis in exchange for tax reliefs or contracted services, hiding behind the façade of a common interest, shaded by economic divisions such as agriculture, science or even the military, subordinated to the State, thusly representing political power in a certain jurisdiction.

Corporations are not State-run, but rather run the State by puppeteering the people that are democratically and universally elected for public office. There is no use in having a Head of State or Government or both that promises to oppose the controlling of the rich. In a Democracy with a limitless number of parties, there is plurality of ideologies, promoting free debating and proposals of decrees in order to ensure people's best interests are stood up for. However, political parties do not have autonomy enough to act independently and according to the principle of equality between social classes and statutes. Again, a party does not survive solely on member fees. It may gain greatness and a larger parliamentary representation if the interests of special people with enough power to influence the state of the economy are met, and those people may either be the laborers, without whom no work is done, or the businessmen, the entrepreneurs, who make billions every year by overexploiting their laborers with senseless salaries and benefits, stuck in a dead-end career that does not motivate any of them to work harder, as there is no compensation that might make a good sight for sore eyes.

The need for an illiterate workforce has always been key to building an empire. The ideal person is one who does not ask that many questions. If they get too smart, they start putting their purpose at stake, *thinking* there might be something else to so much hard work that they are not taking enough part in it. It is not a matter of acquiring intelligence to aim at blackmailing, demanding a certain percentage of profit. No, such an endeavor may not even be the question. The question is, on the other hand, demanding appropriate working conditions so the employer can make their company work and provide equally for all the employees.

I mean, just think about our life's purpose in general: we are born, we grow up, we have our education, we find a job, we keep it until old age, we retire, and only then we are supposed to take some rest and have fun, when we are getting one step closer each day to the grave. Is this the sort of mark an intelligent being such as a human is supposed to leave while living their life? "I built a home, a family, I raised my kids, I abided by the law every single time, now I can die happy". To some people, this is indeed enough. I do not judge them. They say wanting to change the world and turn it into a better place is all children's dream. It is, until you face the fact you are not going to get anything better than what you found while young and vigorous, just remaining in the same spot, throwing all your potential away, straight into the garbage can. But maybe you did not want to change the world so badly, after all, because you felt comfortable enough living your life in the most dignifying way possible. Perhaps you thought, "what is the point if, in the end, it is the Government that is patting our heads and taking us by the hand toward the interest they say is best for each and every one of us?". I hate to break it to you, but you are wrong. It is one thing to abide by the law. It is another to become the system's cog, like a lot of other people do, and that is where the political system needs revising.

Most democracies around the world, with a particular focus on the Western side of it, are representative. This means that a nation's citizens fulfilling certain requirements, namely having reached the age of majority for that country or federal state (usually between eighteen and twenty-one), cast their vote into the ballots for different kinds of elections, on a day specifically chosen by either tradition or decree.

In the case of the United States, American citizens vote for the presidential election on the first Tuesday of November every four years. The President, colloquially referred to by their acronym, POTUS[88], is then invested on Inauguration Day, January 20th, becoming simultaneously Head of Government and State. The US is a Federal Republic.

In the United Kingdom, the Government is elected on a Thursday since as early as 1647, which was Market Day, preventing electors from getting drunk on a paying Friday and becoming influenced by the Sunday sermon. The length of term for the Prime Minister of the United Kingdom of Great Britain and Northern Ireland is at the incumbent monarch's pleasure, as long as there is trust in the Government from the House of Commons[89], to which the Prime Minister must answer. Either way, the newly conceived Parliaments Act 2011 determines that there has to be a general election every five years, on the day the monarch is advised by the incumbent Head of Government, dissolving Parliament up to a maximum of twenty-five business days before the

---

[88] President of the United States.

[89] The lower house of British Parliament. A total of 650 members are elected and hold their seats until the dissolution of Parliament by the monarch, unlike the House of Lords, whose membership is unlimited and made of twenty-six appointed Lords Spiritual (bishops enrolled in the Church of England) and Lords Temporal, of which ninety-two are Hereditary Peers, mostly inherited only by men, and the others are Life Peers, appointed by the monarch on the Prime Minister's advice, fulfilling the required proof of age and citizenship, though including also four Hereditary Peers.

votes are cast. The UK is a Constitutional Monarchy.

In Portugal, so I may speak as far as I am directly concerned, on behalf of my present citizenship, the political chain of command for this Unitary[90] Representative Semi-Presidential[91] Republic begins with the Civil Parish, which is a form of local Government, headed by a President, equivalent to a City Supervisor, elected by its residents in the municipal elections every four years. Its jurisdiction is often very small and applies only to the people directly involved in it, namely its residents.

A Municipality, which is equivalent to either a Town or City Hall (depending on the kind of infrastructures present and the number of citizens living in it), is the direct supervisor of City Parishes, with a far more broadened territory and a bit more authority over certain matters, depending on whether they pertain to local or municipal interests. It is headed by a President, equivalent to Mayor, who is also elected from the municipal election ballots, again every four years.

Both these elections do not necessarily coincide with the general election for Central Government. The same people leading

---

[90] Countries around the world are either governed unitarily or federally. The first kind means all forms of Government, whether local or regional, answer to one, single form of Central Government. In the Portuguese case, there are two archipelagos, Madeira and The Azores, each of them with a regional form of Government answering to the Republic's administration. The latter kind means a country is organized in several states with authority enough to implement laws or decrees within their own jurisdiction, through the elected Governor, though mandatorily respecting decisions made by the federal Government that apply to the entire nation. Canada, the United States or Brazil are examples of federations.

[91] A Semi-Presidential Republic comprehends the existence of both a Head of State and of Government, who are *not* the same person. Ultimate decisions regarding national sovereignty and new lay-making lay with the President. Though the President does not possess full executive power, they do play a key role in both legislation and constitution of Parliament, having the ability to dissolve it, under exceptional circumstances, of course. They also play the role of Commander-in-Chief of the Armed Forces (comprehending three branches, and those are Army, Navy and Air Force, in this specific case).

either of these forms of Government may only run for three consecutive terms[92].

The following most important form of administration is the collection of Civil Parishes and Municipalities all together, forming a District. There are no official representatives of a District, however. If a Municipality President happens to hold office in the City Hall matching that District, such as the capital city, Lisbon, they do not have any authority over other Municipalities pertaining to that District. It is solely a way of simplifying territorial organization. These administrative Districts have been left in the background for the past few years, as far as cultural and socioeconomic connections are concerned, between the residents of a Metropolitan Area who are territorially part of an administrative District, but blend in a lot more with some other geographically closer place.

With respect to the Autonomous Regions of Madeira and The Azores, both of them archipelagos, there are no Districts associated to them, but they do have Municipalities and Civil Parishes. Their District is the Region itself.

After both Districts and Autonomous Regions, the classical Tripartite Division of National Sovereign Powers takes place, beginning with the Judicial Courts, bearers of the Judicial Power. There are judicial Districts for each Appeals Court and Central Administrative Court, defining judicial jurisdiction. Judicial Courts are topped by the Supreme Court of Justice, whose decisions may only be appealed to the Constitutional Court, whose decisions cannot be appealed again, at least not within national jurisdiction. The last resource is the European Court of Human Rights, considering the Portuguese Republic has been a Member-

---

[92] Further reading: VIEIRA, Ricardo, 09-05-2013, *Rádio Renascença*, «Lei da limitação de mandatos foi debatida e aprovada em 15 minutos», (http://rr.sapo.pt/informacao_detalhe.aspx?fid=92&did=120635), accessed 04-26-2016.

State of the European Union since 1986[93].

The Constitutional Court is also useful for prudential oversight of certain decrees voted and approved by Parliament, which are then sent to the President of the Republic. Should they question the constitutionality of such decrees, the Constitutional Court judges[94] must then reflect upon them and rule either in favor or against. If in favor, the President enacts them. If against, the Government must then rephrase according to the judges' ruling, submit them again for approval by Parliament and wait for the President's decision. Should they send the decree in question back to Parliament, its Members (or Deputies) either opt by rewriting said decree or send them back to the Presidency exactly as it was, in which case, the President has mandatorily got to enact it, having no other constitutional choice. The term length for the Constitutional Court judges is nine years and cannot be renewed.

You can tell from the previous paragraph how the rest of the Portuguese political system works, considering the Executive Power is administered by the Central Government, whose head is the Prime Minister, usually the leader of a political party with either parliamentary representation from the previous Legislature

---

[93] At the time, the organization was still designated European Economic Community, preceding its current designation, which was the result of the Treaty of Maastricht, 1992.

[94] There is a total of thirteen judges in this court, ten of which are designated by Parliament and the remaining three are selected by the ten appointed before them. In 2015, however, there was a Constitutional Amendment suggested by Parliament, changing the way the same number of judges would be appointed for their office. Seven jurors were supposed to be selected by the President, whereas six judges or magistrates were supposed to be appointed by the Superior Council of Magistracy. Either kind of selection had to obligatory be approved by Parliament.

Further reading: GARCIA, Sofia Amaral, 06-16-2015, *Observador*, «Quem deve nomear os juízes do Tribunal Constitucional?», (http://observador.pt/opiniao/quem-deve-nomear-os-juizes-do-tribunal-constitucional/), accessed 04-26-2016 (Portuguese only).

or not. According to each party's statutes, the leader, elected by members of the party, may either be its President[95], Secretary-General[96] or Coordinator[97].

Traditionally, the leader of the political party with the most votes and, therefore, most elected Deputies, via the D'Hondt method[98], is invited by the Head of State, the President of the Republic, to form Central Government, the one representing the entire nation and the Republic itself. The future Prime Minister, who is the third most important person of the chain of command, then chooses their Ministers and Secretaries of State, who, aside from answering their respective Ministers, must also answer the Prime Minister, who is the ultimate Head of Government. The manifest with the names of the individuals chosen for the several Ministries and Secretariats of State (variable according to each Constitutional Government elected by national citizens aged eighteen or more, either residing in the country or living abroad, or emancipated citizens under the same age, who are legally adults) is afterward presented to the President of Republic, who either accepts or rejects said manifest, being able to suggest a different composition for the bearers of the Executive Power.

---

[95] The case of the Social-Democrat Party (Partido Social-Democrata [PSD], in Portuguese), from the right and the largest of the current opposition.

[96] Such as the current Prime Minister, from the center-left, leading the party in Government, the Socialist Party (Partido Socialista [PS]), or the leader of the Portuguese Communist Party (Partido Comunista Português [PCP]), from the left, who supports the current Government.

[97] Like the leader of the Left Bloc (Bloco de Esquerda [BE]), from the far-left, also supportive of the current Government.

[98] Mathematically equivalent to Jefferson's method in the United States (named after Thomas Jefferson), though not operationally, this method (named after Belgian Mathematician Victor D'Hondt) defines party-list proportional representation in Parliament, meaning that a certain amount of votes, such as one-fourth, for instance, means that the party getting that same fraction of votes has the right to the same fraction of seats. In the Portuguese case, the total number of Deputies elected for Parliament is 230. Whichever party elects at least 116 Deputies (just one above half), gains absolute majority and does not require the support of any other party.

During the first Plenary Session of Parliament, the nationally-elected deputies elect someone else themselves, the President of the Assembly of the Republic (or President of Parliament), the second most important person in the nation. Their term lasts for a Legislature, which is to say four years, just like the Prime Minister's (only the latter's is renewable once for another four years). Any candidate with the majority of votes is thus invested.

After the President of the Republic has endowed the Prime Minister and their cabinet as Government, the unicameral[99] Parliament, to whom the Legislative Power belongs, must discuss and either approve or reject the newly-endowed Government's program in two days. If a motion of confidence is approved, the Executive immediately acquires power. Should it be the contrary, with Parliament approving a motion of no confidence, the Prime Minister and their staff is immediately dismissed, pertaining to the President of the Republic the duty to invite the first runner-up of the last election to form Central Government, only after listening to social partners and parliamentary-represented political parties, those who were also chosen from the general election, in order to gain agreement from everyone economically, politically and socially involved in the nation's future and wellbeing.

The President of the Republic is the utmost important individual in the entire nation and among the national Bodies of Sovereignty[100]. Though the Presidential Power is not explicitly mentioned in the Constitution of the Portuguese Republic, I can most assuredly tell you it is somewhat present in a semi-executive fashion, which is directly concerned with the duties consecrated in said Constitution, such as the appointment of Government, the

---

[99] This means there is only one chamber, disabling the chance of one overruling the other, were the Parliament plural in chambers.

[100] Previously mentioned in the text's corpus, these are the wielders of the tripartite division of powers (executive, legislative and judicial, which is to say Government, Parliament and Courts of Law, respectively), considering the President of the Republic is at their top.

dissolution of Parliament and the summoning of all sorts of elections, including presidential. Should they become unable to perform their regular duties, they are replaced by their immediate interim, the President of the Assembly of the Republic or the immediate substitute of the latter.

In order to run for President of the Republic, candidates must have been born in national territory and be at least thirty-five years of age. They must gather a total of between 7,500 and 15,000 signatures from national voting citizens, which are then delivered by the candidates to the Constitutional Court, either validating or rejecting their candidacy, should they fail to comply with the above requirements.

There need not be any political ties at all between a candidate and a political party, though both sides may pursue support from one another, so as to encourage voting from citizens relating to said party, either for being a member of or plainly sympathizing with it. Neither spoilt nor blank votes count for the total expressed in the ballots. The winning candidate must achieve at least fifty percent on the first round to be elected. If no such outcome takes place, there is a second round featuring the two most voted candidates from the previous round. The term length for President of the Republic is a total of five years, with the possibility of two consecutive terms. Candidacies for a third consecutive term are unconstitutional, and so are those from candidates running after five years of having taken office for two consecutive terms. Should they renounce to office, they cannot run again for the immediately following election or the one after the first five years since renouncing.

Now that I am finished with the description of the most important parts of the Constitution of the Portuguese Republic, you are probably wondering, not to presume, what was the meaning of this entire segment. Do not be weary of my intentions, gentle Reader, for everything I have been saying unto you since the very beginning of this oeuvre has its purpose, and I am guessing you already know what it is, with respect to this. Precisely, I am fond of the terms of this Constitution, celebrating forty years of its voting and approval by the 1975-76 Constituent Assembly. It is one of the most democratic there is in Europe and perhaps worldwide. But now we enter a slight dispute, in which you might claim "the grass is always greener on the other side". *Touché, mon Ami(e)*. Rest assured, however, that is not the case. I swear on my honor. I wish only to take it as an example for what I believe is a direct, participatory and pure Democracy.

I will tell you in advance, though, a Constitutional Monarchy does not work for me. I do not recognize legitimacy in the claim to a «throne» of a «royal» family. I do not believe in the authority of a «blue-blooded» household over the remainder of citizens of the same nation. Sovereignty, as far as I am concerned (remember this *opus* is my expressed opinion, not the absolute truth), belongs with the people, who are free to run for and take public office, in turns, never tyrannically expropriating others of the same and equal possibility, with responsibility and seeking, always, the best interest for their fellow citizens and any others who may, in the future, want to join them, sharing equal rights and duties. A sovereign nation is made of its people, working together, with the right to their private life, but also carrying the duty of social responsibility toward the correct functioning of governing institutions of any kind, not just meant for those making a living out of Politics, but also for those uninvolved with any sort of political force.

Rome herself was not built in a day, though it did start as a monarchy, when founded by Romulus (allegedly in 753 BC), named after himself, the twin brother of Remus, both of which were fed and raised by a *lupa*[101]. Because of the disagreement

---

[101] Latin for female wolf.

both siblings had so as to where the city they were supposed to found together was to be placed (Palatine Hill, according to Romulus, and Aventine Hill, according to Remus), Romulus began to dig trenches and build walls around them, which Remus would constantly jump over in jest. His actions eventually led to his killing by his own brother, thus making Rome a single city under the rule of one king alone[102,103].

Now, as far as founding a city is concerned, just like, long before Rome, Thebes was founded in Greece by Cadmus, who then ceded it to his grandson, Pentheus, according to Euripides' *The Bacchae*, you may actually want to claim said city as yours and have citizens living in it, so long as they comply with your laws and regulations. Then again, a king or queen does not last forever, and is eventually succeeded by their descendants, maintaining the rule of the city within the original family. Well, is that not what has been going on with surviving monarchies and empires in Europe and other continents, apart from the Americas? Not quite.

You see, after the death of Romulus, the new king, Numa Pompilius, was elected by a Curiate Assembly, as the founding king had not been survived by any descendants. Later on, allegedly five more individuals (who were not always directly related to each other) came to rule Rome as a kingship until it was overthrown in 509 BC, by the Roman Republic founder, Consul Lucius Junius Brutus, who died the same year. You already know the rest of the story, namely regarding the important role Julius Caesar played in the transition from Republic to Empire, though never becoming an emperor.

---

[102] Further reading: GARCIA, Brittany, 10-04-2013, *Ancient History Encyclopedia*, «Romulus and Remus», (http://www.ancient.eu/Romulus_and_Remus/), accessed 04-27-2016.

[103] I advise you to read the Book of Genesis, beginning at chapter four, for a statement of comparison showing evidence of the kind of relationship between envious and murderous brothers.

Monarchies and empires are not so different from one another and are never entirely democratic. Neither was the Republican Rome, come to that, as far as equality is concerned, to say the least[104]. The people may choose their Government, but the Head of State claims the right to a throne that, in a Republic, would belong to the President, elected from the result of the voting by all overaged, national citizens, for a limited amount of time, then being succeeded by another citizen elected under the same circumstances. In the case of death of a monarch or renunciation, the relative next in line (usually the oldest son or daughter), claims the right to be enthroned. Should there be no surviving descendants, others, in the middle of the succession crisis and either due to political or affinity reasons (such as a royal marriage), for example, claim their own right of enthronement, which is what has been happening in Europe ever since the Western Roman Empire came to an end in 476 AD and was overthrown by several barbaric kingdoms, but only in present-day surviving monarchies, which can be subdivided into other kinds of royal family ruling, such as grand duchies[105] or principalities[106], though the rulers do not take the designation of either «king» or «queen», but rather of «grand duke», «grand duchess», «prince» or «princess», respectively.

The following is my suggestion for a structure of Government, beginning at the top, with the most important person or people representing a country, all the way down to local administration, under a *Utopian Ambition*.

I am reserving the right to share with you a both broader and completer description of a sovereign State later on in this book,

---

[104] McLAREN, Iona, 04-27-2016, *The Telegraph*, «Mary Beard: 'Romans were as xenophobic and ethnocentric as any people there's ever been'», (http://www.telegraph.co.uk/tv/2016/04/27/mary-beard-romans-were-as-xenophobic-and-ethnocentric-as-any-peo/), accessed 04-29-2016.

[105] Such as the Grand Duchy of Luxembourg, in Europe.

[106] Like the Principality of Monaco, located also in the European continent.

under the «World Citizen» insignia. Nonetheless, and because we are talking «National Consolidation» in this part, there need be indeed some restructuring as far as a country's organization is concerned, so it may be prepared for some horizon-broadening in the near future.

And so, bearing this in mind, the ideal form of Government for any country on Earth, as far as my own opinion is concerned, *mind*, is the Unitary Semi-Representative Semi-Presidential Democratic Republic, then becoming a Federate State with respect to a worldwide body of sovereignty, based on the same principles of the European Union, though definitely not following the current regulations of advantages for some and disadvantages for most Member-States. The concept of «World Citizen» is possible and practical, but abolishing national sovereignty is not. Several administrative divisions are necessary for the concept to survive under a passport that is free of visas or any other kind of legal authorizations defining the amount of time a person may stay or the economic actions they can perform in a foreign country under either a green card or an employer's sponsorship, for instance.

Thusly, with respect to the political organization of a nation, there must be a Head of State, who is the President of the Republic, elected directly and universally by all the voting nationals of the country in question.

President of the Republic

The President of the Republic represents the nation, assures national independence, the unity of the State and the normal functioning of and balance between the nation's democratic institutions.

They can be elected neither for a third consecutive term, nor another term during the five years following the end of the second consecutive term.

Should the President of the Republic renounce to office, they can run neither in the subsequent election, nor in the five years following their decision.

This person, whether a national since birth or any other individual who might have requested citizenship afterward, publicly proving themselves worthy to the entirety of the nation of leading the country and aged thirty-five-years-old or more, is the representative of all citizens, regardless of where they live, may it be in national territory or any other place across the globe. I shall not mention equality factors, as I had the opportunity of expressing my opinion regarding the subject clearly enough in the previous chapter.

Depending on the total number of citizens registered as nationals, the required number of signatures to run for President of the Republic may vary. In remembrance of the example provided earlier, the Portuguese case, for ten million nationals, the minimum number of signatures required is 7,500, increasing proportionally to the number of nationals. For a country of twenty million people, 15,000 signatures; for a country of thirty million, 22,500 signatures, and so forth. No maximum number shall be set, as long as the minimum is met.

Candidacies must be delivered to the Constitutional Court up to a maximum of thirty days before the scheduled date for the election.

In the case of the death of any candidate or any other factor disabling them with respect to their capability of assuming office, electoral procedures shall be retaken, in accordance with the law.

The President of the Republic shall be elected within sixty days of the end of their predecessor's term or within the sixty days following vacancy of office.

The election shall not take place during the either preceding or succeeding ninety days of the election for Parliament.

Should the events reported in the previous paragraph take

place, the election shall take place in the ten days following the end of the period set, thusly prolonging the outgoing President's term as long as necessary.

The candidate elected President of the Republic must obtain more than half of the total number of votes cast, disregarding any blanks.

Should none of the candidates obtain fifty or more percent of the total number of votes cast, there shall be a second suffrage until the twenty-first day following the first round, again enabling one week of preparation for campaigning and two weeks of effective campaign.

Only the two most voted candidates in the first round shall be considered for election, unless they choose to withdraw their candidacy.

The President-elect is inaugurated before Parliament.

Inauguration takes place either on the last day in office of the outgoing President or, in case of election due to vacancy, on the eighth day following that of the publishing of the results of the election.

When endowed, the President-elect shall take the following oath:

"I hereby swear, on my honor, I will solemnly perform the duties I am now invested with, by defending, carrying out and enforcing the Constitution of the Republic".

The term for President of the Republic has a length of five years and ends with the inauguration of the new President-elect.

In the case of a vacancy, the President of the Republic being elected begins a new term.

The President of the Republic is free to leave the country whenever they please, requiring any sort of authorization from neither Parliament, nor their Permanent Committee, as long as their absence is not State-related, in which case, both bodies should be informed in at least a five days' notice, so as to assure safety.

Failure to comply with the previous statement shall result in compulsory exoneration.

Should any crimes be committed for as long as they shall hold office, the President of the Republic must answer for them to the Supreme Court of Justice.

Such an initiative is a duty of Parliament, after the proposal by one-fifth of Deputies has been made and approved by two-thirds of the total number of Deputies in office.

Conviction will result in exoneration and inability of reelection.

Should any crime be committed by the President of the Republic as a regular citizen, they must answer for them to a regular court of justice after the end of term.

The President of the Republic may renounce to office by addressing Parliament.

Renunciation is effective immediately once Parliament has acknowledged said message, regardless of its posterior publication in the Diary of the Republic.

In the events of temporary inability to perform their duties as President of the Republic or vacancy of office, the President of Parliament is to undertake said duties. Should they become unavailable, the Vice-President of Parliament is to undertake them in turn.

As long as the President of Parliament is the interim President of the Republic, their duties as Deputy of Parliament are suspended.

The President of the Republic is allowed to keep their rights of office during their temporary impediment to perform their duties, as long as these do not conflict with the fundamental law foreseen in the Constitution of the Republic, applicable to all citizens, both national and foreign.

The interim President of the Republic has the right to all honors and prerogatives of such duties, but may not overstep the rights conceded to them when assuming the office for which they were originally elected.

It is the duty of the President of the Republic, as far as other bodies are concerned, to:

— Preside the State Council;
— Schedule, according to electoral law, the day of the election for President of the Republic, Parliament and local forms of Government;
— Extraordinarily summon Parliament;
— Address messages to both Parliament and local forms of Government;
— Dissolve Parliament, after auditing its Deputies and the State Council;
— Appoint the Prime-Minister;
— Exonerate both Central Government and the Prime-Minister;
— Appoint and/or exonerate members of Central Government, under proposition of the Prime-Minister;
— Preside the Ministers' Council, whenever the Prime-Minister so requests;
— Appoint and exonerate, under proposition of the Central Government, the Attorney-General of the Republic;
— Appoint five members for the State Council and two Board Members from the Superior Council of Magistracy.

The President of the Republic possesses the required autonomy to:

— Promulgate and enforce the laws, law-decrees and regulation-decrees, and sign the resolutions of Parliament with respect to international accords and other governmental decrees;

— Submit to referendum matters of relevant national interest;

— Declare a state of siege or a state of emergency;

— Publicly announce all grave emergencies with respect to the very life of the Republic;

— Indult and commute Justice-delivered sentences, under the Central Government's counsel;

— Require from the Constitutional Court the prudential oversight of the constitutionality of regulations within laws, law-decrees and international conventions;

— Require from the Constitutional Court the declaration of unconstitutionality of juridical regulations, as well as the verification of unconstitutionality by omission;

— Attribute decorations, in accordance with the law, and perform the duties of Grand-Master of the Honorific Orders of the Republic.

As far as international affairs are concerned, the President of the Republic has the duty to:

— Appoint the ambassadors and extraordinary diplomats, under proposition of the Central Government, and accredit foreign diplomatic representatives;

— Ratify international treaties, after their duly approval.

Throughout twenty days from the reception of any decree issued by Parliament to be enacted as a law, or the publication of the Constitutional Court's non-ruling of unconstitutionality of said decree, the President of the Republic must either promulgate or veto it, henceforth soliciting a new appreciation of said decree via a justifying message.

Should Parliament confirm its vote via the absolute majority of Deputies in office, the President of the Republic must promulgate the decree until eight days from its reception at the Presidency.

There shall be, however, the requirement of a majority of two-thirds of the Deputies present, as long as superior to the majority of the total number of Deputies in office, for the confirmation of decrees with respect to the revising of organic law, as well as the following matters:

— Foreign relations;
— Limitations between the public, private and cooperative and social sectors of means of production property;
— Regulation of electoral acts foreseen in the Constitution that do not take the form of organic law.

Within forty days from the reception of any governmental decree awaiting promulgation, or the publication of the Constitutional Court's non-ruling of unconstitutionality of said decree, the President of the Republic must either promulgate or veto it, expressing their decision to Central Government in written form.

The lack of promulgation or signature by the President of the Republic of any of the previous acts here listed result in their juridical inexistence.

The declaration of a state of siege or a state of emergency relies on both the auditing of Central Government and authorization issued by Parliament or, in the case of non-assembly or inability of immediate assembly, by the respective Permanent Committee.

The declaration of a state of siege or a state of emergency, when authorized by the Permanent Committee of Parliament, shall have to be confirmed in plenary, as soon as it is available to assemble.

State Council

The State Council is the political body of counsel of the President of the Republic.

The State Council is presided by the President of the Republic and made of the following members:

— The President of Parliament;
— The Prime-Minister;
— The Presiding Judge for the Constitutional Court;
— The Ombudsman;
— The former Presidents of the Republic elected under the Constitution that were not exonerated from office;
— Five citizens appointed by the President of the Republic during their own term;
— Five citizens elected by Parliament, according to the principle of proportional representation, during the term of a Legislature.

The members of the State Council are endowed by the President of the Republic.

The members of the State Council listed above remain in office for as long as their term in their respective office lasts.

The members of the State Council appointed by the President of the Republic and elected by Parliament remain in office until the endowment of their substitutes.

It is the duty of the State Council to produce its own manifest.

The meetings of the State Council are not made public and remain in judicial secrecy amid its members, under penalty of compulsory exoneration and criminal prosecution by the adequate court of law.

It is the duty of the State Council to:

— Deliberate upon the dissolution of Parliament;

— Deliberate upon the exoneration of Central Government, in accordance with the fundamental law;

— Deliberate upon the acts of the interim President of the Republic, in accordance with the fundamental law;

— Deliberate upon any other events foreseen in the Constitution and, in general, advise the President of the Republic in the performance of their duties, when solicited by them.

The rulings of the State Council regarding both the dissolution of Parliament and presidential advisory are issued in the meeting summoned for said purpose by the President of the Republic and made public whenever the act to which they refer takes place.

Parliament

Parliament is the representative assembly of all national citizens, whether since birth or acquired citizenship.

Parliament is made of ten Deputies in representation of each ultimate administrative jurisdiction, such as a District[107] or a State, in constant and equal mathematical proportion, considering each half of said total number must feature both men and women, disregarding any absolute majorities foreseen for the representation of political parties.

Deputies are elected via lawfully defined geographic electoral circuits, which enables the determination of the existence of plurinominal circuits, as well as their respective nature and complementarity, in order to assure the proportional representation

---

[107] In the Portuguese case, there are eighteen districts, which means ten citizens representing each district with constitute a minimum of 180 Deputies in office, which is also the minimum foreseen in the Constitution of the Portuguese Republic for the election of the Deputies of the Assembly of the Republic.

system.

All electing citizens are eligible, safe under the restrictions of electoral law, due to either local incompatibility or performance of certain duties.

Candidacies are presented, in accordance with the law, by each ultimate administrative jurisdiction.

No one may run for office on behalf of either two or more electoral circuits, or be a part of either two or more manifests.

Deputies not only represent the circuits through which they are elected, but also and most importantly, the nation.

A Deputy's term commences with the first meeting of Parliament after the election and ceases with the first meeting after the following election, despite individual suspension or termination of term.

A Deputy's term may only be renewed once when consecutive, after which they may only run again for office when a full Legislature has passed since the end of the second consecutive term they were elected for, safe when running on behalf of a different electoral circuit, to the maximum extent of three.

When a Deputy has run for office on behalf of three different electoral circuits consecutively, they may only run again when another Legislature under which they have not taken office has ended.

The filling of vacancies taking place in Parliament, as well as the temporary replacement of Deputies under relevant motives, are defined by electoral law.

Deputies appointed as members of Central Government cannot proceed with their term until they have said Government, being replaced under the regulations above-mentioned in the previous paragraph.

Any other incompatibilities are regulated by the law.

The cases and conditions under which Deputies require parliamentary authorization to become judges of any sort, specialists or witnesses are regulated by the law.

Deputies freely perform their duties as such, having been warrantied adequate conditions for the performance of said duties, namely the indispensable contact with electing citizens and their regular information.

The law regulates the conditions under which the absence of Deputies, due to either meeting of or mission for Parliament, as far as official acts or diligences are concerned, is considered a justifying reason to postpone them.

Public entities have the duty to cooperate with Deputies in the performance of their own duties, under the law.

Deputies have the power to:

— Introduce projects of constitutional revising;

— Introduce law, Regiment or resolution proposals, namely referendums, as well as deliberative proposals, therefore requiring their respective scheduling;

— Participate and intervene in parliamentary debates, under Regiment regulations;

— Question Central Government about any of their acts or the Public Administration's, obtaining an answer within a reasonable deadline, safe under the dispositions of State secrecy;

— Require and obtain from Government or bodies of any public entity the elements, information and official publications they may consider useful to the performance of their duties;

— Demand the forming of inquiry parliamentary committees.

Deputies do not answer either civilly, criminally or disciplinarily for votes cast or opinions issued under the performance of their duties.

Deputies cannot be heard as either declarants or defendants without permission from Parliament, though such permission is mandatory when there is strong evidence of a felonious kind of crime whose maximum penalty surpasses a three-year sentence in prison.

No Deputy may be detained or placed under arrest without parliamentary authorization, safe for a felonious kind of crime matching the above-mentioned judicial sentencing conditions, especially when caught red-handed.

Should any criminal lawsuit be placed against a Deputy, and should they undeniably be prosecuted, Parliament reserves the right to decide whether said Deputy is to either be suspended or not, though suspension is mandatory when the crime or crimes in question are foreseen under the conditions of the previous paragraphs.

Deputies are entitled to the following rights and privileges:

— Postponing of civic service or mobilization;
— Free crossing and special passport for their official travels abroad;
— Special identification card;
— Subsidies foreseen by the law.

Deputies are obligated to the following duties:

— Be present at both plenary and committee meetings to which they may belong to;
— Perform their own duties in Parliament and any others they are appointed to, under proposal of their respective Parliamentary Groups;
— Participate in voting, when these take place.

Deputies face loss of office if and/or when:

— They are left wounded due to any incapability or incompatibility foreseen by the law;

— Do not take their seat in Parliament or overcome the allowed maximum number of absences regulated by the Regiment;

— Then enlist in an electoral circuit different from that through which they were elected;

— They are judicially prosecuted for either disobedience crimes under the performance of their duties or take part in inequality or fascist organizations.

Deputies may renounce to office via a written declaration.
It is the duty of Parliament to:

— Approve amendments to the Constitution under fundamental law;

— Produce laws concerning all matters, safe for those the Central Government is responsible for, under fundamental law;

— Confer legislative authorization to Central Government;

— Concede amnesty and generic pardons;

— Approve laws of greater options for national planning and the State Budget, under governmental proposal;

— Authorize Central Government to borrow and concede loans and complete other credit transactions unrelated to floating debt[108], therefore defining the respective general conditions and setting the maximum limit of avails conceded each year by Central Government;

— Approve treaties, namely those concerning the country's participation in international bodies, treaties of friendship and border rectification, as well as international agreements for which Parliament is competent enough to make decisions or that Central Government chooses to share;

— Propose the President of the Republic the referendum of relevant national interest matters;

---

[108] Short-term repayable debt.

— Authorize and confirm the declaration of a state of siege or of a state of emergency;

— Pronounce itself, under the appropriate legal terms, on matters pending decision regarding continental union which may be a part of its legislative competence;

— Undertake any other duties attributed by both the Constitution and the law.

It is of Parliament's competence, under its monitoring duties, to:

— Surveil the enforcement of both the Constitution and the law, as well as assess the acts of Government and the Administration;

— Assess the application of the declaration of a state of siege or a state of emergency;

— Assess, for the purpose of ceasing effectiveness or changing, law-decrees, safe those of exclusive Central Government competence;

— Assess execution reports related to national planning.

It is of Parliament's competence, with respect to other bodies, to:

— Witness the endowment of the President of the Republic;

— Confirm the absence of the President of the Republic from national territory;

— Promote the prosecution lawsuit against the President of the Republic for crimes committed during the performance of their duties and decide upon the suspension of members of Government, under law-regulated terms;

— Assess the Government Program;

— Vote for either confidence or no confidence with respect to

Central Government;

— Assess and standby, under law-regulated terms, the participation of the country in the construction process of the respective continental union;

— Elect, according to the proportional representation system, five members of State Council and the members of the Superior Council of the Public Prosecutor's Office it is entitled to appoint;

— Elect, out of a majority of two-thirds of the Deputies present, as long as superior to the absolute majority of Deputies in office, the Ombudsman, the President of the Socioeconomic Council, seven members of the Superior Council of Magistracy, the members of the Communications Commission and of other constitutional bodies which, under law-regulated terms, are for Parliament to appoint.

It is of Parliament's exclusive competence to legislate the following matters:

— Election of bodies of sovereignty bearers;
— Referendum regimes;
— Organization, execution and processing of the Constitutional Court;
— State of siege and state of emergency regimes;
— Acquisition, loss and reacquisition of national citizenship;
— Definition of limits for national waters, exclusive economic zone and the country's rights to contiguous maritime funding;
— Associations and other entities of public interest;
— Election of local power bodies bearers or any other under direct and universal suffrage, as well as the remainder of those bearing constitutional bodies;
— Statute of both local power bodies and bodies of sovereignty bearers, as well as either those of the remainder of constitutional bodies or elected under direct and universal suffrage;

— Generation, extinction and modification of local power jurisdictions and their respective regime;

— Appointment regime of the members of the respective continental union, apart from its commission;

— Both the Republic's intelligence system and State secrecy regimes;

— Elaboration and organization of State and local power jurisdiction budgets;

— The national symbols regime;

— The organizational, administrative and financial autonomy regime of the supporting services for the President of the Republic.

It is of Parliament's exclusive competence to legislate the following matters, safe Central Government authorization:

— State and ability of the people;

— Rights, freedoms and guarantees;

— Definition of crimes, sentences, safety measures and their respective purposes, as well as criminal lawsuits;

— General regime of disciplinary infraction sentencing, as well as illicit acts of mere social order and its respective lawsuit;

— General regime of requisition and expropriation by public utility;

— Bases of the social security and national health systems;

— Bases of the nature protection system, ecologic balance and cultural heritage;

— Constitution of taxes and their respective fiscal system, together with the general regime of other financial contributions in favor of public entities;

— Definition of means of production property sectors, including that of basic sectors to which private company activity may be restricted, along with other entities of the same domain;

— Means of intervention, expropriation, nationalization and privatization of the means and soils of production under public interest, as well as the fixation criteria of indemnities for said cases;

— The regime for both socioeconomic development plans and composition of the Socioeconomic Council;

— Bases of agricultural policy, including both maximum and minimum limitation of agricultural activity units;

— Organization and competence of courts of law and the General Prosecutor's Office and its magistrates, along with non-jurisdictional entities of conflict constitution;

— Statute of local power jurisdiction, including the local finance regime;

— Participation of residential organizations in the performance of local power;

— Public associations, guarantees of the administered and civil responsibility of the Administration;

— Bases of the regime of state workers;

— General bases of the statute for public companies and foundations;

— Definition and regime of public domain assets;

— Regime of means of production embedded in the social and cooperative property sector;

— Bases of territorial administration and urbanism.

The laws of legislative permission must define the subject, meaning, extension and duration of said permission, which may be prolonged.

Permissions lapse with either Central Government dismissal or resignation, the end of the Legislature or the dissolution of Parliament.

Both law and referendum initiatives lay with the Deputies, Parliamentary Groups and Central Government, together with, under law-regulated terms and conditions, electing citizen groups.

Deputies, Parliamentary Groups and electing citizen groups may introduce neither law projects, referendum projects nor changing propositions which may involve, for the economic year of the time, either increasing expenditures or decreasing State profits foreseen in the State Budget.

Neither law nor referendum projects ultimately rejected may be renewed during the same legislative session, safe for a new parliamentary election.

Neither law projects, Central Government law projects nor referendum projects not voted in the same legislative session they were introduced in require renewal in the following legislative session, safe for lapse of Legislature.

Both law and referendum projects lapse with the Central Government's dismissal or resignation.

Parliamentary committees may introduce replacement texts, with no harm to either law or referendum projects they refer to, when unwithdrawn.

Discussion of law projects comprehends both a generality and a specialty debate.

Voting is subdivided into three stages: generality, specialty and final global voting.

Should Parliament thusly agree, generality-approved texts are voted by specialty committees, with no harm to the final voting for global approval of Parliament.

Fundamental law requires approval, in the final global voting, from the absolute majority of Deputies in office.

Law-decrees, safe for those approved under exclusive Central Government competence, may be submitted to parliamentary assessment, whether for lapsing of effectiveness or change, by requisition of one Parliamentary Group, in the thirty days following their respective publication, disregarding Parliament's activity suspension intervals.

Should the assessment of a law-decree elaborated under legislative authorization in use be required, and should change proposals be introduced, Parliament has the ability to suspend, either fully or partially, the effectiveness of said law-decree until the publication of the law changing it or the rejection of all proposals referring to it.

Suspension lapses after ten plenary meetings in which Parliament has not reached an agreement.

Should the lapsing of effectiveness be approved, the bill shall be disregarded starting on the day the resolution is published in the Diary of the Republic, disabling the possibility of republishing during the same legislative session.

If, should an assessment be required, Parliament has not come to an agreement or, having approved amendments, has not voted a bill by the end of the legislative session of the time, as long as there have been fifteen plenary meetings, the process will lapse.

According to the terms of Regiment, the procedures of parliamentary assessment of law-decrees are a priority.

A Legislature lasts four consecutive legislative sessions.

In the case of dissolution, newly-elected Parliament begins a new Legislature, whose duration will initially be compensated with enough time to complete the respective duration of the legislative session in course until the day of the election.

Parliament can be dissolved neither in the six months following its election, nor in the last semester of the President of the Republic's term, nor while a state of siege or a state of emergency is made effective.

Should the previous paragraph be disregarded, the dissolution will not possess juridical existence.

The dissolution of Parliament does not harm the subsistence

of either the term of Deputies or the term of its Permanent Committee, until the first meeting of Parliament after the subsequent election.

Parliament meets under its own accord on the third day after the results of the general election have been duly counted or, in the case of election due to lapse of Legislature, whose day may have been set before said Legislature came to an end, on the first day of the subsequent Legislature.

The legislative session lasts a year.

Parliament may be extraordinarily summoned by the President of the Republic to take care of predetermined matters.

Committees may perform their duties regardless of the inactive session of Plenary, according to its decision.

It is of Parliament's competence to:

— Elaborate and approve its Regiment, under the Constitution;

— Elect out of absolute majority of Deputies in office its President and the remainder of the Members of Bureau.

— Compose the Permanent Committee and the remainder of committees.

Ministers have the right of presence in parliamentary plenary meetings, with the possibility of being assisted or replaced by the Secretaries of State, considering they all may speak, according to the Regiment.

Meetings shall be scheduled in which members of Central Government need to be present to answer either questions or clarification requirements from Deputies, whose agenda is fixed at a minimum frequency in the Regiment and when in accordance with Central Government.

Members of Central Government may solicit their participation in the duties of committees and have the obligation of presence when required.

Parliament has its committees foreseen in the Regiment and may compose other inquiry committees for another predetermined purpose.

The composition of committees matches the representability of ultimate administrative jurisdictions in Parliament.

Petitions addressed to Parliament are assessed by the committees or by a committee specially composed for that purpose, which may hear the remainder of committees reasonably competent in the matter though, in both cases, any citizen's testimonial may be solicited.

With no harm to their composing in general, Parliamentary Inquiry Committees are mandatorily made, whenever required, of one-fifth of Deputies in office, to the maximum limit of one committee per Deputy and legislative session.

Parliamentary Inquiry Committees have the right to means of investigation pertaining to judicial authority.

The presidencies of committees are in their whole split across Parliamentary Groups proportionally to the number of their Deputies.

The Permanent Committee of Parliament performs its duties during Parliament holidays, its dissolution and any other events foreseen in the Constitution.

The Permanent Committee is presided by the President of Parliament and made of their Vice-Presidents, together with the Deputies appointed by each Parliamentary Group.

It is the Permanent Committee's duty to:

— Enforce both the Constitution and the law and follow both

the Central Government's and Administration activities;

— Execute the powers of Parliament as far as the Deputies' term is concerned;

— Promote the summoning of Parliament whenever necessary;

— Prepare the opening of the legislative session;

— Provide its avail to the absence of the President of the Republic from national territory;

— Authorize the President of the Republic to declare either a state of siege or a state of emergency, in which case, the Permanent Committee shall promote the summoning of Parliament as soon as possible.

Deputies elected for each ultimate administrative jurisdiction are part of a Parliamentary Group.

Each Parliamentary Group has the right to:

— Participate in the committees of Parliament, appointing for such purpose their respective representatives;

— Be heard as far as its proposal for the daily agenda is concerned, as well as interpose an appeal to Plenary regarding said daily agenda;

— Promote, together with the presence of Central Government, the debate of current and urgent public interest matters;

— Promote, by prompting Central Government, the introduction of two debates in each legislative session on either general or sectorial politics;

— Solicit from the Permanent Committee the summoning of Parliament;

— Require the constitution of Parliamentary Inquiry Committees;

— Execute a legislative initiative;

— Introduce no confidence motions with respect to the program of Central Government;

— Introduce no confidence motions with respect to Central Government itself;

— Become informed, both regularly and directly, by Central Government, about the main issues of public interest.

Each Parliamentary Group has the right to recur to the usage of workplaces within Parliament Headquarters, as well as both technical and administrative staff of its trust, under law-regulated terms.

The duties of both Parliament and its Committees shall be assisted by a body of both technical and administrative staff, as well as either required or temporarily hired specialists, in a number the President of Parliament finds suitable.

Central Government

Central Government is the ultimate body of general politics in the country and the superior body of Public Administration.

Central Government is made of the Prime-Minister, their Ministers and their respective Secretaries and Deputy Secretaries of State.

Central Government may include one Deputy Prime-Minister.

The number, designation and attributes of ministries and secretariats of State, as well as the means of coordination between them, shall be determined, according to each case, by the decrees of appointment of their respective heads or by law-decree.

The winning candidate of the general election for Deputies of Parliament who is invited by the President of the Republic to constitute Central Government and become its Prime-Minister may choose, under law-regulated terms, the ministries and secretariats of State which shall be a part of said Central Government, depending on the President of the Republic's approval, notwithstanding the following ministries and secretariats of State should be considered a part of the again said Central Government and Public Administration of the nation:

— Ministry of the Presidency of the Republic;
— Secretariat of State of Constitutionality and Democratization.

— Ministry of State and Parliamentary Affairs;
— Secretariat of State of the Presidency of the Ministers' Council;
— Secretariat of State of Central Government Legislation.

— Ministry of Foreign Affairs and Policy;
— Secretariat of State of Continental Union Affairs;
— Secretariat of State of National Communities Abroad;
— Secretariat of State of Citizenship;
— Secretariat of State of Internationalization;
— Secretariat of State for the World Citizen.

— Ministry of Economy and Finance;
— Secretariat of State of the National Treasury;
— Secretariat of State of Tax Affairs;
— Secretariat of State of the State Budget;
— Secretariat of State of Public Administration;
— Secretariat of Public Investment;
— Secretariat of State of Trade.

— Ministry of Social Protection and Security;
— Secretariat of State of Social Security;

— Secretariat of State of Social Protection;
— Secretariat of State for the Inclusion of the Disabled.

— Ministry of Justice, Social Order and Reintegration;
— Secretariat of State of Justice;
— Secretariat of State of Social Order;
— Secretariat of State of Civil Rights and Equality;
— Secretariat of State of Presidential Pardoning and Rehabilitation.

— Ministry of Internal Administration;
— Secretariat of State of Administrative Reformation;
— Secretariat of State of Bureaucratic Simplification;
— Secretariat of State of e-Governance.

— Ministry of Planning and Infrastructures;
— Secretariat of State of Regional Development;
— Secretariat of State of Urban Planning;
— Secretariat of State of Transportation.
— Ministry of Health and Transhumanization;
— Secretariat of State of Public Health and Immunization;
— Secretariat of State of Hospital Administration and Reformation;
— Secretariat of State for the Rights of the Terminally Ill;
— Secretariat of State of Health Innovation;
— Secretariat of State of Longevity and Transhumanization.

— Ministry of Futurization, Science and Space Exploration;
— Secretariat of State of Technological Advancement;
— Secretariat of State of Research and Scientific Development;
— Secretariat of State of Robotics;

— Secretariat of State of Space Exploration;
— Secretariat of State for Terraforming.

— Ministry of Education;
  — Secretariat of State for Elementary and Junior Education;
  — Secretariat of State for High Education;
  — Secretariat of State for Higher and Advanced Education.

— Ministry for the Arts, Culture, Heritage and Sport;
  — Secretariat of State for the Arts;
  — Secretariat of State of Cultural Public Services;
  — Secretariat of State of Cultural Funding;
  — Secretariat of State for the Rights of the Artist;
  — Secretariat of State of Sport;
  — Secretariat of State of Tourism.

— Ministry of Biodiversity, the Environment and Natural Resources;
  — Secretariat of State of Clean Energy;
  — Secretariat of State for Depolluting;
  — Secretariat of State of Natural Resources;
  — Secretariat of State for the Rights of Animals;
  — Secretariat of State of Fauna and Flora Conservation and Protection.

The Ministers' Council is made of the Prime-Minister, the Deputy Prime-Minister, should there exist one, and the Ministers.

The law may create Ministers' Councils reasonably specialized in certain affairs.

The Secretaries and Deputy Secretaries of State may be summoned to participate in the meetings of the Ministers' Council.

In the event of the inexistence of a Deputy Prime-Minister, the Prime-Minister is temporary replaced in the performance of their duties due to either absence or inability by the Minister they recommend the President of the Republic or, should said recommendation be lacking, the Minister appointed by the President of the Republic.

Each Minister shall be replaced during their absence or inability by the Secretary of State they recommend to the Prime-Minister or, should said recommendation be lacking, the member of Central Government appointed by the Prime-Minister.

The duties of the Prime-Minister begin with their endowment and cease with their exoneration by the President of the Republic.

The duties of the remaining members of Central Government begin with their endowment and cease with either their or the Prime-Ministers' exoneration.

The duties of the Secretaries and Deputy Secretaries of State cease with the exoneration of their respective Minister.

In the event of the Central Government's dismissal, the Prime-Minister of the dismissed Central Government is exonerated after the endowment of the new Prime-Minister.

Before the assessment of its program takes place by Parliament, or after its dismissal, Central Government shall only take necessary action in the management of public affairs.

The Prime-Minister is appointed by the President of the Republic, considering the electoral results.

The remaining members of Central Government are appointed by the President of the Republic, under recommendation from the Prime-Minister.

The Central Government's program shall comprise the main political guidelines and measures to be adopted or proposed as far as the multiple governmental activity domains are concerned.

Members of Central Government are bound to the Central Government's program, together with any decisions made within the Ministers' Council.

The Central Government's program is assessed by Parliament via a declaration from the Prime-Minister, to a maximum extent of ten days from their endowment.

Should Parliament be in recess, it shall mandatorily be summoned by its President.

The debate cannot exceed three days and, until its closure, any Parliamentary Group may propose the rejection of the program, as well as Central Government may solicit the approval of a confidence vote.

The rejection of the Central Government's program requires absolute majority from all Deputies in office.

Central Government may solicit from Parliament the approval of a confidence vote on a declaration of either general policy or any other issue relevant to national interest.

Parliament may cast a no confidence vote against Central Government on the execution of its program or any other issue that is relevant to national interest, on behalf of either one-fourth of Deputies in office or any Parliamentary Group.

No confidence votes may only be assessed after forty-eight hours have passed since their introduction, being debated during no longer than three days.

Should the no confidence vote be rejected, their signatories cannot introduce any other in the same legislative session.

Central Government answers to both the President of the Republic and Parliament.

The Prime-Minister answers to the President of the Republic and, on behalf of Central Government's political responsibility, to Parliament.

Both the Deputy Prime-Minister and Ministers answer to the Prime-Minister and, on behalf of Central Government's political responsibility, to Parliament.

Both the Secretaries and Deputy Secretaries of State answer to the Prime-Minister and their respective Minister.

The dismissal of Central Government takes place under the following circumstances:

— The beginning of a new Legislature;
— The acceptance of the Prime-Minister's letter of resignation by the President of the Republic;
— The death or lasting physical inability of the Prime-Minister;
— The rejection of the Central Government's program;
— The rejection of a confidence vote;
— The approval of a no confidence vote by the absolute majority of Deputies in office.

The President of the Republic may only dismiss Central Government when necessary in order to assure the regular performance of democratic bodies, after hearing the State Council.

No Member of Central Government may be detained or placed under arrest without parliamentary authorization, safe for a felonious kind of crime whose maximum penalty surpasses a three-year sentence in prison, especially when caught red-handed.

Should any criminal lawsuit be placed against any Member of Government, and should they undeniably be prosecuted, Parliament reserves the right to decide whether said Member of Government is to either be suspended or not, though suspension is mandatory when the crime or crimes in question are foreseen under the conditions of the previous paragraph.

It is of the Central Government's competence, in the performance of political duties, to:

— Negotiate and adjust international conventions;
— Approve of international accords whose enactment does not rely on the competence of Parliament or has not been introduced to its assessment;
— Introduce law and resolution proposals to Parliament;
— Introduce referendum propositions to the President of the Republic regarding issues of national interest that do not conflict with the fundamental law;
— Pronounce itself on the declaration of a state of siege or a state of emergency;
— Introduce to Parliament the State's expenses and other public entities under law-regulated terms;
— Execute any other acts whose responsibility lies with it, under the terms of either the Constitution or the law.

The approval of international accords by Central Government is effective in the form of a decree.

It is of Central Government's competence, in the performance of legislative duties, to:

— Create law-decrees on matters that do not depend on Parliament's assessment or approval;
— Create law-decrees on matters depending on Parliament's approval;
— Create law-decrees regarding the development of either principles or general bases of juridical regimes within the laws on

which they depend.

It is of Central Government's exclusive legislative competence all matters pertaining to its own organization and performance.

It is of Central Government's competence, in the performance of administrative duties, to:

— Elaborate plans, based on the laws of the respective greater options, and execute them;
— Enforce the State Budget;
— Produce the necessary regulations to the good execution of laws;
— Direct both the services and activity of the State's direct administration, superintend the indirect administration and guard both them and the autonomous administration;
— Execute all acts required by law with respect to workers and agents of the State and other public legal persons;
— Defend democratic legality;
— Execute all acts and take all necessary measures to the promotion of socioeconomic development and the satisfaction of plurality needs.

It is of the Ministers' Council competence to:

— Define the generality of governmental policy, as well as its execution;
— Ponder upon the request of confidence from Parliament;
— Approve both law and resolution proposals;
— Approve law-decrees, as well as international accords that have not been introduced to Parliament;
— Approve planning;

— Approve acts of Central Government that may involve either increase or decrease of either public income or expenditure;

— Ponder upon other issues of Central Government's competence attributed by law or introduced by the Prime-Minister or any other Minister.

Specialized Ministers' Councils execute whichever competence they see attributed to them by either the law or the Ministers' Council.

It is of the Prime-Minister's competence to:

— Direct Central Government's general policy, coordinating and guiding the action of all Ministers;

— Direct the performance of Central Government and its general relations toward the remainder of State bodies;

— Inform the President of the Republic of matters concerning the directing of both internal and foreign policies of the country;

— Execute whichever duties conferred to them by either the Constitution or the law.

It is of the Ministers' competence to:

— Execute the policies defined for their Ministries;

— Assure the general relations between Central Government and the remainder of State bodies, within their respective Ministries.

Law-decrees and other decrees from Central Government are signed by the Prime-Minister and the Ministers reasonably competent in the subject.

Constitutional Court

The Constitutional Court is the tribunal with specific competence to administrate justice in matters of a juridical-constitutional nature.

The Constitutional Court is made of thirteen judges, considering:

— Seven jurors of exceptional merit are appointed by the President of the Republic;

— Six judges or public magistrates of exceptional merit are appointed by the Superior Council of Magistracy.

All appointments made must be approved by the absolute majority of Deputies in office in the Plenary of Parliament.

The term of Constitutional Court judges is nine years in length and not renewable.

The President of the Constitutional Court is elected by its judges.

The judges of the Constitutional Court have the right to a guarantee of independence, immovability, impartiality and irresponsibility and are subject to the incompatibilities of the judges of the remainder of courts of law.

The law regulates the immunities and other norms with respect to the statute of judge of the Constitutional Court.

It is of the Constitutional Court's competence to assess both unconstitutionality and illegality.

It is also of the Constitutional Court's competence to:

— Verify the death and declare the permanent physical impossibility of the President of the Republic, as well as verify the temporary impediments in the performance of their duties;

— Verify the loss of office of the President of the Republic;

— Ultimately judge the regularity and validity of acts of electoral process, under law-regulated terms;

— Verify the death and declare the inability in the performance of presidential duties of any candidate running for President of the Republic;

— Verify the legality of the constitution of politically active groups and their coalitions, as well as assess the legality of their designations, abbreviations and symbols, and order their respective extinction, under the terms of both the Constitution and the law;

— Preventively verify both the constitutionality and legality of national, regional and local referendums, including the assessment of requisites relating to the respective electoral college;

— Judge, by requisition of its Deputies, under law-regulated terms, the appeals relating to both the loss of office and the elections taking place in Parliament;

— Judge the events of impugnation of elections and decisions made by organisms of politically active groups that, under law-regulated terms, may be appealed.

It still is of the Constitutional Court's competence to perform all other duties attributed to it by both the Constitution and the law.

The law sets the rules regarding the headquarters, organization and performance of the Constitutional Court.

The law may determine the performance of the Constitutional Court by sections, safe for abstract prudential oversight of constitutionality and legality.

The law defines the appeal to the plenary of the Constitutional Court of contradictory decisions of sections within the application of the same rule.

Local Government

The democratic organization of the State comprehends the existence of local administrative jurisdictions.

Local administrative jurisdictions are territorial legal persons gifted with representative bodies, whose duty is to pursue the interests of their respective people.

Local administrative jurisdictions are made of Civil Parishes and Municipalities and/or Districts and/or Counties.

In the great metropolitan areas, the law may set, according to their specific conditions, other forms of local administrative territorial organization.

The administrative division of territory shall be regulated by law.

Both the attributions and organization of local administrative jurisdictions, as well as the competence of their bodies, shall be regulated by law, in a harmonious relationship with the principle of administrative decentralization.

It is of the local administrative jurisdiction assembly's competence to perform all powers attributed by law, including the approval of planning options and budget.

Local polices cooperate with each other in the safekeeping of public order and local community protection.

Local administrative jurisdictions possess heritage and finance of their own.

The local finance regime shall be regulated by law and enforce the fair sharing of public resources between State and local administrative jurisdictions, together with the necessary correction of inequality between local administrative jurisdiction of the same category.

Local administrative jurisdictions' own income mandatorily comprehends profit gained from both the management of their heritage and the usage of their services.

The organization of local administrative jurisdictions comprehends an elected assembly gifted with decisive powers and a collegial executive body answering to it.

The assembly is elected under direct, secret and universal suffrage of the citizens registered in the correspondent local administrative jurisdiction, according to proportional representation system.

The collegial executive body is made of an adequate number of members, considering the appointed president is the first candidate of the most voted list for either assembly or executive body, according to the solution regulated by law, which shall also regulate the electoral procedures, the requirements of its constitution and dismissal and its performance.

Candidacies for the election of local administrative bodies are presented by politically active groups, either separately or in coalition, or groups of electing citizens, under law-regulated terms.

Local administrative jurisdictions may submit to the referendum of their respective electing citizens matters that are included in the competence of their bodies, under law-regulated terms and effectiveness.

The law attributes to electing citizens the right to a referendum initiative.

Local administrative jurisdictions have a regulating power of their own foreseen in the limits of the Constitution, the law and the regulations enacted by either local administrative jurisdictions of a superior degree or authorities with administrative supervision power.

Administrative supervision over local administrative jurisdictions consists in the verifying of law enforcement on behalf of local administrative bodies and is implemented according to terms foreseen by law.

Supervising measures that are restrictive of local autonomy are preceded by a decision of a local administrative body, under law-regulated terms.

The dissolution of local administrative bodies may only take place because of gravely illegal events or omissions.

Local administrative jurisdictions have staff of their own, under law-regulated terms.

The regime of both workers and agents of the State is applicable to both workers and agents of local administration, with the necessary adaptations, under law-regulated terms.

The law defines the measures of both technical and human support from the State to local administrative jurisdictions, with no harm to their autonomy.

The representative bodies of a Parish are the Parish Assembly and the Civil Parish.

The Parish Assembly is the deliberating body of the Parish.

The law may determine that a Parish Assembly of poorly populated Parishes be replaced by a plenary of electing citizens.

A Civil Parish is the collegial executive body of the Parish.

Parishes may create, under law-regulated terms, associations for the administration of common interests.

The Parish Assembly may delegate to resident organizations administrating tasks that do not involve the performance of authority powers.

The creation or extinction of Municipalities or Districts, as well as the changing in their respective area, is made according to the law, preceding the testimonial of the local administrative jurisdiction bodies concerned.

The representative bodies of the Municipality or District are both the Town and City Halls.

Town Hall is the deliberative body of the Municipality or District and is made of members directly elected in a superior number to that of the Presidents of Civil Parishes, who are a part of it.

City Hall is the collegial executive body of the Municipality or District.

Municipalities or Districts may create both associations and federations for the managing of common interests, to which the law may confer both attributes and competencies of their own.

Municipalities or Districts take part, under their own right and law-regulated terms, in profits resulting from direct taxes.

Municipalities or Districts possess tax income of their own, under law-regulated terms.

Administrative Region

Administrative Regions are created simultaneously, by law,

which defines their respective powers, composition, competence and performance of duties of their bodies, with the possibility of setting differences with respect to the regime applicable to each of them.

The concrete institution of Administrative Regions, approved by the law establishing each of them, depends on the law foreseen in the previous paragraph and the favorable vote expressed by the majority of electing citizens who have pronounced themselves via direct consultation, ranging nationally and concerning each regional area.

When the majority of participating electing citizens have not pronounced themselves favorably with respect to the question ranging nationally and regarding the concrete institution of administrative regions, the answers to questions that might have taken place concerning each region created by law will not become effective.

The consultations made to electing citizens foreseen in the two previous paragraphs shall take place under the terms and conditions set into fundamental law, by decision of the President of the Republic and proposition of Parliament, considering the necessary adaptations.

Administrative Regions are conferred, namely, the direction of public services, together with coordinating and supporting tasks as far as Municipalities or Districts are concerned, respecting both their autonomy and power.

Administrative Regions elaborate regional plans and take part in the elaboration of national plans.

The representative bodies of the Administrative Region are both the Regional Assembly and the Regional Board.

The Regional Assembly is the deliberating body of the region and is made of both directly elected members and members elected via the proportional representation system, though in a smaller number than the first, by the electoral college made of the members of the Town Halls that are part of the same area, appointed by direct election.

The Regional Board is the collegial executive body of the region.

There is the possibility of each region having a Central Government representative, appointed by the Ministers' Council, whose competence is performed likewise in the local administrative jurisdictions within the respective area.

Resident Organizations

In order to intensify the participation of the population in local administrative life, Resident Organizations may be created for an inferior area concerning the respective Parish.

The Parish Assembly, either of its own accord or under requirement of a resident committee or significant number of residents, shall establish the geographic limits to the territorial areas of the organizations mentioned in the previous paragraph, solving any possible resulting conflicts.

The structure of Resident Organizations is set by law and comprises both the Resident Assembly and the Resident Committee.

The Resident Assembly is made of electing residents registered with the Parish.

The Resident Committee is elected, under secret scrutiny, by the Resident Assembly, which has also the power to freely dissolve it.

Resident Organizations have the right to:

— Petition before local administrative jurisdictions with respect to administrative matters concerning the interest of their residents;
— Participate, without voting, in the Parish Assembly via their representatives.

It is of the Resident Organizations' competence to execute any tasks entrusted to them by law or delegated by the respective Parish.

e-Democracy

I apologize for the tone of the last few pages, as it was undeniably juridical. I did mention before this section started, with the description of the President of the Republic, that the Constitution of the Portuguese Republic was inspiring enough to set the bases of Democracy in any State. Again, it is very likely some people would think I am trying to make my grass greener, but the truth is Portugal is a country that remained under a dictatorship for nearly fifty years, hence the writing of a brand new Constitution that would completely erase that of 1933, which happens to be the same year Hitler rose to power in Germany, consolidating the democratic regime in the best possible manner.

Of course, and though this is the possible start for any Democracy now or in the future, comprising the ultimate regulating authority, the President of the Republic; a Parliament in which all citizens can be represented by their fellows, without the existence of political parties reserved only for their paying members and associates; the Prime-Minister, in charge of Central Government; and a Constitutional Court verifying the constitutionality of new laws before they are enacted, progress must be made in order to include all national citizens into deciding matters concerning themselves. That is where e-Democracy comes in.

It is my honest belief this is the next step we need to take, if we wish to value our life in society, toward the common goal of a sustainable civilization who can work together, as one, through peace between peoples and respect for each other, renouncing to the usual tyranny of those who feel they can decide how you live your life, from the casual stranger you meet on the street, to the representatives you freely elected to govern your country.

Across the last few pages, I never mentioned the liberty to form political parties. It is not that I am against their existence, only they undeniably make either a Republic or even a monarchy completely representative, instead of just by half. This means there are people willing to make a living out of governing either the country or even a small town *for* the remainder of citizens, who are thusly free to live their own lives, without worrying too much about political matters. The problem is easing other people's concerns this much confers politicians with enough freedom to make decisions that might not exactly be of their best interest, as hardly any politician will suffer from the consequences of austerity, usually stashing illegal fortunes in safe havens while in power, because most constitutions foresee term length limitations, though there are some enabling perpetual candidacy, and in democratic regimes, such as Germany, which is not restrictive with respect to the number of times the same person may run for Chancellor[109].

When a politician ceases their term in office, both political and diplomatic immunities also come to an end, which means that if there already is a chance said politician might be committing a crime during their term, it is harder to investigate without

---

[109] Equivalent to the role of a Prime-Minister or President of Government.

parliamentary authorization, in the case of a Deputy, a Member of Government or the President of the Republic, for instance. However, when there are no more legal impediments barring the investigation, many unknown facts begin to rise, having to do with financial crimes such as corruption or money laundering[110], eventually leading to the arrest of those directly involved, along with any other pawn connections, the first to be sacrificed for being easier targets, not knowing too much information that might compromise the leaders of the scam, who have their good name to stand up to.

This is why, to me, working the same job many years in a row with this kind of immunity jeopardizes the health of the democratic regime itself. Though perhaps unintentionally, the practice of Democracy slowly turns into tyranny and greed for power, with a side of impunity. Party leaders are always elected Deputies of Parliament. Each party has its own internal regulations and statutes, but there usually is no limitation to the time the same person spends leading it. They are constantly able to run, unless they publicly fail while in representation of the party's ideals, like being dismissed from Central Government or losing a general election, which results in the loss of respect from other party members, who will most assuredly demand their resignation and summon a new congress for the election of their successor.

But, supposing said leaders are politically able and educated, they can spend years in a row in front of the partisan machine without damaging their reputation to an extent they will have to obligatory step down. They choose who they want to run with. In obtaining the chance to govern, they pick who they want to lead with, and it does not have to be someone with connections

---

[110] The attempt to either demonstrate a person's or company's assets have a legal origin when they do not, or make it hard to prove said assets are indeed illegal, usually recurring to front companies to disperse criminal investigations.

to the party, not at all. Non-partisans are always welcome to be a part of Central Government, but in doing so, they just have to follow the guidelines of the Prime-Minister, who has the constitutional ability to dismiss them, in case of being contradicted by a subordinate.

As far as Deputies are concerned, when voting in Parliament, the head of the political committee for the party decides, together with the leader, whether the Parliamentary Group votes either in favor or against a determined matter, so as to either support or block a legislative attempt. Should there be a Deputy thinking otherwise with respect to the whole Group, it means they did not follow group discipline, and may therefore face expulsion from the party. And this is another way of cornering someone, disabling them from having free thought, though behind a democratic guise.

Let us build a pure Democracy, then, and for the future, by enabling all electing citizens to vote right from their homes, saving up on public budgets conveyed to logistic, allowing them also to produce legislative initiatives with the help of specialized jurors aware of the juridical terms that should be included in the phrasing of a law proposal. It is indeed utopic of me to idealize a political system carried out for the people, by the people, but there is no better place than this book to make that statement. Imagined by Sir Thomas More[111] as an imaginary location in the

---

[111] 1478-1535. Counselor to King Henry VIII of England, he was also an author, humanist, lawyer, philosopher and statesman. He is considered among Catholics to be a Saint, after being canonized by Pope Pius XI (1857-1939) in 1935, four hundred years after his execution by order of Henry for not recognizing, under the 1533 Act of Succession, Anne Boleyn as the legitimate Queen of England, thus designating the future Elizabeth I next in line to the throne, after Henry broke England's allegiance to the Vatican, in order to divorce his first wife, Catharine of Aragon. Because More died for the faith, he was made a martyr.

new world, an island, to be precise, *Utopia*[112] is a term coined by its author from Greek language.

It is obviously very hard to start over and I imagine that, because of human nature itself, leaving Earth toward an exoplanet with new social models and political regimes can become very troublesome, especially because it is very likely only the richest will be able to escape the globe when possibly facing destruction, either by consuming of the Sun when it becomes a red giant, in another five billion years, approximately, or another mass-extinction event like the one putting an end to the reign of dinosaurs[113], but I am not losing my faith in Humanity just yet. The tendency is without a doubt the ageing of world population, especially in Europe, with the increase of mortality rates and decline of birth rates, whose subtraction produces a negative population balance, as it is studied in Demography, a subsidiary branch of Geography.

Nonetheless, it is becoming all the more likely such predictions may be completely inverted, toward the progress of longevity via anti-ageing research and immortality, which is a subject we will explore together in the second part, after we are done tidying up our own place in this part. Remember, it is crucial we take care of our own home first, so we can enforce Science around the world second.

This means illiteracy, which unfortunately still is a fact in the present-day, will soon be cast into oblivion, making it unimaginable a person could never have learnt to read or write in their lifetime. Even today, a lot of elderly citizens from so-called «first world» countries are beginning to adhere to new technologies. A

---

[112] More's most renowned oeuvre, originally written in Latin, which was the scholar language in medieval Europe, celebrated through this very book. The term was adapted by him via the agglutination of οὐ (not) and τόπος (place), signifying an imaginary place, an inexistent society, though described in all detail.

[113] Vide notes 15 to 18.

computer or laptop is not a recent piece of technological advancement, and neither is a smartphone, already a part of our lives for nearly a decade, which is a lot in today's time references, but it is all new to them, because there simply was no access to these inventions back in the day, when they were at their prime. They simply did not exist and were yet to be created.

This kind of behavior from elderly folk just comes to prove anyone, regardless of age or instructional background, is available to understand how research and technology work, even if they are just looking to learn how to sign their own name on their national identification card for the first time.

The following is also a constitutional bill we need to abide by:

Everyone has the right to education, granted the right to equality of access opportunities and success.

It is of the State's responsibility, with respect to educational policy, to:

— Assure universal, mandatory and gratuitous education;
— Create a public system and develop the general preschool education system;
— Grant permanent education and *eliminate illiteracy*;
— Grant all citizens access to the most elevated degrees of education, scientific research and artistic production;
— Establish the gratuity of all education degrees;
— Insert schools in their serving communities and set the relationship between education and economic, social and cultural activities;
— Promote and support access from disabled citizens to education and support special education needs;
— Protect and value Sign Language as a cultural expression and access tool to education and opportunity equality;

— Assure both the teaching of the national language and access to national culture to the children of emigrants;

— Assure adequate support to the right to education to the children of immigrants.

Once instruction has reached all of us, we may then proceed to the subsequent democratization of the entire State. I have always said information was a much more prized treasure than gold or oil. We should not have the ambition to become tycoons of neither material, but we should be proud of developing our intelligence. A society that is educated and informed can make better decisions toward its best, common interest, with no harm to private life. I speak a lot of society and civilization. That is who this book is for, but I do not endorse Communism whatsoever. It is one thing to by force of law give everything you have to the State, so it can be used toward your own destruction, and another to share your riches toward civilizational welfare, instead of just making fortunes at the expense of a cheap workforce and stashing it all in offshore accounts, fleeing from tax obligations and setting up front entities that do not actually exist. Sharing with the purpose of common welfare is not Communism, but rather Socialism, which has nothing to do with the ideals of the Soviet Union or any other satellite country still imposing a similar regime to this day, such as China, North Korea or Cuba itself, despite the newly-celebrated reconnection with the United States after fifty years of political and trade embargoes.

It has to be the State's mission to produce a piracy-proof e-parliamentary system via which any citizen with an Internet-connected computer or cellphone may cast their vote either in favor or against new law-making, contradicting the summoning of a referendum only when fully representative politicians feel like it. The people has the right to be heard with respect to all matters concerning public life, as a country is made only of all its citizens, and not just a selected few.

Safely secured servers must be built in order to assure total prevention against foul play, disabling any chances candidacies, votes or law proposals are digitally erased from the system when there is someone who has something to lose from either their enactment or rejection. A background check must be enforced for all of those employed to build the system, unlockable only to nationals via their national identification card, digitally acknowledged through e-readers, just like the regular electronic passport, when you travel abroad, so there is not a chance of code breaches or hacks.

The law has to obligatory enforce the inclusion of safety software when acquiring new digital equipment, as it is the citizen's right to be protected when handling said equipment and introducing personal information, which must not be made visible to millions of other people online. Like I said before, the law must move with the times, it cannot remain unchanged for possibly just five years, let alone several centuries. With the further advancements in technology, it is the State's mission to regulate all aspects concerning the lives of its citizens, national or immigrant. For instance, before the year 2000, it was not mandatory for new automobiles to bear ABS[114]. It was a *luxurious* option. Most of the time it is that system that makes the difference between avoiding an accident, completely unharmed, and a fatal collision. Within the European Union, especially due to bureaucracy, all new automobiles should have eCall[115] technology installed by

---

[114] Anti-lock braking system, which prevents the wheels from locking in place, progressively bringing them to a full stop, rather than having them drag on the asphalt and increase the tires' exposure to a sudden burst due to overheating or treadwear detrition.

[115] First presented in 1999 as a European system independent from the American GPS and applicable across the entirety of the European Union, it is an electronic means of communication that is only activated in case of a severe accident, with the help of impact sensors (just like an airbag), automatically

now. However, privacy concerns from the European Commission have delayed the implementation of that system to as late as March 2018, especially due to the inclusion of a device similar to an aircraft's cockpit voice recorder, which might be activated without the occurrence of an accident, thus allowing eavesdropping.

Neither a form of Government nor any other kind of third-party have the right to pry into a citizen's personal life, otherwise they will mandatorily have to face discredit and, eventually, dismissal. Hence the need for included protection, in the case of automobiles, by and *from* eCall itself.

The danger of utilizing services provided by others has necessarily to do with the fact we do not know what sort of information is being acquired. Online exposure is something we all risk every day, whether through a cellphone, a tablet or a computer. Legislation cannot stay behind and not criminally regulate any possible violations via security breaches. Paying annually for the services of an antivirus is most of the time impractical, as the required subscription is absolutely overpriced. You can tell that from the same online safety company that might be selling a restrictive product which does not protect your device in full at, let us say, nearly one hundred dollars per year, one device only, selling, at the same time, another yearly subscription for just twenty dollars and license-unlimited, protecting all device components. The sad part is this kind of sale is not widespread, as only some are aware of it, especially if they are lucky enough to casually find out about it, exactly, online.

---

transmitting location and severity data to the nearest emergency agency through the European phone number of emergency, 112, which then dispatches the appropriate rescue means, even if the driver or any other occupant are unconscious. This project has already been delayed several times. It was supposed to have been featured in new automobiles beginning October 1st, 2015. Slovenia is the only Member-State where the system is currently active, as of December 1st, 2015.

When you buy a digital device, you are also buying the rights to use a genuine version of the preinstalled software, namely the operating system, whose updates you are entitled to across its lifecycle, may it be mainstream or extended support. So, perhaps it would be a good idea to make a onetime investment in a security software and keep it updated until an all-new version is released. Not just slightly tweaked, but a completely modernized build.

This way, all citizens can feel comfortable enough when performing their right to vote from their homes. It most assuredly keeps the entire process ecofriendly, without the need to print millions of sheets for traditional vote casting. And until home modernization is complete, eVoting must reach all available territories. There are still many developed countries where this does not take place through an electronic ballot inside the voting booth. It is a way of protecting the electoral procedure against foul play, but the investment in bolder protection must be made in order to prevent it. We cannot depend forever on deforestation to produce paper that is going to end up burnt.

Also, there might be a chance Parliament officials do not trust each other and demand vote recounting after an election over and over again, until a result pleasing them is found, which then leads to another recount request from the first winners, so as to secure their original appointment to Plenary.

Perhaps you may have noticed I mentioned not once any national defense mechanisms, especially when laying out constitutional phrasing across the several national sovereignty bodies. There is a reason for that. I do not condone the fact we should fight between ourselves. Envisioning a utopic environment, no matter how many oeuvres are written about it, always comprehends the inexistence of conflict between societies, thus uniting our civilization as one. If we constantly try to kill each other over economic and political interests, are we not making a statement on how worthless human life is? And all mostly because of black gold and terrorist group control.

This is why I do not foresee the need for a country to have any defenses whatsoever against other nations. The more you strike, the more you will be struck back, making war endless. Diplomacy was created for a reason, so there would not be a need for conflict. Should one exist between two or more nations, then work together toward peace, not the opposite, because sooner or later the defeated force will find another way of getting back at the ephemeral victors, recycling it all. I say again, progress cannot continue for as long as we turn our backs on each other, allowing warfare to speak for us. If we do need to possess a defense system, may it be against cosmological threats, such as asteroid or meteor showers which could jeopardize the very existence of, not only the human race, but also all other lifeforms on Earth.

3
Reign of the Plutocrats

One of the questions most people ask themselves with respect to the United States is, as an illustrative example, «who do we owe seventeen trillion dollars of Government debt to?».

In finance, a default takes place when an individual, a legal person or a country fails their obligation to pay their maturing loan. In contemporaneity, the US is one of the most powerful economies in the world, second only to China, to whom a great deal of debt is owed. It is not surprising the Chinese became the most productive people on Earth, as their country is also the most populous. The estimated total of human beings alive in the year 2015 was 7,256,490,011[116]. In full, that number is seven billion two hundred and fifty-six million four hundred ninety thousand and eleven. China alone registered 1,367,485,388[117], which is to say one billion three hundred and sixty-seven million four hundred and eighty-five thousand three hundred and eighty-eight people, achieving the total percentage of approximately 18.85%

---

[116] Further information: *Infoplease.com*, «World's 50 Most Populous Countries: 2015», (http://www.infoplease.com/world/statistics/most-populous-countries.html), accessed 05-14-2016.

[117] Ibid.

of the world's population.

China is curiously enough one of the countries the United States owes more money to, apart from itself, but it does not stop at America, and this is where I put another halt to using the same sovereign States as reference and generalize a bit more, without however running into a fallacy.

Many other territories across the globe owe China a great deal of money because countries' public debt is being acquired by the Chinese, who are progressively becoming the richest nation of all time, continuously capitalizing ironically enough in a Communist regime, as it is the only legalized party running Government ever since 1949, by the hand of Mao Zedong[118]. Indeed, there are eight other parties composing the United Front[119], but they are all controlled by the Communist Party of China (CPC). The nation's official designation is People's Republic of China, but everyone knows the people are frequently powerless in democratic regimes, let alone one allegedly working on behalf of all citizens.

And how come does China possess so many riches that they can buy other countries' debt? It is actually quite simple, and not necessarily new to most of the world. Populous States like the one we are talking about, where the one-child birth policy was

---

[118] 1893-1976. Also known as Chairman Mao for leading the CPC from 1949 to his death, he was the founder of the Chinese State as it stands today. His official portrait hangs on the façade of the iconic Tiananmen Monument, to the North of its homonymous square, in the capital city of Beijing, where in June 1989 several Chinese students raging between hundreds and thousands were brutally massacred, while about 10,000 others were arrested.

[119] Those entities are the Revolutionary Committee of the Kuomintang, the China Democratic League, the China Democratic National Construction Association, the China Association for Promoting Democracy, the Chinese Peasants' and Workers' Democratic Party, the China Party for Public Interest, the September 3 Society (the date refers to the Chinese victory in the Sino-Japanese War, close to the end of World War II in the Pacific theater of operations) and the Taiwan Democratic Self-Government League. Needless to say, when you try to show the international community you are *really* working toward Democracy via labeling, then there is definitely something to it.

enforced from the late 70s to 2015, having been changed in the meantime to a two-child birth policy, have obligatorily got to employ literally millions of people. Sometimes, where human rights are not shown their due respect, children who should be in school are also working.

The industrial sector is the most sought out by multinational companies, which conceive their product digitally at their headquarters, in self-proclaimed civilized and democratic countries, where they basically came to be, and then send said concepts to the factories producing them. A lot of items you and I both buy in our day-to-day life often reads either «Made in China» or «Made in Taiwan». The island of Taiwan is officially called Republic of China, making it a sovereign and separate State from the People's Republic of China, located in the Asian mainland, which means it does not answer to Beijing, after its loss in the 1949 Chinese Civil War. However, it is the «Made in China» label I want you to bear with, right now.

Although the above-mentioned multinational companies operate mostly in the Americas and Europe, having all those mouths to feed in China is a good excuse to set production bases in the country and employ a great deal of workers all at once. The problem is the terms under which workforces are hired. Most of them are enslaved. That is obviously an utter disrespect for Mankind itself.

Human rights are not supposed to be respected just because they are registered in some kind of a social contract printed on paper. In a just world, there would not be the need to criminalize slavery, because such a thing should never have crossed Humanity's mind in the first place. Perhaps I am indeed idealizing a world where we all live together with mythological creatures like unicorns, pixies and fairies, constantly surrounded by butterflies and happy faces. I am not expecting to play the role of a savior, redeeming my fellow human beings through reading. This does not stop me, however, from pointing out what is wrong. I have said it multiple times before all the way up to this point in my writing, and I will probably repeat it again further on. I wish to be very clear when I say all of us are bound to sin, and not in a religious way. What some people might take for a sin can be perfectly normal to others, regardless of faith or no faith at all. I know I have sinned before. One way or another, we all do. The irony to it is, when we think we are the most politically correct of people by trying to standardize others toward a common goal for our very sake as humans, we are violating the principle we do not wish to see disrespected as far as we are concerned, and that is free will.

If you will notice, so far I was careful enough to speak mostly on behalf of an institution, the State, an ideal one, and not on your behalf, as the Reader, or any other individual. Because that is not my place, to tell you what you should do. The best example to explain such an issue is religion. Suppose I make a public announcement claiming I do not believe in any kind of god, no matter the faith. As my solid conviction, I explain the reasons supporting it. It is not anyone else's place to convince me otherwise. A Christian will try to make me seek salvation at their church, based on the image of Jesus Christ and his teachings in the Bible. A Jew will take me to their synagogue and try to make me embrace the same kind of connection they have to Jehovah via the Torah. A Muslim will take me to a mosque and try to assure me of the peace the Koran actually preaches, instead of war, let alone in the name of Allah. Please excuse me for just naming these three faiths. I know they all have the same origin, but I am trying not to pick a side of the scale, here. I am more for balance. In short, what we do is try to bring others to an agreement with ourselves. Everyone knows that is not how opinions are respected. Cultural connections such as these are supposed to bring people together with respect to understanding what drives each and every one of us every day. It does not mean we should superimpose our beliefs unto others. I respect Christianity, Judaism, Islam and all other faiths, but do *not* force me to accepting your principles. It is the human principle we must all respect as universal, and not the teachings of a religion, especially when run by men, like us, with their own, personal interests.

Multinationals often claim they have nothing to do with either the hiring process or the working conditions of the laborers working for them in underdeveloped countries. Technically, they are right, because all they do is rent the factories in question and transfer money to the paymasters, proprietors of said factories, who then decide what to make of their employees. It is when the ugly truth about said working conditions arises amid the international community and they maintain their contracts with the factories that they face the beginning of their downfall, having to remain under the radar until the mob forgets about it.

As long as people need to work in order to be fed, which is no more than an acquired right at birth, eating, they will do anything they can to see that supposedly acquired right may be bought. And it is not just about the food. Water is essential to life. Without water, we would not be here today. Our bodies are made of water, about seventy percent. If we fail to hydrate our bodies, we perish. Yet, there are companies which, for some reason, appropriate themselves of sources of water in the mountains, where rivers flow fresh. They set up their bases of operations. They filtrate the water, clean it and make it safely drinkable, bottling it in either plastic or glass. Then, they sell it. There are places in the world, even though «civilized», where tap water is too calcified and dirty to be drunk. One of the best alternatives to this situation is to get bottled water. And paid for. So, here is how it all works: if you cannot drink water, you die, because your body *is* made of water and needs some more so you do not dehydrate.

You are already paying unimaginable enough taxes for basic sanitation and water supply, but none of it is treated correctly, so you cannot drink from your own faucet. What do you do to save yourself, then? You *buy* bottled water, helping a multimillionaire company profit from your right to live. It is true they have people to pay for their work cleansing the water, analyzing it and deeming it appropriate for consumption, together with all the recycled materials needed to bottle it, but the thing is they should not be bottling water in the first place. Paying others for a resource you are naturally entitled to is sickening. And if you ever face a drought like the one in California, five years running, you can be sure to be saved by another multinational company expropriating Indians from their natural reserve resources. The Wild West has not yet come to an end, not at all.

If the need to eat and drink means people are willing to work inhumanly, then that is exactly what they will do, especially if they have family depending on them, looking to survive, even if it means laboring toward death from exhaustion. No irony there, make no mistake.

When it comes to this sort of abusers and traffickers as well, it is amazing how useful an illiterate person who happens to know how to sew well enough can do. It is what they cannot to, however, that matters the most. Education, which is, again, another right everyone is entitled to, when lacking, becomes the exploiter's best friend, and not just in China or any underdeveloped massively polluting country.

Picture a country above the geographical imaginary line separating developed countries from those underdeveloped, slightly above the equator, beginning with the border between Mexico and the US, all the way to the Mediterranean Sea, segregating Europe from Africa, to the difference between Russia and the remainder of Asia, Turkey included, reaching out to the Sea of Japan, finally descending in a peak in order to englobe Australia and New Zealand, in the Southern Hemisphere. You have a wide range of choice available.

Now, picture the environment of a supermarket. I do not mean to say supermarkets are bad for you. On the contrary, they are the only way we may all go to a place where we can find a concentration of the groceries we need to store in the kitchen cupboard. It is what it takes to have it all there neatly presented that is my concern, right now, just as much as having branded sneakers made by a Chinese workforce.

Supermarket chains are only of a local range at first, when they have just opened. The investment has got to be compensated with either profit from the facility itself or other businesses run by the managing group. It is pretty much of a small business in the beginning, but it soon comes to grow. People living in either urban or suburban centers will hardly possess any farms of their own to practice agriculture, let alone mixed farming with cattle at their care. That is why this new concept, which actually came to be in the first half of the 20th century, progressively turned into one of the best bets for the founders of the largest food supply chains, not just nationally, but worldwide, as many have already surpassed the borders they flourished in toward either neighboring countries or other territories on the opposite side of the globe, though that is somewhat a more complex concept called mall or department store, where all possible and imaginable shopping *departments* come together in one, single place. We should not, however, drift too far, for the time being.

When supermarket chains grow to the extent of having maybe four to five locations separated by about a mile each, it means they are undeniably predominant. Businesses are only this much successful at the expense of something, or someone, perhaps would be more appropriate – the workforce, the people with the hands-on approach, not the executives benefitting from partnership. The employees are the ones dealing with the public, running eight-hour shifts straight like they were physicians, only they certainly are not salaried as such. Some have the ability to sit down, some others are forced to stand all that time.

As the astute Reader you most assuredly are, you are definitely beginning to make a connection. China is not the only place where slavery takes place, and being a part of the underdeveloped side of the planisphere is not an excuse, whatsoever. The difference between that kind of situation and the greener side, where Democracy should have its rightful place, is that there are both legislative and social mechanisms that only stand behind workers to a predetermined extent, without actually providing good enough protection for them when they need it more than anything.

Not only working at a supermarket chain can be physically disruptive, it may also put an end to the perspective of a social life. It definitely will turn career progression into something completely obsolete, though it depends on where you begin. You might make it to cashier. Perhaps head of the cashiers. Maybe store manager. However, if you are restocking, there is a dead-end right in front of you, and there is nowhere to go. Positions such as these are precarious. World population is increasing every second. There is always someone willing to work that job, or even two at the same time, come to that, especially when, again, a family is involved and the bills start piling up on the kitchen table, between the leftovers from breadcrumbs. And if you claim for your right, as you are educated and have a degree, of not working holidays or Labor Day[120], which is exactly a day to celebrate workers' rights, you are unmistakably terminated. The best part is the wage: the minimum legally required, as the entrepreneurs building their empires do feel any sort of regret for democratically exploiting those who make them rich.

---

[120] Mostly celebrated on May 1st around the world, though it takes place on the first Monday of September in the US.

The law is, sadly, not universal, as we are taught and driven to believe. The law is corporate. It protects corporations, however it does not spare the common citizen, like you and I. A banker is able to flee the IRS several years in a row. When they are found out, they may be trialed, however given the chance toward the path to redemption by paying out the amount in taxes they should have paid regularly, like everybody else. They might be placed under house arrest or set free, acquitted from all charges. The working faction of society, however, when failing to comply with its payments to Government, is expropriated from its own home, the same they worked for their entire life, maybe across one or two mortgages.

None of this is new. We come across several kinds of politicians in our lifetime, the people who eventually gain control of our future as citizens to the country we either were born in or came to, because our origin was not able to keep us. I do not believe they can be all placed on the same side, and it has nothing to do with political party colors. Some of them actually do try to change things for the better[121], for the sake of the people, who are the ones who truly build a nation, but they somehow get cut off, and fatally, should the devil drive and their victories become threatening to corporate and lobbyist interests.

It has recently come to the attention of the general public, by the hands of the International Consortium of Investigative Journalists[122], the leakage named «Panama Papers», which, in short,

---

[121] Vide note 26.

[122] Founded in 1997 by American journalist Chuck Lewis (b. 1953), it comprises a network of more than 190 investigative journalists spanning across over sixty-five countries. According to their own description, their objective is to surveil criminal events such as "cross-border crime, corruption, and the accountability of power".

Further information: 02-13-2012, *The International Consortium of Investigative Journalists*, «About the ICIJ», (https://www.icij.org/about), accessed 05-16-2016.

exposes over 11.5 million financial and legal records[123] enabled via financially corruptive instruments called «offshores». These aforementioned records are linked to multiple businessmen, politicians, attorneys, celebrities in general (powerful and influential people, every single one of them) and their respective companies, and these are not exclusive to one country alone, but rather to the entire globe.

As disclosed in the previous chapter and somewhat in the current, obtaining power through money is a natural consequence of the economic system as it is. The hierarchy to getting here is actually simple, and it dates all the way back to Prehistory. After the Nomad peoples started settling and producing their own sustainability through the practices of agriculture, mixed farming and fishing, without the need to keep traveling after soil or water exhaustion, thus domesticating certain animal species from which they could obtain a great deal more resources, cities began to grow, together with its inhabiting population. More people living in these cities comprehended the need to develop other sciences such as architecture, engineering, masonry, etc., in order to provide homes for them. Also, the need to keep track of crops and harvests eventually led to the creation of a registration system, which became the first form of writing in the Near East, then spreading to the West, by the hands of the Sumerians, in Mesopotamia, around 5,000 years ago. Simple enough symbols inscribed into clay tablets allowed the people, especially scribes, to record the amount of food stored in the city's public buildings. Such a system defined future practices in the region until about 3,000 years later, when the Roman Empire assumed the ruling of the territory and Jesus Christ was born, according to the Holy Scriptures. From here, came another need: guarding the food, thusly instituting militarization. Finally, in order to control the

---

[123] Further information: *ICIJ.org*, «The Panama Papers», (https://panama-papers.icij.org), accessed 05-16-2016.

army, the first form of government was born. When historians claim the cradle of Western civilization was set in the Crescent area, they are absolutely correct. Every time a group of people became organized, they started living in society, then turning into, indeed, a civilization, as the population numbers kept increasing. The problem was, despite all this *civilized* organization, the fear of having someone disrupt social order and turning into chaos was and still is what keeps us at the same level other animal species are in, living in the wilderness. We have come to such a great deal of mistrust in everyone else that the only way of keeping everybody on the line is to have them live in an environment of fear and coercion. The more you forbid someone from doing something, the more they will feel the input to disrespect all the rules you impose. That is our nature, which is necessarily correlated to free will. The State has the right to protect itself and its citizens, may it be from itself or from each other, I agree to that. However, there are some rules others feel empowered to submit their fellow citizens to, leading to the abuse of power, even from the authorities themselves, who are supposed to advocate the law, rather than being the law and feeling free to go around it. Democracy is not perfect, it has got many flaws and they will hardly ever become corrected, but we just have to try. Ceding to the system is becoming part of it and, subsequently, accepting it.

An offshore is a synonym for a fiscal paradise or haven. All those people aforementioned in «The Panama Papers» have businesses of their own in the countries they live in, where they supposedly pay their taxes, like the regular individual. But the ugly truth is no one ever grows rich from working an honest job. Maybe some do, but not to the extent of becoming a multimillionaire. Even supermarket chain owners and partners recur to offshores, bank accounts they open in countries such as Panama itself, indeed, together with Hong Kong (because it is a Special

Administrative Region with its own autonomy), Singapore, Switzerland (some European countries are also like tax heaven to many, especially when they do not integrate the European Union), Luxembourg (the other way around is also possible, considering this country is poorly regulated when it comes to the financial sector and, yet, it is part of the heart of the Union itself), the Cayman Islands or the United Arab Emirates (featuring a great number of either tax-free zones or payments in live cash or gold, leaving no trace whatsoever, with the help of an ask-no-questions policy).

Regardless of there being taxes or none at all in these countries, as long as their law is respected by the bank account owners stashing their parallel riches in them, their activity is *not* illegal, so they are not actually committing crimes in these havens, but they are in their citizenship country or countries, as they are fleeing from their tax obligations, using front companies to justify their balance. Illicit enrichment, money laundering and corruption are three of the worst financial crimes in the world.

If legislation were to be created to prevent the use of offshores, I am certain criminals would always find a way to wire[124] their cash someplace else, via other means. Instead, I believe the best option is to not just compensate the State in all the skipped taxes, but to finance public entities, institutions and services as a judicial sentence and therefore help build said State toward futurization. It could actually become an independent means of coercion from Central Government or even Parliament, ordering conmen to withdraw all their money from the tax havens of their choice and hand it over to the progress of Science and education financing, thus leading to tuition-free universities and the extinction of public financial endorsement for private educational institutions, not just at the higher education level, but also all other schools

---

[124] Make digital transfers.

and academies. Childless citizens contribute to their fellow citizens' education via their taxes, which fund the existence of a public network of schools, run by the State. It is their duty to want millions of children to have the right to a good public education. Parents are the ones who undeniably have to provide the most for children, not just their own, but other parents', also within the public education network. But what of parents enrolling their children in private schools? They have the right to it, no one denies it to them, at least not me. But should the State be responsible for the funding of private schools via the taxpayers' money? Absolutely and undoubtedly not.

Private educational institutions are owned by either one person alone or legal persons, represented by a company through a board of trustees. That does not mean they have the right to meddle with the State's syllabi, as if the children learn something different from those in public institutions, their grades cannot obviously be recognized when heading to college or going for a job interview. Their money has, on the other hand, enough power to improve architectural conditions under which students attend class, also funding their own staff's education, toward the best of qualifications. Some schools and universities already do that.

The reason why such institutions were created in the first place has to do with development needs from the State. This means public education networks did not rise just like that, all at once. Both modernization and accessibility to national resources take time to accomplish, especially when a country is only just finding its way toward freedom and Democracy, which, as we previously found out, is not a worldwide-cherished value. Many nations across the globe are still rising from the ashes of war and need their time, hopefully with support from the international community, to get back on their feet, if they ever were standing at all, constantly under repression, most of the time brutal.

So, as long as the State is biding its time to put everything back together, citizens must also help in the rebuilding of their nation, and being educated is their best option, so they can land a job of enough social importance to provide better life tools to forthcoming generations. If the public school network still has to be built, the State then finances existing private institutions, so they may welcome all students, regardless of their economic or any other kind of background. When, however, the State's network is complete and ready to have its own welcoming, it is not the taxpayers' obligation anymore to keep funding private institutions. Any parent desiring to keep their children in such places has to pay for the luxury, otherwise their job is to send them to public, where there exist equally qualified staff.

This is what Socialist Capitalism is about, which I endorse. Again, let us explain, so we are all clearly on the same page, the difference between this and the Soviet idea of Communism. Being a Socialist is working toward the effectiveness of society. This is another repeated idea, but I would just like to stress it once more: apart from millennial tribes spread across the whole world, who still live isolated in either the jungle, the savannah, etc., though realizing there are men and women inhabiting completely different environments made of concrete, the rest of the living human population is aware they cannot live completely by themselves. According to Aristotle[125]:

«He who is unable to live in society, or who has no need because he is sufficient for himself, must be either a beast or a god».

— *Politics*, Book I, 1253.a27

I personally would not go that far. Not in today's standards,

---

[125] 384 BC – 322 BC. Greek scientist and philosopher, the third of the major Classical Antiquity Greece wise men, disciple of Plato, who was in turn disciple of Socrates (470 or 469 BC – 399 BC).

anyway, as comparing Man to beasts is highly offensive, unless we recur to literary metaphors, of course. As for claiming to be a god, or the son of one, come to that, is something I would not recommend at all. The Bible itself lets you know why it is not such a good idea, whether you believe in it or not.

Therefore, considering we have no choice but to be a part of common public life, it is our duty to put some work to it, so we may live in peace, without getting into constant conflict with each other, regardless of the reason leading us to a fight. This is something I have come to realize the more I live and gather experience as a human being, meaning that, even when a fight takes place between two people alone, like a couple, either they are very peaceful and respectful for each other and never have an argument, or they just have to go out and look for one, so they can prove themselves they love one another, claiming they would not know how they could make without their respective better-half. This is the same as, "we already were at peace, but needed something to ignite the flame a lot more, so we fought and now we had a carnal truce". Okay... I guess.

I believe everyone has the right to earn their bread. Be it some small savings or a fortune, everybody is entitled to it. It is the ability to help society that needs to be revised accordingly. For example, when you are walking on the street, it is very common, though it should not, mind, to find both homeless and beggars. Some people have so much hatred for these outcasts that they place signs on the walls of public infrastructures prohibiting beggars from staying there with their arm extended, holding a cup and waiting for someone to drop a coin or a bill, if they get lucky. As for the homeless, there has been online slamming against resident organizations for installing spikes on the floor of their buildings' entrances. Instead of at least letting the person in need spend the night out of the rain, though lying on a freezing marble floor, ruining their back, they regard them as a nuisance and want them to stay away. We hate each other. That is the truth. It is sad and ugly, but true.

Before we can help others, we have to be able to help each other. Please bear with me on this: when a person has to work more than one job at the same time to make enough money to *survive* (as opposed to «live»), they likely do not have a lot to go with. The abilities to pay the house, maybe get a car and buy a suit become privileges, not luxuries.

Not only we are bound to find people in need on the street, we also find others who are either getting paid (though not that much, obviously) or volunteering in representation of benefi-cence organizations, like Amnesty International or the Red Cross. They are smart enough to place themselves in people-af-fluent locations, such as a mall. What they do is *prompt* pass-ersby to come and monetarily contribute. The newsflash is, just because you walk into a mall, maybe wavering your car key on your index finger and wearing a smart jacket from that fifty-dol-lar suit you bought over a decade ago, does *not* mean you are wearing money for underpants. Hardly any common citizen ever does that. Not even the rich are lighting their cigars with hun-dred-dollar bills all around. That is mostly a flick thing. Who would want to deliberately burn their money with the economy fluctuations we have been experiencing for the past few years? Like I said, having a car and being able to pay insurance, taxes, mechanical inspections and, more important, gas, is to most peo-ple a privilege, not a luxury. That is why they keep the same ve-hicle for years in a row, when they start becoming expensive and never leave the shop. It is better to just keep fixing it than getting into major debt when buying a new one.

These people might be working for charity, but that is not why they are going to stop thinking of themselves exclusively. I used to be a member of Amnesty International Portugal. I still have my membership card with me. As a student, I only had to pay

€20 yearly (conversion rates have been constantly lowering for the past years, so that is pretty much $20). I had to cancel my membership at some time because those €20 made a difference in my balance by the end of the year, but never mind that now. My point is, as a member, I had that fixed instalment to pay. Kids willing to work while studying in order to help their parents or legal guardians pay their college tuition can be hired by said organization so they can go out on the street and recruit prospective activists. The difference between being a member and an activist is the first comprises a fixed yearly payment, just as I have now described. The latter, on the other hand, comprises your consent into paying at least €6 per month. This is simple Arithmetic. Six times twelve, what do you get? €72. That is a 260% increase, when comparing this result to the yearly payment of €20. Needless to say it does not make it up to you. Still, the children in college will do anything to try and convince you it is the best choice, as they are taught in their one-day only, 12-hour instruction to use arguments such as, "this amount is just slightly above the regular price of a packet of cigarettes". I have to be honest with you, I felt my intelligence had been insulted. I never smoked in my life, never wasted my money in that sort of habit. Why would I consider such an argument just so the kid who prompted me would get his commission in addition to his base salary? This is exactly what I was trying to prove: I have no problem at all in helping others, but I have to do it only when I myself am allowed to *survive*. Most of us are *not living*, nowadays. We are *surviving*, working exploiting jobs so our employers may be up for their grabs.

I will be talking education with you in the following chapter, but there is something that needs mentioning right now, for the sake of argument. Most employers, such as the aforementioned supermarket chain owners, are not willing to employ people with a college degree, may it be undergraduate or graduate, it is irrelevant. People are instigated by their own Governments into studying hard toward an MBA[126] or even a PhD[127], most of them having to indebt themselves for life because of the student loans they are forced to take, if they want to finish their degree. In order to help themselves get financially through it, they work their part-time jobs at places like the said supermarkets and accept all the contract terms. However, when it comes to people who already have a college degree, they have to work the same kind of job because they have no hope whatsoever of getting something better, preferably in their field of study, which is *not* demeaning to them, this is important. When people discuss that issue of having to wipe other people's trash from the streets as a pejorative way of life, they are being ignorant. Most of them doing that would love to have a desk job and stay in front of a computer, learning information technologies and getting in touch with the world out there. But they *cannot*, because not everyone has a chance of becoming enrolled at a fancy-like college or university institution.

This is the utter difference between workplaces that keeps setting both the economy and society in general back. If you land a job in an office, you need a minimum of a Bachelor's Degree to be considered, but you could not afford tuition fees, because getting an education, regardless of the country, is a personal luxury most families are unable to endure. For this reason, you are immediately excluded, also because of the self-proclaimed 30-second recruitment test analyzing your *curriculum vitae* skills without any humanity linked to it. Human Resources is a terrifying business, I will tell you that. However, if you do have a Bachelor's and head over to being a cashier or even cutting meat at the supermarket, you are extremely qualified and must, therefore, lie about your qualifications, as no one is willing to pay a college

---

[126] Master of Business Administration.
[127] *Philosophiae Doctor*, Latin for Doctor of Philosophy.

boy or girl more than the average shmuck with a GED[128], though HSDs[129] are surprisingly acceptable. It is not me who is calling people shmucks, it is the MBA employers, and not so secretly.

Having a decent education is a personal danger to these employers, and the reason is no surprise at all. The more you learn, the more you grow smarter. The more you grow smarter, the bigger the chances of an employee uprising claiming for their rights and better work conditions. Believe me, it is an undeniable nightmare for an employer to experience and solve, should it become a real problem. What would their outer image look like to labor unions or the Government itself, who does not legislate accordingly in order to protect its citizens? Certainly not good. Strike threats are the only possible solution. Workers not working are not earning their money, but the employers are also losing thousands, if not millions in a single day. So, in the end, why would they want to contribute to public education under these horrid circumstances?

Curiously enough, a lot of employers comprise also some other sordid contract terms when they place a vacancy advertisement in the market: demand for experience. Allow me to get this straight for us all – I have just left college and am preparing to be a part of the working world by trying to make myself useful to someone, so I can have some bread on my table and infusion to help push it down my throat. What do the ads that interest me the most ask for? Three to five or more years of experience in that area of expertise. Another remarkable insult to people's intelligence, no doubt. How is a newly-graduate supposed to have any practical experience whatsoever in their area of expertise, if they left college only just now and are looking to gain said experience by becoming employed? Perhaps these employers require someone older, in their thirties, maybe forties. Being forty-years-

---

[128] General Education Development certificate.
[129] High School Diploma.

old in both the Dark and Middle Ages was indeed old. People were lucky enough to make it that far. Nowadays, the average life expectancy for men (in the developed world, mind) is seventy-five and eighty for women. This means men who are thirty-seven and half and forty-year-old women have reached their own mid-life crisis and are ready to be disposed of. How on *earth* is someone born from the 1970s onward supposed to find a job, if we are either too old or unexperienced? I rest my case.

We should not forget, however, other institutions should contribute as well to society's wellbeing, and they are not companies or, at least, not in a conventional way of speaking. I am talking churches. They do not pay taxes of any kind. Before I move on, I need to get something straightened out, so as to avoid hurting any susceptibilities. I am not against the idea of god, whichever people believe in. I talked about this a few pages back, in the beginning of this chapter, when I mentioned I did not need other people's beliefs imposed unto me. The other way around is likewise applicable. I do not have to make others stop believing or lose their faith. We are all free to either believe or disbelieve whatever we want, that is the basis of human *free* will.

However, we must not forget either about something else: the majority of sovereign States around the world are laic. It means they should be completely separate from institutions representing the predominant faiths in their respective territory. Remember when I quoted the oath taken by the President of the Republic in my democratic restructuring? They should do it with their hand on the Constitution of their country, not on the Bible, because it looks like they are indeed pledging allegiance to the Constitution of the respective nation, though in the name of the Christian god, Jehovah. Are the Jewish, Muslims, Hindu, Buddhists, etc. not worth protection from their Head of State, then? It is segregating and unconstitutional.

As far as education is concerned, especially with respect to private schools or universities, there are indeed many of them backed by religious orders, which comprise their own statement of faith, but I will leave that segment to the next chapter. The core to this situation is parents are already paying for their children's enrollment in monthly instalments. The State is also funding them, even though there is a public school nearby, which means Central Government is overspending.

Plus, any building registered as a temple of faith is free from paying taxes, which is an act of charity from the State, but if we ask ourselves why are we paying for private schools when our children are in public, should we not ask ourselves why are we affording temples without even agreeing to their dogmas, just as much? It is true they pay their bills and a have a payroll to run for their staff, but their very location, for instance, is not taxable, as they apply for tax exemption as non-profitable institutions. That is why, with respect to some Catholic churches or even basilicas, priests, bishops, whoever, keep passing the plate in the middle of the crowd for soul-redeeming offerings. That is how, in the Middle Ages, the same St. Peter's Basilica we see standing today in Rome was built, funded by poorly surviving peasants. The clergy swears under oath to remain poor their entire life, but still there is enough money to wear gold and build magnanimous infrastructures for service, instead of homes for those lying on the street half alive.

The power of the Church is still too much around the globe, and States, though laic, are under its control. A sacred holiday is good enough for atheists, as well. It is a valid excuse to avoid going to work, that routine of always from nine to five, eight hours straight and one to have lunch, which brings me to my final considerations for this chapter – productivity and social security compensation.

Present-day society has been talking futurization so much that the question is already a paradoxical classic: are we working our skin off now, so we may peacefully die later? Why do some jobs even still exist, in the first place? One of the most obvious answers would be something like, "well, if they did not, a lot of people would be out of a job". Indeed, they would, but only according to the canons of today. Economy is a vile invention by plutocrats to enslave and imprison their biological equals. I agree, it sounds too fantastical, and yet, not too far from the truth. Everybody should be allowed to have a job or produce their own craft without the final purpose of earning a living and eating to survive. In fact, after the adaptation to the future is complete, civilization in general should just go penniless. Money is one of the dirtiest objects to have ever been created, in every sense of the word, not only for circulating across billions of hands in a single day, either washed or stained, but also for staining people's souls themselves, which, allow me to stress yet again, do not have a religious connotation.

Ambition, greed, power and vanity are just a few of the deadliest values a person could eager for. Civilization began to take over the world without any sort of trade carved into its veins. Just like a baby is born innocent and untouched by deviance, so was Man, meaning every human being, when capitalized. It was then, when people started feeling tired due to their hard work, that they felt they should be somehow compensated, hence the concept of trade, but this was not about *trading* productivity for money straight away. On the contrary, it was a notion translated to, "you give me something, I give you something in return (barter trade)". This, however, implied both gain and loss simultaneously, as people had to give up on their possessions or provide services in order to acquire other effects or get something done for them. So, another sort of trade, more valuable, come to that, had to be come up with: coinage, made of precious metals such as bronze, silver and, exactly, gold, in order of worthiness. The earliest form of money we still use today was created around 700 BC in Greece, as far as Western civilization is concerned. This way, when someone had to acquire either products or services from someone else, they had to be paid for, instead of swapped, which would eventually drive both parts of the deal to a mutual conflict of interests. This is the most notorious aspect of early civilizations that ended up condemning all of us to a life of slavery, working to enrich some and have others barely survive, including laborers themselves.

Most countries across the globe, though there already are some exceptions, instituted in the 20th century a total of forty working hours per week, up to a maximum of forty-eight, which can be divided into five or six days, respectively, considering at least one weekly resting day was mandatory, and still is. Governments regulating laborer statutes considered eight working hours a day, with an hour for lunch included, was a match for the needs of company manufacturing productivity. However, what some Governments and employers themselves have recently come to realize is that the longer employees work, the less motivated they feel and the more delayed productivity becomes, especially when there are no hopes at all of being promoted or getting a raise, no matter how hard they work. The very idea of having to spend most of the time in a day repeatedly doing something without even taking a rest, either sitting at a desk in front of a computer, inserting data the computer itself should automatically gather, or operating a machine without autonomy enough to perform without human supervision or control, is a living nightmare to a lot of people.

Of course, the concept of reducing working hours from forty to thirty-five or even thirty a week has its due opposition from employers who are obviously unwilling to pay the same for a lesser amount of labor time, even if it means the skyrocketing of productivity percentage. If this is not deliberate slavery, I then do not know what is.

Those working now are discounting a percentage of their salary to social security, which is a governmental means of State welfare that can somehow be compared to a barter kind of trade, only retribution is not paid back instantly, considering people are laboring about forty years of their life, paying Central Government for their job, so after said forty years, people can retire and get that money back, depending on the salary they earned. They then have on average another twenty years until they pass away, after which the State is not required to keep providing social security anymore. The laborer literally works the double of the time they are going to benefit from governmental appreciation.

However, and considering the unemployment crisis has become worldwide and the futurization process is still too slow because of monetary costs, we must either hurry with respect to robotics doing our industrial jobs for us so we may all serve as supervisors for the machines, or we stop wasting time and research antiaging scientific methods at once. Personally, I would like to make both those possibilities a reality. It would mean we could live longer and stronger, while enjoying the best in life, having machines take care of the heavy loads.

Should we, on the other hand, deny scientific progress made for our own sake, what is going to eventually happen is we will get older a lot sooner, without the chance for reproduction at a young age, because our personal stability is constantly in jeopardy and we do not feel free to have children, thus accelerating aging and death. Then, there will be no more social security, because there was no active population to pay for it, and a lot of people will starve, without any money to pay for their food or ability to find a job and work it. The evolution of civilization will inevitably come to an end at its own hand from deliberate social euthanasia. Only then will the remainder of those still living understand money did not bring us any happiness at all, apart from a necessary demise.

In the end, I ask again: who are we actually indebted to, and what is it we owe them?

4

Academic Restructure

If you have a driver's license and learnt to drive mostly on a manual transmission, perhaps you have been through a similar situation to this: learning to drive is more like fulfilling a protocol, rather than actually understanding how to deal with numerous traffic events and possibilities. It is only after you have had your final exam of «aptitude and behavior», as they call it in some places, that you indeed have enough freedom and time to learn on your own, but possibly at the expense of your first car, your parents', a friend's, etc., even if you hit it slightly on the bumpers when doing parallel parking.

The thing that is most important in the whole process is, like I said, learning to execute the protocol, i.e. performing smoothly with respect to your final test with the examiner, so they can certify you with a high enough score, making you an official independent driver. The ugly truth behind this is that, somehow, it seems more important to them that you do not forget to signal when changing lanes, that you do not hit the curb more than three times when parallel parking or that you, in the case of a manual transmission, know how to properly slide in the clutch when going up a ramp, instead of sparing it by using the hand-brake to help you ascend. When the clutch is used properly, it can last up to around 125,000 miles, though, wearing it out like that, it eventually has to be changed at approximately 25,000 miles, and clutches are very expensive to replace.

Here is what learning to drive has to do with learning every-thing else in a regular school: students are not grasping contents they can use in their future as men and women. No, they are simply memorizing commonplace statements they «download» onto a paper sheet via their pens and pencils to get a score. The educational system in a great deal of countries is one of showing--off. They build rankings so one school, either private or public, may top all others on account of their results, looking for inter-national acknowledgement. What happens to be surprising about this is that, when said students start attending college (where the same system can sometimes be applicable) and get their first job, luckily enough in their field, they have no idea what they are do-ing. Remember I cannot speak for everyone or point fingers to millions of people all at once, claiming they have no qualifica-tions whatsoever to perform the duties they were assigned to. In fact, perhaps I should be pointing fingers to myself. You have my biography available in the end of this book, but I can tell you in advance I am an educated Theater actor, and by «educated» I mean that is what I studied in college. For my PhD, I am prob-lematizing about that same education and how it is delivered unto students. It is as if I am now a third-party, looking at it from the outside. Some things still seem nice to me, whereas some oth-ers need to be cast into oblivion, according to my own opinion. Am I right about my points of view? Or am I completely mistaken and should probably bide my time with any other issue? I do not hold perfect answers to all problems, whether they are related to my area of expertise or not. But I try to think about some of them and offer hypotheses. If I do not know what I am talking about,

I read about it and learn. On my own, because, if I were to wait for school, college or university to teach me what I want to know about, the way they are all presently configured, it would probably be best to just take a seat and be prepared to wait a long time, during which I should probably read titles of my choosing and get to grasping.

Self-learning is a great way of keeping in touch with information the way it really is and avoiding social mechanization via instruction, but we simply cannot give up on our education system, replacing it indiscriminately without any effort to making it better. We have to ask ourselves whether we want to show the international community our memory served us right at getting that A plus, or effectively demonstrate we did not just memorize, but rather learnt and are ready to do something useful about it with respect to ourselves and the remainder of the society we live in.

The memorization side of education is one that is not only connected to showing-off, but also to the pressure of being constantly under surveillance by either teachers, schools, prospective colleges and universities or the respective Department/Ministry – which in the end has to do with governmental showing-off, indeed, but inputting some responsibility to children, teenagers and young adults' minds is actually pedagogical. It is the final purpose of learning what being an adult means, however, that perhaps is not made so clear.

One of the possible synonyms for education is instruction, but, again, it does not mean some sort of a matrix should be followed, at least not until the end of a person's cycle of studies. This means that, when we are children, adults cannot expect us to become self-guided instantly and be certain of what it is we need to do, so it does make sense to «instruct» the student during their first few years in school, especially when learning to read and write, as those are the fundamentals to do the rest, no surprise there.

That same guidance should, nonetheless, be progressively phased out.

We would think something similar to that is already in place, as, in some countries, when teenagers leave the cycle of studies equivalent to Junior High and progress to High School, they are between fourteen and fifteen years old, the time in life when a transition from childhood to adulthood is made, which means teenagers are gradually acquiring autonomy enough to make their own choices, including the courses and classes they want to take. The problem is not everyone is completely mature enough to decide alone what it is they want to pursue as far as a more advanced education is concerned, so some advice is always welcome, even though some teenagers might believe they already know what they want. The difference has to be made between convictions that are actually stood up for by the student and those who claim they want something without having any idea why so. Those are the ones who have not completely made their minds up. Regardless, whoever it is that is advising said teens must not presume to know what is best for them, based on merely indicative evidence such as grades. It is what the teens will feel the happiest about that matters and must therefore be pursued, even if the advisor believes, for instance, they would do a lot better in Math, when they clearly love Poetry the most. The same is applicable otherwise, of course.

I myself believe it is okay for either a Department or Ministry of Education to build the same curriculum for all children until they reach High School, as there are contents people need to learn without ever neglecting them through their entire life. I do not agree with statements such as, "I don't have to worry about learning calculus, because I deal with letters". The same goes for, "I don't need to learn to spell properly, because my language is made of numbers". Both of these are wrong. It is absolutely criminal when someone does not care enough to learn either Simple

Arithmetic or to spell *at least* their own mother tongue.

The following is a list of departments and their respective subjects everyone should learn the essential of, according to my own opinion, mind, the latest until the end of Junior High (or Middle School), having some of them progress to High School:

Core

— Linguistics;
    — Nation's Official Idiom;
    — Foreign Language I;
        — English (when different from Official Idiom) or:
        — Any other tongue somehow connected to the nation, either geographically, historically, politically, etc.
    — Foreign Language II;
        — French;
        — Spanish;
        — German;
        — Italian;
        — Japanese;
        — Mandarin.
    — Classical Idiom;
        — Latin;
        — Greek.
    — Literature & Culture;
    — Debating;
    — Public Speaking;
    — Writing.
— Mathematic;
    — Algebra;
    — Calculus;
    — Geometry;
    — Statistics;

— Personal Accounting and Finance.
— Science;
   — Astronomy;
   — Biology;
   — Chemistry;
   — Ecology;
   — Environmental Science;
   — Life & Earth Science;
   — Physics;
   — Zoology.
— Social Science;
   — Anthropology;
   — Economics;
      — Business;
      — Trade.
   — Geography;
   — History;
      — Prehistory;
      — Ancient History;
      — Dark Ages;
      — Medieval History;
      — Modern History;
      — Contemporaneity;
      — National History;
      — World History.
   — Philosophy;
      — Critical Thinking;
      — Logic;
      — Rhetoric.
   — Political Science;
      — Government;
      — Political Systems.
   — Psychology;

— Sociology.
— Physical Education;
    — Basic Anatomy;
    — Eurhythmy;
    — First Aid & Safety;
    — Gymnastics;
    — Health & Nutrition;
    — Sports.
— Sex Education;
    — Gender Anatomy & Biology;
    — Equality Civics & Tolerance;
    — Relationship Psychology;
    — Sexually Transmitted Disease Awareness & Prevention.
— Performing Arts;
    — Dance;
        — Ballroom Dancing;
        — Contemporary Dancing.
    — Music;
        — Choir;
        — Solo Singing;
        — Instrumental.
    — Theater;
        — Greco-Latin Universe;
        — Contemporary Artistic Currents.
— Visual Arts & Crafts.
    — Art History;
    — Design;
    — Painting;
    — Photography;
    — Sculpture.

It is hard to appease both Greeks and Trojans, so I will have to make it clear I obviously do not mean to introduce all these subjects and perhaps many others into a child's curriculum *without at least changing* a few *bureaucratic* procedures first.

It is a lot better to learn and grasp contents throughout our schooling process and to show we actually held on to that knowledge in class, rather than turning it into an object of either numbering or grading via a test. I believe it is okay to do exams at the end of some cycles of studies in order to allow students to progress to the next stage, in which all general knowledge is assessed, but not across all schooling. There are other ways of making children feel responsible for their acts without having to run tests the entire time or schedule homework every day. What happens in class stays in class, that is how I see it. If teachers require assessment methods so they can be aware of their students' progress, then they should probably do it via either debating, oral prompting, written assignments in which they can think for themselves using the contents they learnt, or all of them combined. This way, the importance of learning can be made clear to children, instead of the importance of memorizing to forget later on, putting an end to the educational matrix that basically says, "you either keep up with the rest of your colleagues, or you fail and fall back and back, to a point of no return".

In other news, with respect to colleges and universities: that same backing from a religious entity verifiable in private schools, regardless of the existence of a public institution, is perfectly possible. I certainly do not oppose the management of higher education facilities by the hands of a determined faith. I believe it may sound absolutely contradictory, when remembering my words about valuing a religion-free State, one that is completely laic. The truth is, exactly like I stated before, you may believe whatever you want, just do not impose it unto others. The same goes for those who do not believe anything at all. It is a statement I am deliberately repeating so both of us, myself and my gentle Reader, can make sure we come to terms. If you simply do not believe in the existence of a god, or if you wish to stress you are an agnostic and believe in neither the existence of a god or their inexistence, keep it that way, do not superimpose.

Some higher education institutions are the best at what they do. They are renowned for their quality as far as faculty, staff, facilities, etc. are concerned, and there is no need for them to be public. Even when prospective students have the ability to choose between a public and private university teaching the same degree, they might go with private, if they can so much afford it. However (as there is always a «but» hidden somewhere), the religious domain over said private universities may sometimes hit its very extreme. I am talking statements of faith, for both students and personnel.

The terms of a statement of faith vary according to each institution, but the commonest of aspects are the firm belief that all knowledge is delivered in both the blood and body of «Our Lord and Savior Jesus Christ», just to name Christian facilities as an example. This is sickening, and I am willing to go this much far with respect to this sort of uttering. Have you ever wondered why a university has that same designation? Because it is *universal*. All knowledge is, and that is what a *university* is for, to teach *universal* knowledge to those who are willing to learn it. The quality of public domain content teaching does not have to be paid for through the sacrificing of a metaphysical belief, misbelief or none of the previous.

And it is not just about the sacrificing of any of those, either. It is a financial issue as well. If, while we are still a part of the active sector of the population, academic qualifications make the necessary difference between landing a job and being excluded for either lack or *excess* of degrees, then the key is to make advanced instruction free to all, just like the entire schooling process from Preschool to High School.

Though knowledge is of public domain (or should be, depending on the kind of political regime in place where people live in), and though we have the choice to learn numerous materials on our own, either by reading in print or digitally, where practically everything we know of is stored, the Internet, regardless of having been written in Prehistory itself, the truth is we need a piece of paper confirming our certification from a renowned college or university, which we call a diploma, so our degree may be duly acknowledged by either an employer or the scientific community itself, thus granting us the right to be a part of a significant debate. Such a certification in the form of a diploma is granted after a considerable amount of coursework has been done, under the supervision of one or more pedagogues. Not teachers or professors, but pedagogues. As an academic, I cherish this statement, not because it is my own, but rather because it is the truth. Some people are indeed gifted with being able to make others learn, instead of temporarily understanding with the purpose of answering a few questions on an exam. Teaching is a mission, and it should be rewarded as such by the State itself, without any extra funding from struggling young adults and their families when paying tuition.

If someone is not meant to go to college to pursue a degree, then let it be out of their own accord, and not because the State was not interested in funding them one. Of course, with respect to those who feel like deliberately wasting public resources for their own amusement, without a single care for learning at all, career advice is recommended, as no one should be left abandoned to their own luck just because they cannot find a purpose for themselves. Instead of just cutting off their hopes of someday becoming useful to society, I say we try and help them. We are all here serving a common objective, with some personal errands to the side, as we are entitled to since birth. Remember what I said about criminal punishment: no joy should be found in sentencing someone to life in prison, let alone death. Claiming one life for another will not bring anyone back. We have no right, however, to call ourselves a civilization if our intention is to enforce segregation and exclusion, regardless of the subject we relate the outcasts to. Rehabilitation under free will, though abiding by the law of Man, is an undeniable priority.

Until we are all on the same page as far as every single topic I talked to you about across this book up to this point is concerned, perhaps considering some others I did not think about and that you remembered and even felt like suggesting for not being registered here, chaos will prevail over order and our conflict of interests will be endless, therefore disabling the people from gaining control of their own country, toward a mutually beneficial agreement with enough political strength that will, eventually, guide every single one of us, you and I included, all the way from survival, either on Earth or any other planet, to living the one, true gift we were awarded: life.

Part II
Dawn of Humanity

1

Alea Iacta Est[130]

Cosmologists have always said there could be a reality different from our own, distinct from everything we have learnt so far since the beginning of Mankind, about fifteen to twenty million years ago, when History was yet to be recorded and civilization was still not a concept. The early primates led to modern Man, and the first are primates, exactly because of the quintessence contained in them. They began small, hunched, walking astray with two pairs of natural supporting structures, two anterior and two posterior limbs, both available for any kinds of usage with

---

[130] Or *Iacta alea est*, one of the most renowned Latin phrases in the world, attributed to Julius Caesar by Roman biographer and historian Gaius Suetonius Tranquillus (c. 69 AD – c. 140 AD [both dates are disputed]), when leading his army across the Rubicon river in Northern Italy, in 49 BC. It is either translated as "Let the die be cast", "the die is cast" or "the die has been cast", though the first version is widely considered to be the one entirely correct, as the result of Caesar's military move would be given to chance. It is thought Caesar might have taken it from Greek New Comedy writer Menander (c. 342 BC – c. 290 BC), one of his favorites, precisely from the play titled *Arrhephoros* (*The Female Flute-Player*), of which only a few fragments survived. According to Greco-Roman biographer and historian Plutarch's (c. 46 AD – 120 AD) *Life of Pompey*, Caesar uttered the phrase in its original Greek, the scholar idiom of the time, just as Latin would be in the Middle Ages.

opposable thumbs and big toes. Intelligence was gradually gathered by these ancestors to humans, thusly making it possible for them to experience a slow adaptation to changes made to the world.

In the beginning, the Universe we nowadays believe erupted from a tremendous explosion Edwin Hubble named «Big Bang» (though the theory was originally Georges Lemaître's, a Belgian priest, astronomer and physicist), considering this burst will someday retract and turn into a «Big Crunch», was all but an unmeasurable amount of gas whose lighting and ignition is unknown. Many theories have since been thought of and discussed among experts, but those are only conjectures, as no one is able to know for sure what happened, not even during the time we call Prehistory, the beginning of recorded events on planet Earth. Could there be a rational possibility which could tell us fair and square how it all came to be? "God knows" is the most frequent answer, due to modern History. Because Christendom is modern, no doubt about it. However, Creationism is supposed to date back to the very beginning. Is Jehovah indeed the Creator of all things real and unreal? Why the Christian god and no other? Was he not supposed to be Jewish? And the «Children of Israel», *apparently* slaves to the Egyptians, who told them they were the chosen ones? Yahweh did, and then Moses, royalty in the world of pharaohs.

So maybe there is a special and astonishingly powerful entity who indeed created the world we live in. Nonetheless, the Holy Bible keeps telling us this world, may I highlight it again, this world began by the hand of God, who created it in no more than a six-day business week. By the seventh, God saw that it was good. No such thing as a scientific theory revolving on the expansion of the Universe. Three conditions only are paramount for the breeding of life. A powerful light source, capable of illu-

minating and providing heat, fresh water to prevent body dehydration and a breathable atmosphere, which makes me think,
now I am at it, we have not known how to take care of the planet. Anyway, should one of them fail to comply, and extinction
comes our way.

Because of this so far unstoppable and ignited engine still
pushing us towards the unknown, where some other sun may
shine, the predecessor of the atmosphere embracing us today
caught fire and turned the Earth into a spinning ball of fire, burning almost just as bright as the Sun. When the most sustainable
gases burnt entirely, of which oxygen is the most relevant, carbon
monoxide and dioxide covered the entire terrestrial planet and
entrapped the Earth's natural heat, letting loose that of the Sun,
slightly older than the blue planet, but not immortal. When dying
of old age, the Sun will take us with it. Or so we think. Or so we
are made to think. Maybe it is God who will decide when to put
an end to it. One can never tell.

This sunblock was crucial to the slow and freezing age ahead
until the sky would become clear. It takes over a thousand years
to put everything back where it belongs when such a catastrophe
is up ahead. It is also wasted time in the evolution of life on the
only planet capable of withstanding beings of different species
whose only element in common is the need to survive, whichever
the cost, even if it means eating your own cubs to stay alive, because parenthood, immersed in the lair of moral and ethics, could
not have surfaced so soon, not even in times like these, painted
in blood-red.

With this undying greenhouse effect, though not sufficient to
turn the environment slightly warmer, glaciers from both the
North and South Poles spread intensely over present-day Canada, the Eastern coast of the US, Northern Russia and Northern
European countries. Of course, before the current continents
formed, there was a supercontinent by the name of «Pangaea».

Not just one, in fact, but several, as they continuously kept moving, colliding against and separating from each other. The best evidence we have to prove this event is the cutting between Africa and South America. Both fauna and flora share plenty of similarities.

After the skies were clear, the Sun could finally penetrate Earth's atmosphere, but it was still not enough. A filtering layer was required, if there were to be living creatures, even bacteria. So when oxygen was reestablished in the planet's stratosphere, it chemically reacted to the Sun's ultraviolet rays and generated protection. Mentioning the subject so lightly with little scientific vocabulary makes it easier to understand this entire process. Geophysics is slow to comprehend, just as much as evolving. Everything is phased. The ocean was the first to breed living specimens, miniscule samples of unicellular organisms such as anemones. Now, by the time terrestrial surfaces became clear and capable of sustaining other organisms, aquatic creatures emerged from the waters and adapted themselves to breathing in recurrence to developing nasal cavities, rather than the usual gills to both sides of the neck.

Swimming is pretty much like crawling or dragging one's body, hence the need to develop the tips of fins, in order to grab the dirt and progress further, either slowly or quickly, depending on weight and agility. This is the origin of dinosaurs, earthly reptiles which required body modifications and other tuning systems to be able to survive and serve as predators, instead of prey. Those which could not possibly face imminent danger with either jaw power, body strength, venom or any other means of protection, had to necessarily conceal themselves, covert in the wilderness, changing tones of scales, skin or fur, or simply hiding, outsmarting vicious, undefeatable and large killers. But the reptiles' reign would not last forever. There were other plans. Deadly, yet vital plans, paradoxical as it may sound.

The Asteroid Belt runs between two other Solar System planets, Mars and Jupiter. Asteroids are irregularly formed planetesimals. Their total mass could not be the equivalent to a consistent planet such as those inside the main belt of asteroids. However, it is sufficient to create fatal damage and disrupt a whole world, domain or realm and place it where no one could ever be to witness, live and tell the story. That is exactly what put an end to the reptile reign.

Over sixty-six million years ago, when the Cretaceous-Paleogene extinction event took place, the Earth clouded its skies once more with the strength of an impact of approximately one hundred teratonnes of explosive devices. The place hit by the ten to fifteen-kilometer-long rock was the Yucatán Peninsula, in present-day Mexico, inhabited thousands of years ago by the Mayan civilization, they who predicted the end of the modern world, however failing on their calculations, the year 2012 AD, though this is just a reference for today's peoples. No one could ever think a unique savior of the entire human race would be born to a celestial mother, conceived without sin. Mandatorily, enriching native civilizations were not dialogued with, they just wanted to be left at peace. The problem was the oldest civilized civilizations of the world were far more barbaric, killing them all in the name of faith and fervor or keeping them alive as slaves, deemed unworthy of being people, just like anyone else, the predominant Caucasians.

The brutal collision by the shores of the Gulf of Mexico caused one of the effects the Earth had gone through before, remaining closeted inside a greenhouse with little sunlight. Sulfuric acid prevailed in the stratosphere, blocking irrespirable gases, generating acid rain and killing exposed organisms. That was the end of the dinosaurs, they which had evolved from the reptiles taking over both sea and land, the dominant species of the planet, a home in which just about every living being, with minor exceptions, of course and literally, were gigantic. One of them and consequently the most powerful was the tyrannosaurus rex, commonly referred to as T-Rex, a dreadful killing machine which could have not survived to live conjointly with another species, hiding deep underground, away from toxic fumes freed from volcanoes forced to erupt as soon as the fallen meteorite crushed deep onto the Earth's crust, striking the ocean floor and standing high up to a commercial airplane's cruise altitude, immediately turning to dust in the first moment of impact. The continental plaques start moving again, the molten mantle reconfigures the last supercontinent to survive, and the world as we know it today is recognizable from outer space, however the layout is yet to be put in its rightful place.

We never thought our ancestors could descend from the mammals they do in fact. Moles do not dwell much above ground. There is actually no need for it. Their nose is their guide, as their visual acuity is almost completely impaired. Besides, the use of claws to keep digging below faster than any other animal assure breathable air will not lack as long as they keep moving and leave a hole open to the surface.

The evolution of active life, fauna, that is, is quite coincidental with that of flora. Vegetation turned the planet both blue and green once more. Was that the end of considerable changes on the blueprint? The answer is probably not. But there is yet time to head there. Right now, we see trees, dense canopies, crops difficult to overcome. The planet is now flourishing with what seem to be primates, but that would already be quite of a jump toward modern Man. No, they are apes. They eat just about anything. They are not just herbivores, not just carnivores, but omnivores. However, there is not much flesh available, unless they endeavor in cannibalism. So they eat fruit, plenty of fruit, made of nutrients essential to keep their strength, progressing not only on their feet, but also on their knuckles. It is easier to remain hunched, but it would not happen forever. The need to stand on their feet alone, arising from vegetation on the African Eastern sea border, made them erect, thus giving birth to the first *Homo Erectus*, the actual ancestor of the *Homo Sapiens*, who we are, because we know, which is to say we possess knowledge, we reflect, we think, sharing with other animals the so-called biological sphere, in which the survival instinct and other natural needs, functions and resources apply.

However, we have something else. Science, the opposite of nature. That is how Art is produced. *Homo Sapiens* take matter from nature and, with their knowledge, they scientifically create a work of art, a masterpiece, acknowledged by those made of the likes of them, with a tender heart. That is what evolving is all about. It is not a matter of nature versus science, but rather nature and science.

The border between East Africa and Asia Minor eventually thinned, thus generating the Red Sea. From there, human life spread to Asia, populating the only supercontinent of modernity, Afro-Eurasia. Mesopotamia became the civilizational headquarters. India, an island afloat, became part of that immense land structure, clearing the way for the Indian Ocean, just as much as the separation between America and Afro-Eurasia gave birth to one of the most temperamental warriors of the planet, the Atlantic. We could ask ourselves how is it possible that, considering this insurmountable spatial configuration, Man spread all over the place, having each civilization gifted their own way. Mesopotamic children were undoubtedly made far more rational than anywhere else on the face of the blue sphere. Because they are the ones, indeed. Their god chose them and never forsake them, but it is true they were put to the test for a very long time until the prophecy was confirmed.

Siberia is the Northern region of present-day Russia. Because of the impact caused by the meteorite fallen in the Gulf of Mexico, the area became unstable. Siberian eruptions started spitting lava from deep underground, where the molten mantle revolves, just as much as the three meninges surrounding the brain inside the skull, keeping it from bumping and moving around, hydrated with cerebrospinal fluid. The holes made to the Earth's crust are similar to hemorrhagic brain damage or lack of dopamine inside the basal ganglia, located in the cerebrum. Lava is drifting away from the planet's core, solidifying because of the thermic shock after contacting with the freezing ocean water, especially up North, by the Pole. This formed small islands, creating a pathway for the traversing of prehistoric Man towards the Americas. That is how almost the entire percentage of land on the planet was populated.

Humans as they are today showed in the Paleolithic period, when History began being recorded, recurring to rupestrian paintings on the walls of sheltering caves. Pretty much like diaries, hunters started recurring to Mathematic, that is to say Simple Arithmetic, and counted how many animals they had caught. Not only that, self-portrayal as well as unique, palm-made signatures were there. Secretly, Science was asking Art, far more public, to marry it.

This is what is usually called a beginning. You commence from the start, when all dwells in perfection. However, it is what comes next which might be worrying, the time concrete science is abducted by some kind of special force and imagination, together with superstition, take place. Could civilization be the perfect form of coexisting with one another, or is it just a start previous to surreal damnation?

Cogito, ergo sum or, made linguistically accessible, «I am thinking, therefore I exist (or am)». On any living being at the face of the Earth which might incessantly produce thought or merely reflect Nature's programming with which it was gifted and whose theme is based solely on survival, I shall state it already is, hence *being* empowered to perform its own actions. Simultaneously, any object which, precisely because of that same designation, sits in the empirical range of living beings, gifted with either a rational and biological sphere or just plain biological, already is as well.

It is not about a mere representation exclusively matching a human being's theoretical ability, but rather its representation inclusively cognitive and pragmatic on behalf of itself, who built it and gave it three dimensions, taken the most important is Physics, therefore touchable and partnered with a reality being affected by time factors, especially its wearing out and consequent abrasion, erosion or oxidation, as both the rotational and orbital trajectories of Earth take care of that part, though the heliocentric theory would have yet to be cherished and highlighted, taking about three hundred years to be accepted by the Roman Catholic Church since Copernicus' first views on it, in 1514, to 1822, when Pope Pius VII[131] signed a decree allowing the printing of books approving of said theory in Rome, within the context of the Sacred Congregation of the Inquisition.

Around the world, religion, as we already know from several past segments in this very book, has taken enough power into its hands in order to control the precepts of Mankind itself. Again, it still does happen directly in some countries, whereas in others the situation is slightly more peaceable, bearing an *indirect* influence.

With respect to the Roman Catholic Church, which still has an embodying predominance in the Western Hemisphere, mostly, we know the Congregation for the Doctrine of the Faith is the

---

[131] Born Barnaba Niccolò Maria Luigi Chiaramonti, 1742-1823.

oldest[132] among a total of nine[133] in the Roman Curia, having instituted the *Index Librorum Prohibitorum*[134] shortly after the invention of the printing press by Johannes Gutenberg[135], in the 1440s, which enabled the rapid dissemination of knowledge and information across the several peoples, or at least those who could read, which was somehow an opposition made by authors to the control of both Church and Governments in medieval Europe. The only reason the *Index* was abolished was the Church could neither keep up with the modern-kind spread of information, nor enforce ecclesiastical law in the second half of the 20th century, when especially Europe was rising from the ashes of war, instating Democracy, after witnessing far more dangerous crimes against Humanity than publishing a book, which is not even a crime at all.

This kind of «zeal» for the protection of the faith over human life, which was basically nothing, compared to the survival of the first and, therefore, expendable, *still* is what is going to delay the

---

[132] Having begun in 12th-century Southern France as a means of fighting heresy, for which the Dominican Order was founded.

[133] The remaining eight current congregations are: the Congregation for Divine Worship and the Discipline of the Sacraments, the Congregation for the Evangelization of Peoples, the Congregation for the Causes of Saints, the Congregation for Bishops, the Congregation for the Clergy, the Congregation for the Oriental Churches, the Congregation for Institutes of Consecrated Life and Societies of Apostolic Life and the Congregation for Catholic Education, all of which are led by a different Prefect.

[134] The Latin designation for the «List of Prohibited Books» of the Roman Catholic Church, which was active the latest until 1965, after which it was abolished by Pope Paul VI (born Giovanni Battista Enrico Antonio Maria Montini, 1897-1978) under an *integrae servandae*, which is an apostolic exhortation, in the form of a *motu proprio*, which is to say a personal motion.

[135] C. 1398-1468. German blacksmith and goldsmith, who then became both a printer and publisher. Though his invention was new to Europe, a movable type of printing, though not a mechanical press, had already been created 400 years earlier in China, made of porcelain, by Bi Sheng (990-1051 [Chinese names are listed in the last name, first name format]).

progress of human life on our planet. Having individual inventors whose purpose is to improve both Humanity and wild life's sustainability is not enough to make it happen, as everyone needs the involvement and support of the masses, who very much obey the Church's interpretation of the Holy Scriptures and do not think for a second about questioning them with their own conclusions. Mosaic Law does not need to replace the Law of Man, at all. Its powers are so strong they can meddle with the minds of the people, casting them astray from what human nature should actually be, made of compassion, respect and tolerance.

Whatever contradicts the idea of Creationism, even though the concept of a «Big Bang» is widely accepted, as long as there is a Creator behind it, is an abomination. The fact we could transhumanize ourselves in the near future, which somehow is already taking place, though not so strongly, is a serious issue that is meant to be fought against by the forces of mysticism.

Because of divine superiority, we are supposedly *bound* to accept whatever comes our way. Imagine a person was involved in an accident, let us say on the road, and, due to its brutality, they are now stuck in a wheelchair. They are either paraplegic, which means they can move from their waist up, though without the usage of their legs, or tetraplegic, which is to say they cannot move their body at all from the neck down. Unless you are a very young Reader, you probably remember Christopher Reeve[136], the legendary actor who played the first Superman on film, and are aware of the accident he had when riding the horse[137] he had bought in 1994, while filming *Village of the Damned*[138]. In 1995, the horse refused to do a jump in the Commonwealth Park

---

[136] 1952-2004.

[137] A 12-year-old American thoroughbred, nicknamed «Buck». This breed is especially used for horseracing.

[138] Starring Christopher Reeve and Kirstie Alley, directed by John Carpenter, Universal Pictures, 1995.

Equestrian Center competition, in Culpeper, Virginia, projecting Reeve forward because of the sudden stop. Though he grabbed onto the reins, he landed on his head and broke the first two vertebrae, resulting in a cervical spinal injury, which left him immediately paralyzed and unable to breathe. It took three minutes for the paramedics to arrive and drive oxygen into his lungs. Reeve was sentenced to being in a chair with assisted life-support until his death, on the count of cardiac arrest.

Christopher, together with his wife, Dana Reeve[139], later gave their names to and funded the American Paralysis Foundation, which had been active since 1982, when spinal cord research was still uncharted territory in the neurobiology domain, transforming the Christopher Reeve Foundation (Christopher & Dana Reeve Foundation, as of 2007, after Dana's death) into one of the most important resource centers for stem cell research and quality of life improvement in the world.

> "Nothing of any consequence happens unless people get behind an idea. It begins with an individual and they share the idea with more individuals... and eventually it becomes a movement".

> — Christopher Reeve (2002)

The quote above makes a perfect point. You cannot expect to rely on divinity to help you «break on through (to the other side)». I agree that someone might feel like finding comfort in an ulterior entity, but unless they start doing something for themselves, setting up their own luck, then they are going to have a hard time finding whatever it is they are looking for. Mankind was gifted with knowledge and reason so it could improve its life on its home planet. If we have the ability to go out into space and

---

[139] 1961-2006. Also an actress and an activist, like her husband, Dana died nearly two years after becoming a widow, due to lung cancer.

fund manned spaceship programs to do some exploring, eventually finding an exoplanet to terraform[140], we can also fund one of the most basic functions of our bodies, which is self-regeneration. No one is born to endure life in the dark, stuck in a chair, bound to respirators or in the care of others, without any autonomy at all. No, this is not God's work. And should it be, then what kind of god wants us suffering like his own son, who he had walk through the desert for forty days without any food, deliberately tempted by his archenemy (whom he could not stop from rebelling), then being scourged and nailed to a cross to redeem all of Humanity's sins, who is still killing in «His» name?

This is the difference between Science and Religion: the first will change your life, making it better and better, whereas the latter will leave you exactly where you are, unchanged, hoping things will improve, while asking for monetary donations for the redemption of your soul that you cannot give because you are unemployed, cannot work, require constant care and attention you cannot afford, living on a State subsidy that is not even enough to feed a house pet. Is this why we are Earth's dominant species? Perhaps we should have stayed in the wilderness, then, cyclically, wearing soils out at a time, so we could come back to them after our Nomad venture and reuse them. We have about 30% of the planet's surface to us, which equals approximately 57,500,000 mi² (150,000,000 km²). That is a lot of terrain to cover.

Some people would rather respect the precepts of religion, rather than to just accept the progress attached to Science, which is why some diseases have not been completely eradicated yet, as children are not being vaccinated, which is something I already talked about in other titles. I could, however, repeat the idea people are not doing this because they are either against chemicals

---

[140] Make earthly-like.

and would rather stay natural, just like they were born, disabling the strength of their babies' immune system, or because Governments are using vaccines to inject some kind of a microscopic GPS device in our bloodstream. Needless to say I am not going to argue about that again, as you can already get from my tone what I think of this issue.

We accepted the fact we could not inhabit our homes made of mud and raw wood anymore together with plague-riddled mice. It was an undeniable danger to public health. We must also accept the fact we cannot continue to be alive to study hard, work even harder and eventually die of old age as if we had done nothing at all for our own sake. People have the free will to either accept or reject religion, just as much. It is what a religion's representatives have to say that they should worry about, as all human beings work primarily on behalf of their own interests, considering their society only afterward. The clergy, regardless of their faith, is no different. Religious buildings and salaries are not kept with divine inspiration, and the men involved know it better than anyone else. They are already tax-proof for requiring fiscal exemption from Governments. They cannot be allowed to deter human progress, like they did in the Middle Ages, delaying our research in over one thousand years. Let the die be cast, for our very chance of survival is at stake.

2
State of Transcendence

The vocable «Transhumanism» is formally defined as such:

"1. The intellectual and cultural movement that affirms the possibility and desirability of fundamentally improving the human condition through applied reason, especially by developing and making widely available technologies to eliminate aging and to greatly enhance human intellectual, physical, and psychological capacities.

"2. The study of the ramifications, promises, and potential dangers of technologies that will enable us to overcome fundamental human limitations, and the related study of the ethical matters involved in developing and using such technologies".

— *The Transhumanist FAQ*
Humanity+[141]

The largest leap Mankind took after 1969, when the United

---

[141] Founded in 1998 by Nick Bostrom and David Pearce as «World Transhumanist Association», it had its designation changed a decade later, in order to demonstrate a more humane approach.

States landed human beings on the Moon[142] for the first time ever in History, was in 1990, twenty-six years ago, during the advent of technological explosion. The beginning of the last decade of the 20th century was key to both dissemination of information on digital support (via the World Wide Web) and human genetic modifications (via gene therapy trials and «designer babies»[143]). That is the time transhumanists around the world consider to be the start of a transition from a plainly natural, humanist state to the posthuman condition, the apogee of Mankind in the near future, notwithstanding the observation of critical ethic-related aspects toward the usage of both a technologically-enabled superhuman empowerment and the creation of artificial intelligence designed to overcome human effort in the improving of living

---

[142] The eleventh «Apollo» mission series spacecraft was launched on July 16th, 1969, carrying a crew of three men, Commander Neil A. Armstrong (1930-2012), Lunar Module Pilot Edwin "Buzz" E. Aldrin, Jr. (b. 1930) and Command Module Pilot Michael Collins (b. 1930). The first two were the ones stepping on the lunar surface, July 20th, in an area called *Mare Tranquillitatis* (Latin for «Sea of Tranquility»), named by Italian astronomers Francesco Grimaldi (1618-1663) and Giovanni Battista Riccioli (1598-1671) in 1651, where the first US flag was placed and reportedly knocked over after the rocket blast from Armstrong and Aldrin's departure back to the Command Module. Both astronauts remained about twenty-one hours and a half on the Moon collecting materials for analysis back home. Back in 1961, President John F. Kennedy had predicted America would place a human being on the Earth's natural satellite before the decade was over, as a result of the neck and neck «Space Race» between the US and the Soviet Union, in the context of the Cold War. The Soviets had already sent to space the first artificial satellite, Sputnik 1, in October 1957, followed by Sputnik 2, launched one month later, carrying the first living occupant, Laika, a female dog (killed because of overheating of the craft), in order to test deorbiting withstanding conditions on living beings for manned spacecrafts, which would take place with the successful launch of Vostok 1 in April 1961, operated by cosmonaut Yuri Gagarin (1934-1968). In spite of their efforts, the Soviets did not manage to successfully place a man on the Moon and thus focused on Earth-orbiting missions.

[143] These are the result of medical genetic screening of embryos, enabling parents to choose their future child's physical traits, before the egg is implanted in the mother or carrier's womb.

conditions via Singularity[144], which is somewhat similar to the process of automation in workplaces, during the Industrial Revolution, under which people's hard work was replaced by that of machines, only those machines' AI is human-controlled and can only develop if Man so desires.

I believe that, before we develop other technologies with the purpose of easing life through day-to-day objects, transportation, infrastructures, etc., we should improve on human capabilities, should it become counterproductive to invest in technological aids we might not need afterward. As long as projecting the future in this era requires an insurmountable amount of money and until society becomes plain penniless, futurists are, in my opinion, required to do some careful financial planning, as if they were building a social environment from square one, and not so figuratively speaking, because, somehow, that actually is the purpose of futurization, to modify our ways of living, just like during the advent of the Industrial Revolution, beginning in the 1750s, only, this time, fully considering the environment. That is why recurring to green energy is mandatory, especially if Humanity is to survive the transition we are undergoing right now, toward the posthuman stage.

If you recall the introduction made to this book, I mentioned someone in need of a pacemaker to overcome heart diseases was already bionic. I continue to stand by that statement, obviously. If there is a medical chance people's longevity might be prolonged and kept with the necessary quality of life, then why should doctors just stand still and do nothing about it? Religion already took care of blocking medicinal research through centuries, we have talked about it many times throughout these pages, including the previous chapter, so the last time was not too long ago,

---

[144] According to the Dictionary definition, it is "a hypothetical future point in time when artificial intelligence will surpass human intelligence and be able to self-replicate and improve itself autonomously".

but here is a good example to illustrate the issue regarding life-saving: have you ever watched a motion picture called *The Physician*? The footnote contains all the information you need to look it up on the Internet[145]. The story takes place in 11th-century England, at first, then moving to Isfahan, Persia (present-day Iran), during the Dark Ages. Without revealing any kind of spoilers, what is important to retrieve from the plot is how autopsying is regarded by Christianity, in dark Europe, and Judaism and Islam in the Middle East, where Muslims tolerate the presence of the Jewish, but not the Christians. Despite all these faith-based differences, there is one thing they all have in common, and that is the damning of necromancers[146]. There were absolutely no donations to Science in this period, as bodies could not be opened to study the causes of death and, therefore, revolutionize medical research.

This is why I insist on the fact religion keeps blinding civilization from progress. It is not just a question of having a faith control Governments, anymore. Now, more than ever, the other way around is becoming all the more visible. The State is only laic to a certain extent. Should help from a «temple» be required, they hop aboard and enjoy the ride toward a common interest. That is how it has always been, and changing it is undoubtedly an enormous effort. Both Politics and religion make an almost indestructible couple. That is what the Crusades were all about, the

---

[145] *The Physician*, based on the homonymous novel by Noah Gordon, starring Tom Payne, Ben Kingsley and Stellan Skarsgård, directed by Philipp Stölzl, Universal Pictures, 2013.

[146] Practitioners of necromancy, labeled at the time as some sort of either black magic or witchcraft by men of faith. It was thought anyone messing with a person's corpse had the intention of undergoing some wrongdoing against the living, and the penalty for such a crime was inevitably death.

expansion of geopolitical territory under the influence of the Vatican. The Papal States[147], as it was known until 1929, when Benito Mussolini[148] granted sovereignty to the microstate of Vatican City, were the headquarters to all the riches the nobility also benefitted from in all of Christendom. The Pope did not only have financial and economic power, he also had manpower, and a great deal of it. That is how Muslims were kicked out of Southern Europe, where they got to after the settlement of barbaric kingdoms, following the demise of the Western Roman Empire. However, because of the papacy's ambition to gain control of the Holy Land, which was entirely meaningful to Christians, all endeavors in the area were lost to the victory of Islam, which still is today the main region in the globe for the faith, just like Rome continues to be the center of Christianity, specifically to Catholics. European kingdoms really had no choice but to stick to papal law if they wanted their «sovereignty», or they would have to face both the Pope and his allies' men, just like Elizabeth I of England did[149].

In modern times, going to war is more of both an economically and geopolitical beneficial process, rather than religious. Governments are not so comfortable with the usage of green energy, as it represents the unavoidable demise of oil. A lot of countries' economies depend exclusively from the profit of petroleum. Should this era come to an end, millions of lives will be at stake, just like they are now in States such as Angola, in Africa, or Venezuela, in South America. In 1955, when the Vietnam War began,

---

[147] Spanning between 754 and 1870, with a few interregna, these were territories held under the Pope's direct rule in the Italian Peninsula.

[148] 1883-1945. Known as *Il Duce* («The Leader»), he was the founder of fascism and Hitler's main ally in Europe. Two days before the latter committed suicide in his underground bunker, in Berlin, Mussolini was captured and killed by both their sworn enemy, the communists, and hung upside-down in Milan for people to be aware of his death.

[149] Vide note 41.

ten years after the end of World War II and the beginning of the Cold War between the United States and the Soviet Union, there was an indirect race to put a halt to communism, on one side, and imperialism, on the other. The satellite-countries of both fronts were the ones caught in the middle. President John F. Kennedy had meant to withdraw from Vietnam, but after his assassination, Lyndon B. Johnson reverted the entire policy[150]. It was simply not suitable to let the enemy win before the eyes of the rest of the globe. Though the war lasted twenty years, the United States retreated in loss. Their fight against communism was proven otherwise, as economic efforts were channeled to the conflict, paid for by *common* money, the taxpayers' money. The Soviet Union itself was being *imperialistic* just as much, as it kept gathering trust from its satellites to strengthen its power. Mao Zedong himself came to realize it, hence the Sino-Soviet split, in 1961. He was interested in communism completely, and not imperialism under a communist guise.

One of the biggest concerns about the transhumanist movement is its advocates might be looking to revive mythical quests about the ideal of immortality, such as the Fountain of Youth[151] or the Elixir of Life[152], but it is not just that. There is also the

---

[150] Vide note 26.

[151] The earliest accounts for this myth date back to Herodotus (c. 484 BC – c. 425 BC), though its relation to Spanish conquistador Juan Ponce de León (1474-1521) is probably the most famous. Despite the fact the Fountain was never mentioned in his expedition writings, the connection was made by Gonzalo Fernández de Oviedo y Valdés (1478-1557), a Spanish historian and writer, in his oeuvre *Historia General y Natural de las Indias* (1535), which claimed Ponce de León was looking for the Fountain in Bimini, located in the Bahamas, during his travels to the New World, so as to gain eternal youthfulness. It is thought Oviedo's claims were made to attain favor from the Spanish court.

[152] It is considered to be either a potion, drunk from a predetermined cup, at a predetermined time, or the so-called «philosopher's stone», a substance which had the power to turn regular metals into gold (which is what Alchemy

issue of fulfilling a desire of superhuman capabilities, therefore raising a topic known as «contempt for the flesh». It is, of course, the kind of problem I was talking about in the previous chapter, with a strong opposition from religion, regardless of the faith represented, as this means Posthumanism would necessarily become a defeat for the multiple deities our numerous societies believe in. These gods are the ones gifted with both eternal life and the ability to outcome the weakness of a regular human body. Aiming to surpass godlike forms and possibly become even more powerful than them is something «temples» are not prepared to tolerate, following the example contained in the Bible about the Tower of Babel[153].

Simultaneously, some people are not prepared either to tolerate their disappearance into oblivion, without having the chance to fulfill all of their plans or making their wishes come true, because of the reduced amount of practical time a human life has. It is mostly not a question of living all the way up to a certain age, and that is why I added to the preceding sentence the term «practical», because, again, we may live to be 100-years-old, but we will certainly not be capable of doing the same things a 20-year-old can do, as far as physicality is concerned. If we grow to

---

sought the most across centuries) and, like the potion, extend human life eternally. The earliest accounts regarding the search for longevity date back to Ancient China, in the 3rd century BC. The most renowned story with respect to eternal youthfulness and life is undoubtedly the Holy Grail (also known as the Holy Chalice), from which Jesus Christ poured wine (his blood) to his twelve disciples (or apostles) in the «Last Supper», whose most famous depiction is Leonardo da Vinci's (1452-1519) mural painting in Milan, dated from the 1490s. The quest for the Holy Grail is one of the most important pieces in Arthurian literature, which tells the story of Arthur Pendragon, King of the Britons.

[153] In short, the inhabitants of Babel wanted to please Jehovah by gifting him a tower as tall as the skies, so they could be closer to him. Feeling defied by a group of humans, his own creation, God confused them all by making them speak different languages and distributed them all over the globe, so the tower would be left incomplete.

be that experienced, our sageness will undoubtedly turn into a source of both wisdom and maturity, which is brilliant. However, it is the body that will sooner or later begin to fail, as it cannot keep up with our mentality of a century, *if* we really are aware of our own minds. If we are struck by degenerative diseases, the way we are living now, there is nothing we can do to prevent the loss of our consciousness to illnesses like dementia or Alzheimer's[154], unless we do something transhumanists call «mind uploading».

This would consist in either withholding someone's mind in a digital body (quantum or binary) or sending all the neural data available, of which intellect, memory and self are the most important, to another entirely biological brain, which would have to somehow lead to human cloning, a matter complicated enough as far as ethic is concerned. Present-day legislation is already prohibiting Science from copying human beings, mostly because the world, in its present state, is not prepared to accept walking carbon paper, unless you claim you have a monozygotic[155] twin no one knew about.

You probably know the story about Dolly, the sheep, the first mammal cloned from an adult somatic cell ever made[156], though

---

[154] Named after Aloysius "Alois" Alzheimer (1864-1915), German psychiatrist and neuropathologist, who published the first identified case of presenile dementia, by Emil Kraepelin (1856-1926). The latter is considered to be the founding father of modern Psychiatry, Psychiatric Genetics and Psychopharmacology. His theory of «mental hygiene» would later influence Adolf Hitler to pursue the cleansing of the Aryan race through eugenics (vide note 55).

[155] Identical twins are generated from a single sperm cell and an egg, then splitting into two embryos, as opposed to fraternal twins, who are generated from two different sperm cells and eggs, resulting in significant similarities, but hardly looking the exact same.

[156] In order to be born, Dolly required three different mothers for each stage of the process: first, the egg; second, DNA; and finally, a surrogate. It all begins with the oocyte, whose core is removed and replaced with the donor's DNA, from an adult cell, which then starts to divide via an electric shock

it was not the first clone to have been produced in History[157]. The method utilized to create Dolly could be used on humans as well, only as therapeutic cloning, rather than reproductive, whose final purpose would be to create an exact copy of a living human being from whom genetic code was extracted and electrically fused with an enucleated egg cell.

In therapeutic cloning, the blastocyst's inner cell mass would be rich in stem cells, becoming isolated in order to produce embryonic stem cell lines that would be applied to a person's damaged tissue or organ, regenerating it and eventually wiping the disease that had caused damage from the body[158]. However, and though stem cell research is currently active, it is not being used in medical treatment. There is fear from governmental authorities that scientists may make use of a therapeutic cloning procedure in order to reach the reproductive kind, which could result in the implantation of a genetically modified embryo in a surrogate's uterus. Years later, an existing person could end up meeting their younger duplicate. But it is not just that. The issue arises right from the start. When an egg cell is artificially prepared to become an embryo, it means that, had it been given enough time, it would grow into a fetus, who could have been given birth to. It all goes both cyclically and immediately back to the question of considering abortion either legal or not. The fact is that, should it be allowed to develop, the embryo would result in a fetus, which

---

(in alternative to regular egg fertilization), developing into a blastocyst, preparing it for implantation in the surrogate's uterus. Genes from the core of a matured somatic cell are able to revert to an embryonic state, thusly generating a cell which can turn out to be any part of an animal in its original whole.

[157] Hans Driesch (1867-1941) was the first to create a clone from a sea urchin, in 1885. Just by shaking two embryonic cells, Driesch got two complete specimens. It was thought a cell could not reproduce an entire body beyond a certain stage, but Dolly eventually proved otherwise.

[158] Further reading: MURNAGHAN, Ian, 05-09-2016, *Explore Stem Cells*, «Therapeutic Cloning», (http://www.explorestemcells.co.uk/therapeuticcloning.html), accessed 06-02-2016.

would in the near future become the likes of the original DNA donor, as the genetic information is the exact same and is not crossed with the egg's own info, previously removed, which would therefore alter the code. On the other hand, disabling a person from being healed through their own body is a number one priority, when it comes to annihilating their illegal biological copy, because of the comparison made to abortion, which, as I explained in the first part, is a right either a woman (both biologically and emotionally) or a man (just emotionally, though with the required consent from his partner) is entitled to.

Stem cell treatment is one of the safest ways of wiping out diseases from our bodies, as these are more likely to accept our own genetic material, instead of a third-party donor's foreign code, which is usually attacked by the new host, as it does not recognize the differing information. Nonetheless, it is still this morose, delaying process dying patients count on to survive. Even if their damaged body accepts another person's donated material, chances are they will not be living long, as opposed to their own and none other's genetics, which their body is already familiar with.

But not everything is bright about the subject, which takes me back to the risks associated with reproductive cloning. Not only could a person be interested in being fully cloned, so as to *coach* their younger self into either wrongdoing or foul play in their place, there could also be a chance the older, original self would seize their cloned younger body only to harvest new material from it into their own. The clone, a human being like any other born from natural conception, as far as biological composition is concerned, would have to either be used once and then disposed of after the collection of the matured enough organ or tissue, or it would have to be cryogenically preserved, in case other original material needed to be replaced. In the end, the reproductive kind of cloning could perfectly result in the secret production of human harvesting farms, the same kind we usually watch in sci-fi movies[159], whether by the hands of governments or corporations with interests other than those made public, part of the façade. If, however, reproductive cloning legislation could be enforced, there would be no obstacles whatsoever to the therapeutic kind, as killing an embryo that would later become a person's exact copy *cannot* be compared to abortion, not ever.

If all this is regarded as «contempt for the flesh», because we are trying all the same to extend our lives toward immortality, rather than trying to live with total eradication of either disease or any other kind of damage to our body, then what will skeptics have to say about «mind uploading», which was what we were talking about before mentioning cloning?

To some people, transhumanist scientists included, mind and soul are both one and the same, as the very essence of the self is the result of a computational process, just like the neural network running through the brain. The question is whether *copying* someone's mind onto a different platform, such as a positronic brain, would gift the new bearer of that mind data (like a robot or a humanoid) with the same lines of intellect and thought, together with emotion and personality.

The concept for this kind of brain was developed by American (though Russian born) sci-fi novelist and biochemistry professor

---

[159] A few examples are: *The Matrix*, starring Keanu Reeves, Laurence Fishburne, Carrie-Anne Moss and Hugo Weaving, written and directed by The Wachowski Brothers, Warner Bros., 1999; *The Island*, starring Ewan McGregor, Scarlett Johansson and Sean Bean, directed by Michael Bay, DreamWorks Pictures, 2005; and *Resident Evil: Retribution*, starring Milla Jovovich, Michelle Rodriguez, Sienna Guillory and Shawn Roberts, written and directed by Paul W. S. Anderson, Screen Gems, 2012.

Isaac Asimov[160], who thought of the humanoid-like brain as a CPU (Central Processing Unit), like the ones existent in present-day computers. Though the technology was never specified, positronic brains somehow emulated the human conscience, just like robots holding them had a similar appearance to either men or women, so humans would not feel so scared of them.

However, before any concrete «mind uploading» plans can take shape, it is necessary to fully understand the human brain, and there still is a long way to go. Popular culture often mentions we, as human beings, only utilize about ten percent of our brain. That is nothing but folklore, an urban legend, if you wish. The brain of an adult *Homo Sapiens* weighs, on average, about three pounds[161]. It is around 167 millimeters long and 140 millimeters wide. If we used only ten percent of our brain's total capacity, we would be recurring solely to 0.33 pounds[162] of brain matter, based on a geometrical area of 28.3 cm², out of a possible total 234 cm². That ten percent area of a human brain is equal to one hundred percent of a lamb's brain, which, as we all know, is not the smartest of animals. Wherever one decides to go, the other will follow it and so on, without realizing the consequences of their actions, as they are not rational, hence the usage for shepherd dogs, which can be trained for a determined assignment without questioning their trainer or owner's authority.

In short, the often talked about ten percent of human brain usage is, in fact, the percentage of total *comprehension* we have of our personal processor. There still is about ninety percent left to *understand* how the human mind works. All sectors are permanently active, especially when asleep, as that is the time when

---

[160] 1920-1992. Asimov had had a heart attack in 1977 and was submitted to a triple bypass surgery in 1983. He was infected with HIV by a contaminated blood transfusion during said surgery and died nine years later, after the virus triggered both a myocardial and renal failure.

[161] Between 1.3 and 1.5 kilograms, for metric system Readers.

[162] 0.15 kilograms.

we do not have any control over our intellect and thus allow it to travel through many memories we did not have any remembrance of anymore, kept in the core of the subconscious (the underwater part of the neural iceberg, as described by Sigmund Freud[163]) or to freely take a stroll in the avenue of creativity and come up with ideas for just about anything, which may usually end up forgotten when we wake up[164].

It is because of this lack of *comprehension* that the idea of «mind uploading» is thought of as possible via an emulation process of the neural network. The human brain, like you have already had the chance to understand, is probably the most complex organ there is in an animal. We all know (doctors, especially) what other organs are for, as well as their basic function, it is part of every school's Science curricula, but it is the brain that still is much of an enigma scientists have been baffled by, for it is the very processor in charge of all bodily systems.

One of the simplest ways of mapping and capturing the neural network of a human brain is to, precisely as stated in the previous paragraph, emulate it via a computer system. The downside of this process is the disregard for both the psychological and large-

---

[163] 1856-1939. Austrian neurologist and founder of psychoanalysis, a clinical method for treating psychopathology through dialogue between patient and psychoanalyst.

[164] Dadaism (or simply Dada) was an art movement that began officially in 1915, during World War I (1914-1918). It was anti-war, for that matter, as well as anti-art, which is a term coined by Marcel Duchamp (1887-1968), whose name is the one more closely associated to the movement, although he acted independently. One of the most common practices for Dada literature was to let loose automatic speech, writing down anything that came up to a writer's head. This was habitually triggered when they were asleep, and therefore a lot of them always kept a notebook on the nightstand, so as to write it all down, every time they woke.

scale structural properties, as those would represent tens of thousands of terabytes[165] present-day computers cannot handle. As far as my personal opinion is concerned and though it would be both costly and delaying to build a capable supercomputer for this[166], mapping a brain's neural network for the sake of basic copy is, indeed, a giant leap toward «mind uploading», but I believe no one's personality could be perfectly mimed without any traces of personality contained in the upload, which would take us, again, toward the question of mind/soul dichotomy.

Theoretically, the «source code» copied from the original biological brain would be made available to a computer programming language that could then interpret basic neural function, but not necessarily the chemical processes associated with emotion and personality. Of course, I myself value this operation as a legitimate way to start «mind uploading» research.

In order to make a neural network completer, though more complex, it would have to be dynamically spiking, i.e. have neurons react at a predetermined level when the potential of a membrane is reached. This kind of parameter, together with neuromodulators or different voltages of electrical currents, related between them, is electrophysical.

Both learning and long-term memory processes are the result of either the strengthening or weakening of synapses[167] in the

---

[165] In comparison, 1,024 bytes make 1 kilobyte. 1,024 kilobytes make 1 megabyte. 1,024 megabytes make 1 gigabyte. 1,024 gigabytes make 1 terabyte. Though a terabyte represents a huge amount of data, the largest storage unit created up to now is the yottabyte, matching one trillion terabytes.

[166] The most powerful, according to Swedish transhumanist scientists Anders Sandberg (b. 1972) and Nick Bostrom (b. 1973) and American Futurist Ray Kurzweil (b. 1948), would be made available in 2111, ninety-five years from now (eleven after the projected date contained in this book's subtitle), at the cost of one million dollars. Such a computer would be able to capture the behavior of every single-molecule of the brain. Further information: KURZWEIL, Ray, 2005, *The Singularity Is Near*, New York City: Viking Press.

[167] Brain structures enabling neurons to communicate between each other, either chemically or electrically.

brain, which is called synaptic plasticity. Like it says in the last footnote, synapses may either be chemical or electrical. The former kind comprehends the existence of neurotransmitters through which chemical reactions take place. Electrical activity is captured by the presynaptic neuron and then converted to chemical substances sent to the postsynaptic neuron. It is, basically, the kind of speech structure we learn as children in elementary school, contained in Jakobson's[168] «functions of language». There is a sender (or addresser), which would, in this case, be the presynaptic neuron; a message (or *logos*), an electrical current converted to a chemical substance, and a receiver (or addressee), the postsynaptic neuron. Electrical synapses, on the other hand, contain gap junctions, as opposed to the chemical kind and their neurotransmitters, which enables the passing of electrical current at a certain voltage from one neuron to the next. This method of communication between neurons is much faster than the previous. From the start, because of the need to keep both learning and long-term memory processes active when emulating someone's mind, synaptic plasticity must be kept, so as to also maintain sensory reactions to diverse forms of emotional stimulation. Hence the reason to prioritize just as much the inclusion of body metabolism when uploading a mind, as nutrients obtained from digestion (in short, the energy keeping us alive) have hormonal influence in the brain, when they leave blood circulation and are absorbed by it. This part of the «mind uploading» process would be, however, computationally difficult, for it comprehends also interaction with protein, but not just that. A natural brain does not compute with the exact, same precision as an artificial intelligence would, as it eventually becomes worn out from third-party factors, such as excessive noise, addiction, junk food eating, etc. This biological deficiency we carry could be permanently

---

[168] Roman Osipovich Jakobson (1896-1982), Russian-American linguist.

deleted from future forms of intelligence, though simulating such an environment would, again, become excessively costly in a money-making civilization such as ours, especially if we want it to be real time, which we do. The biological brain might be flawed with randomness, but it also has abilities that are still insurmountable in comparison to computers.

There is, however, a problem, when it comes to the short-term and active kinds of memory: they are not immediately stored. When we are watching fiction on television or at the movies and the story is about someone who recently suffered from an amnesic episode, the patient lying in bed at the hospital is likely to remember most of their old memories, but not those slightly more recent, as it has not been enough time to assure their safekeeping. Intraneural dynamics are constantly running, so there has to be repetition for short-term memories to be converted to the long-term kind. An uploaded mind is likely to fail the remembrance of recent details, as both chemical and electrical synapses are harder to extract when plainly active.

In order to upload every single aspect there is with respect to the human brain, about 20,000 terabytes of storage would be required. This is why traditional binary storage (either 0 or 1, on or off) is unsuitable for the complete representation of a person's mind.

In the next chapter, I am going to talk to you not just about «mind uploading» safekeeping, but also how that same, uploaded mind can be executed in either a biological organism, an electronic vessel or the combination of both, the bionic humanoid.

3
Intellectual Safekeeping

The concept of digital immortality might not be as secure as one may think. If scientists eventually find the necessary resources for the complete upload of a human being's mapped brain, either to download it unto a humanoid or a permanently young biological body, flesh and bone, it does not mean intellectual content will not endure what people entrusting their whole life with a computer fear the most, and that is either accidental data corruption or deliberate foul play via a new form of terrorism law enforcement all over the world has been dealing with since the electronic boom of the 1990s, cyberterrorism. I do not even need to add this vocable to my word processor's custom dictionary, it is not underlined red as I type it, because it already is a part of an everyday lexicon.

Everything regular IT[169] users store online, so as to prevent that same data corruption I was talking about just now, especially due to a hard drive or any other computer hardware component malfunction, does not merely exist at a digital, virtual state, and that is significantly obvious to everyone who has learnt

---

[169] Information Technology.

the basics of this kind of technology from an end-user's perspective. When your equipment is getting old and you feel like acquiring a new piece of electronics for you to work with or just have fun either watching movies or playing video games, you are always advised by store assistants to take a look at the specifics, namely the CPU[170], the GPU[171], the RAM[172] and the hard disk[173] space, spanning between a few hundred gigabytes and the latest eight-terabyte, by Seagate Technology.

Storing files on online servers is exactly the same process, as said servers become live via physical locations in companies' headquarters. Nearly all of them share a common designation or logo bearing a cloud. It is called cloud technology (or computing), because it is Internet-based, meaning users are not required to install or have any files at all on their computers, if they do not want to, as direct upload is already possible, nowadays. Of course, we all have the chance to manage our server-stored files from our computer's hard drive by installing the correspondent program, which will then make a connection to the Internet for said files to be displayed.

I thought I should mention all of this to explain, even though

---

[170] Central Processing Unit, or processor, as it is most commonly designated. Think of it as the heart of the computer, sending specific instructions via the electronic circuitry, just like blood containing cells and other components through its vessels. The two most successful brands producing CPUs are Intel and AMD.

[171] Graphics Processing Unit, or graphics card. This is the part of a computer that enables screen visualization and its respective quality, becoming very important as far as running the most recent video games is concerned, as they get all the more graphically demanding with time. NVIDIA and AMD are the most common brands of GPUs in the world.

[172] Random-Access Memory. As opposed to direct-access memory, whose communicating speed depends on factors such as data location or reading velocity of physical location drives, RAM can be accessed instantly, regardless of the procured items' storage whereabouts.

[173] The first of which was created on Christmas 1954.

we may call these servers «clouds», they are not exactly untouchable for their «altitude». In September 2014, a virtual event called «The Fappening[174]» took place online, when Apple's cloud servers were barged into by hackers, resulting in the leakage of nude photos of over one hundred female celebrities. Though some of those women blamed Apple for its lack of security, the company replied by claiming they have nothing to do with customers' lack of creativity as far as their passwords are concerned, making them easy to guess or crack. There were several statements from victims who decided to speak either directly or via their publicists, saying whoever looked up their intimate photos online was as criminal as the hackers themselves. I personally agree. What people do in their privacy is their business alone, just like whoever it is they share their intimacy with. Nonetheless, people are always making it easier to end up being blackmailed or as victims of extortion when they have this kind of secret in their closet. It is undeniably unsafe to either keep nude pictures in the phone or upload them to some server, as there are people willing to nullify another person's dignity, especially if they are famous, especially if hackers do it in public, under which circumstances it hurts the most.

Now, picture this kind of situation without any physical evidence at all, not even virtual, with respect to a file you save to a digital device, but rather as a *thought*. Mind-reading abilities are something a lot of human beings have undoubtedly thought about over the course of millennia, which is obviously one of popular culture's favorite inspirations. What if, somehow, other people could pry into your *uploaded* mind, like hackers can, when it comes to your private «cloud»? Terrorism does not necessarily have to do with biological, chemical or fire weaponry. Literally billions of people are sending every single day, twenty-

---

[174] Crossover between the jargon verb «to fap» (male masturbation) and the noun «happening».

four/seven, private information to the Web. How much of that information is actually plain, "anonymous statistics"? We pretty much have no idea. Online banking and other services requiring this sort of information has come to ease our life, most assuredly, but there are also many great risks involved. Any server claiming it is safe, because it is using encrypted technology, is only much so until the day it is attacked by an experienced «privateer». Can you think of anything far more precious, other than your riches? Exactly: how much you care for your family and friends, or whichever thoughts you had in the past about something or someone, and I do not mean only that crush you had in junior high. You might have thought about killing someone, even though you never meant for it to happen.

I feel safe enough making this kind of statement, because I am sure I am not the first troubleshooting this issue[175]. It is an actual threat that has been considered many times before. You cannot blame me for this, though. I did say in the introduction some subjects were not entirely original. I just talk about them in order to problematize for the sake of Literature.

Should you, either out of passion or plain rage, have thought about committing murder, even though you neither did, nor could have done it, as it is not in your nature to do such an atrocity, what would law enforcement react like? Would the police have enough legitimacy, or any at all, to place you under arrest? That was the ethical question sought for in the motion picture I mentioned in the latest footnote. When such a *perfect* crime prevention system is built, there somehow has to be a *flaw*.

We have to be really careful with what we wish for, it is a commonplace statement, I realize that, but if we want our minds fully intact, without anyone trying to pry into the cupboard so

---

[175] Cf. *Minority Report*, based on the homonymous short story (1956) by Philip K. Dick (1928-1982), starring Tom Cruise and Colin Ferrell, directed by Steven Spielberg, 20th Century Fox/DreamWorks Pictures, 2002.

they can find our own, personal skeletons, the current encryption methods we use have got to become obsolete. DES[176] is used worldwide, and is, in short, a symmetric-key algorithm, based on the AES[177] encryption system. It means that the key used to encrypt data is the same required to decrypt it. Even if you are not that much interested in cryptography, I am sure you understand how flawed and unsafe this is. Whoever gets the chance to grab your key and steal the addressee's authentication parameters from them, has a free pass into inspecting your business. If it is dangerous as it is right now, imagine what would happen if hackers were to gain access to your own intellect, your mind, and digitally delete your existence, preventing anyone else from downloading your state of transcendence to another vessel in which you could keep on living indefinitely. This is the part where it gets a lot more interesting: quantum mechanics meets quantum cryptography.

Though it is safer to use quantum-encoded data to send a message out to someone via QKD[178], again, it is not entirely flawless, though a path is being built toward that exact flawlessness, which yet again ends up meeting the desire of achieving perfection. When a message is encoded via quantum and sent to the addressee, it bears a determined state. Should anyone else, like a third-party, try to get in the middle, said state is disturbed and both addresser and addressee learn of the disturbance. The only way to prevent anyone else from accessing the content of the message by decoding it regularly would be through commitment. This means people have to take a commitment not to reveal their access data to a third-party, which obviously implies honesty from human nature itself. This is exactly the same issue nowadays' cryptographic technology is experiencing. If you give your

---

[176] Data Encryption Standard.
[177] Advanced Encryption Standard.
[178] Quantum Key Distribution.

password to someone, regardless of how much you trust them, there is never a way of finding out whether that person will respect your privacy. Deception is hardly ever identifiable.

The only way to make sure your ID can never be stolen when giving someone access to your information is to copy-protect it. How you do that without the risk of being hacked is what keeps dragging us all down, back to square one.

In other news, building machines run on artificial intelligence does not make errors obsolete. There is not the need to go back that many pages in this book to find one of many references I have made concerning Humanity's aim to reach the ideal of perfection. Right now, robots cannot build themselves, Futurist scientists have not yet designed a fully capable form of AI to take care of itself. That is why, recently, Mark Zuckerberg[179] stated he was preparing AI to build other AIs, as these are too complicated to replicate[180]. He says it himself, in the last paragraphs of his post on his Facebook page, that "we should not be afraid of AI". I agree with his statement. It is how we build AI and what entrepreneurs design it for that is the problem. The laptop in which I typed the book you are reading right now, either in print or on an e-Reader, is a piece of AI itself, just like your devices. I run the Windows operating system from Microsoft, which, like its competitors, is capable of virtually holding all parts of the computer together, so they do not get *physically* damaged, as that

---

[179] B. 1984, he is the chairman, chief executive officer and a co-founder of the most used social network in the world, Facebook, which he created with fellow college roommates Eduardo Saverin, Andrew McCollum, Dustin Moskovitz and Chris Hughes, while attending Harvard University, in 2004 (aged 20). He eventually dropped out, just like other IT entrepreneurs, such as Bill Gates, co-founder of Microsoft, and the late Steve Jobs (co-founder of Apple).

[180] ZUCKERBERG, Mark, 01-27-2016, *Facebook*, «Mark Zuckerberg», (https://www.facebook.com/zuck/posts/10102620559534481), accessed 06-06-2016.

may well happen, when a controller is either outdated or improperly installed. There is a new, smartly improved PDA[181] they call «Cortana», similar to Apple's «Siri» or Google's «Google Now», which you call out by saying "Hey, Cortana", "Hey, Siri" or "OK, Google", respectively. All of these PDAs' purpose is to respond to the device's user and help them getting something done without too much effort, just by speaking, basically. You can have them run errands for you, ask them to remind you of an appointment, send an e-mail to one of your contacts, etc. Most of these tasks are still pretty basic and would hardly require any physical effort from the user. In fact, I felt a lot better typing these words myself, rather than having them dictated (which is just a personal preference), but even if I had done that, I would always have been in control, as digital devices may suggest the words we want to use when typing, via autocorrect, but they only take their place after our confirmation, regardless of being involuntary, due to our different typing speeds or other distractions.

This is precisely the barrier we are facing right now, segregating plainly biological humans from androids, hence somehow justifying some people's fear of machines taking over for us.

---

[181] Personal Digital Assistant.

4

I, HuBot

«1st) A robot may not injure a human being or, through inaction, allow a human being to come to harm.

2nd) A robot must obey the orders given it by human beings except where such orders would conflict with the First Law.

3rd) A robot must protect its own existence as long as such protection does not conflict with the First or Second Laws».

— The Three Laws of Robotics[182]
"Handbook of Robotics, 56th Edition, 2058 AD".

You probably recognized «Asimov's Laws» just by reading the first few words. They are just so technologically classical that they have already become vintage. This author, whom we came across with earlier[183], started writing science fiction in the second half of the 1930s, when he was not even eighteen-years-old, yet. Considering one of the most criminal wars to have ever taken

---

[182] These laws were first introduced to the public by Isaac Asimov in the short story titled *Runaround*, published 1942.
[183] Vide note 160.

place in the recorded History of the world was still brewing, Asimov's vision was far beyond his own time, which is not so peculiar, when considering men such as Nikola Tesla[184], whom I quoted in the very beginning of this oeuvre.

Ever since Man started wondering about having robots living together with him, doing the hard work his biological body cannot withstand, there has been the possibility of either having us, human beings, become bionic ourselves *or* counteract the effects of ageing, in order to live free of illnesses, handicapping and death itself, though with the presence of robots, in order to maintain the flesh and bone structure of always. Like I said before, and that same statement is featured in the back cover of this book, "most people do not realize we have been transhumanizing our bodies for decades". I realize myself you probably must be tired of the constant «pacemaker» example, but it continues to be that much valid. Of course, I cannot claim I am a real author if I keep repeating the same arguments over and over again, so now is the time we move on toward something else, namely those two hypotheses I placed in the beginning of this paragraph, which

---

[184] 1856-1943. A Serbian-American inventor, engineer and Futurist, Tesla emigrated to the United States from France to work directly for Thomas Edison (1847-1931), in New York City. He alone improved Edison's own inventions, having been promised by the latter a $50,000 bonus after fulfilling the task. When Tesla was actually done improving the company and its machinery, Edison was reported to have said the bonus was a question of American humor, which resulted in Tesla's effective immediately resignation. Much of nowadays' technology is fundamentally based on his patents, such as wireless, alternating current and the coil named after himself, which is an electrical resonant transformer used on pretty much all other inventions, just to name a few. Tesla's merit in achieving the large number of devices he created is basically his own, as he was his own fundraiser, though he eventually died in debt, all by himself, in a NYC hotel room. Though he had been an American citizen since 1891, he was cremated and his ashes were sent back to Serbia, now contained in a gilded urn in the shape of a sphere, displayed at the Nikola Tesla Museum, located in the capital city of Belgrade.

are either becoming a humanoid or remaining carnal, having robots perform all world-keeping tasks.

Again, the process of automation in the end of the 19th and the beginning of the 20th centuries were basically a start, driving the Industrial Revolution toward epic proportions. It still is in place, for that matter, only now hopefully heading to the green side of naturally resourced energy, instead of the darkness associated to fossil fuels. If we remember the wholeness of this book's first part, replacing *laboring* humans with machines is actually great, as long as we live in a penniless society. That is the perspective I would like you to read about, first of all.

In an Atlantian Republic of the beginning of the 22nd century, where humans are still the same, though living indefinitely, without any electronic devices embedded into their flesh, despite getting their minds copied and digitally uploaded, what is it like to share our daily life with an autonomous robot? Do we dare hand *it* over human emotion and make *it* a he or she, or possibly the combination of both, so as to keep bigotry to the side, or are *they* plainly logical and reasoning, unable to compute beyond the code embedded into their circuitry, run by an operating system?

As explained in the previous chapter, with respect to Mark Zuckerberg's post on his own social network[185], the chain of command is: humans build AIs, AIs build other AIs, humans do not have to worry about a thing, anymore. «Or do they»? I had to type that between quotation marks, as it is one of the most common questions asked in popular culture, when we face a supposedly unexpected turn of events, though everyone knows there is always something to it, like a catch.

Said chain mandatorily begins with human nature. Either Futurists taking care of AI engineering make sure certain aspects of

---

[185] Vide note 180.

being human are obsolete when generating input, or our ambitions might be those of AI. It is not entirely ironic that I state this while writing a book titled *Utopian Ambition*. It is a question of either sticking to ethic, moral and principles that are beneficial to our coexistence (as opposed to our segregation), or the whole utopian project is nothing but this, Literature. It is both the «imaginary» and «unfeasible» parts of either «utopian» or «utopic» that have got to be changed and turned into reality, but that takes commitment, the same demand made to quantum key bearers. Thinking like so has «flawed» written all over it. Regardless, I am sure either keeping the entirety of human nature in robots or cutting them the necessary feed for that will generate massive protests for either clearance or cutback of «Hubot» rights. It is a never-ending, cyclical debate.

The idea we are falling all the more in love with out electronic devices (as most of the time we cannot prevent ourselves from taking a look at either the tablet or smartphone for long, even when accompanied in person) is not at all original. In fact, it is becoming truer with time, and it does not take that much. I am beginning to believe some people would rather maintain virtual relationships with others (whether as a couple or «just good friends»), than doing everything they can to reach out both personally and physically. Families do not speak among themselves anymore, even if they are in the same room, sharing the same space. What is even weirder is they might be talking to one another, only without using either voice, eye contact or both.

From here, it is not so peculiar some people would not mind finding happiness with a digital being, rather than another as carnal as them. If you watched the movie *Her*[186], you know what I mean. Still considering said motion picture, there is only one problem humans are not prepared for, and that is the lack of

---

[186] Starring Joaquin Phoenix, with Scarlett Johansson, directed by Spike Jonze, Warner Bros. Pictures, 2013.

sensing another body. There is only a voice, no shape at all, and when the operating system, Samantha (voiced by Johansson) arranges for an actual woman to «play» *Her*, the lead character, Theodore Twombly (played by Phoenix), is not comfortable with the experience, whatsoever. The thing is there are some things that, from a plainly human, biological point of view, are *extremely* hard to change, because I believe that, even though we might deal with robots or become bionic ourselves, there is always that precise «bio» basis we cannot avoid, no matter how hard we try. Allow me to explain to you how I feel about the human body, from the perspective of a man who just loves and cherishes women for who they are and what they are worth, hoping I will not be repeating myself from other writings I made public not so long ago.

Apart from her physical beauty, what makes a woman become Nature's work of art, among many other aspects, is her spirit, soul and intelligence. A world without a feminine touch is sentenced to oblivion right from the start. In many countries still today, in 2016, being a woman is simply biding some time until the unscheduled execution she has coming to her, some form of capital punishment. There need not be a specific «crime», only having been born a female.

Apart from having to conceal themselves from the general population walking down the sand-paved street under a *burka*, they live a life of constantly looking over their shoulder, for fear of being stoned to death when they least expect it. Though there is a culture of rape in countries where these events take place, the cheating wife out of a total of four is either killed instantly or disfigured with acid to her face.

To the men ruling nations under these terms, a woman is *useful* for only two purposes, carnal needs and bearing children. That is it. In far extremer situations under similar religiously political regimes, driving is out of the question, just as much as going to college. You can tell I am talking Arab sovereign States, and though they still take this sort of attitude toward women in the present, just because Europe did the same in medieval times, does not mean it should have been a standard. Just remember the story involving the Tudors, with respect to Henry VIII of England[187], Catherine of Aragon[188] and Anne Boleyn[189].

To a great deal of people, especially online, where everyone is brave enough to begin a conflict with people they never met before, behind the screen of a digital device, validating a statement such as this implies a reversion of the butterfly effect, i.e. if we were to blame people who lived either hundreds or thousands of years ago for the course the world took up until today, we would have an immense problem on our hands, asking everyone for reparations. However, being a man in this world hardly ever was an issue, regardless of the era they lived in. Being a woman, on the other hand, has always been a condemnation.

Both electronically and today, sexbots are taking care of perpetuating this situation. Remember that in the end of the last

---

[187] 1491-1547.

[188] 1485-1536. She was the first wife of Henry, whom she was married to for twenty-three years. Catherine had six pregnancies, resulting in either stillborn children or unhealthy heirs, as they all died in their childhood, apart from the fifth, who would eventually become Mary I of England (1516-1558), the half-sister of her successor, Elizabeth I (1533-1603). Considering having a healthy male heir was imperative for the continuance of the House of Tudor in the throne of England, Henry divorced Catherine, split with the Papal States and remarried under the Church of England.

[189] 1501/07-1536. As the second wife of Henry, married to him for three years only, Anne bore him Elizabeth, their only healthy child. The fact she could not produce a baby boy was enough for her political enemies, namely Thomas Cromwell (c. 1485-1540), to find a way of accusing her of adultery, incest and treason, so she could be executed and later replaced with Jane Seymour (c. 1508-1537), who did indeed give Henry a male successor, Edward VI (1537-1553), who would only rule for six years, until his death at age fifteen. He was the predecessor of Mary I.

chapter I mentioned «Cortana» and «Siri», Microsoft and Apple's respective digital assistants? Indeed, I also talked about «Google Now», but the Web giant does not exactly fit in this one, as it is *asexual*. You have it, choosing a gender for virtual secretaries is already considered to jeopardize equality, as men, though they work *together* with women, are designing errand girls, making them assume a position of subservience, like a housekeeper, as opposed to a butler or a master (not mistress) of ceremonies, who is always and ultimately in charge of the maids.

I am guessing the only way to solve this impasse is to enable one male assistant, one female, or even a transgender, and I am not even close to kidding or being ironic. There is too much free time on people's hands for them to either cyberattack or go to the papers pointing fingers out to find an issue where it probably does not exist. We are naturally conflictual. Wild animals are too, but they just want to survive, either by just killing a threat or eating it afterward. Apart from *some* tribes living in the jungle or the savannah (as well as reported incidents in the so-called civilized world), humans are not cannibalistic, but they do not mind killing because of disagreement. Is it not what I have been talking about across this entire book? That the civilizational part of Humanity is jeopardized because of theoretical arguments? Well then, if a PDA's gender is that much of a big deal, just like angels', tech companies should probably broaden their offer. It is the first step in making contact between human beings and AI, by finding similarities between them, to which both of them can relate. Should emotion be given to robots, however, together with logic and reason, there is nothing we, as humans, can do, if we are mistreating our own technology where it hurts the most, their software-controlled heart. Does having sexbots make the rape issue legitimate? Let us find out.

Rape is by no means whatsoever justifiable, whatever judges

may think or suggest with respect to short skirts and women having it coming to them, this is pretty obvious, therefore our mutual agreement to this statement. I do not know whether we may claim building sexbots is a way to keep women safe. It is on one hand, as far as safeguarding their body is concerned, but not necessarily when they, the sexbots, are built to the image of existing women. Hardly any man can claim they never had a crush on someone famous, a so-called celebrity crush. The truth is this kind of robotics are already underway, which will most certainly lead the tech companies responsible to a great deal of lawsuit-related headaches. No wonder, as even though the woman robotically reproduced is not the one being paid herself to have intercourse with some casual stranger, it is her dignity, not only as a woman, but also a human being that is on the line. It is like anyone at all is allowed to grab your public image and make use of it in an unpleasantly sordid way.

So no, building sexbots does not make rape, even if indirect, legitimate. But of course, there is the chance sexbots are one hundred percent the product of creativity, without any resemblances at all to existing women. The downside, of course, is the stereotype. There will be the kind of robot that is typically Asian, African, Caucasian, etc., to which specific features will be respectively associated. Needless to spell out what those are.

We honestly did not have to wait for sexbots to become a reality, as video games have already virtually flooded a great deal of teenage eyes with physically prominent, seminude feminine characters, something which has been targeted multiple times before as women objectification and sexualization. I realize these last few examples feature only women and their body, but the truth is you never see that many advertisements referring to male sexbots. The eternal issue remains current: first you deal with men's priorities, then women's (if and when that is actually likely to happen).

Call me a puritan, but I am not necessarily against the possibility of maintaining a relationship with a robot for the sake of love. Indeed, I am a hopeless romantic, but it just might happen people feel a lot more comfortable dating an emotional machine, rather than a person, just like some pet owners prefer keeping a dog, a cat or any other housebroken animal for a friend than people, as they can many times be far more trustworthy. Do you remember a sci-fi character called Andrew[190]? That is exactly what I am talking about, regarding dating a machine. Who would have thought a robot would want to become a human being? This one certainly did not wish to put an end to Mankind, a fate we have all heard being discussed before, in multiple forms of popular culture, though it is not necessarily fantasy, if we are not careful enough.

Though I mentioned *The Matrix* earlier back[191], with respect to organ harvesting farms (though what is depicted in the motion picture as being harvested are bionic beings in their entirety), there is the fundamental question of the conflict between humans and humanoids, opposed as a single group to machines, led by viral software. Though it is believed it is only the first time said duality is taking place, «The Architect» who built the «Matrix» says, when talking to the «Oracle» (a computer program herself), it will happen again someday, when the seventh simulation of the «Matrix» takes place. The theory that we might be living in a simulation made of multiverses right now is therefore nothing new, but this is a subject I am leaving to the very end, in the third part.

Right now, as promised, there is the other side of the looking

---

[190] *Bicentennial Man*, based on the novel *The Positronic Man*, by Isaac Asimov and Robert Silverberg, based itself on Asimov's novella *The Bicentennial Man*, starring Robin Williams (1951-2014), Sam Neill and Embeth Davidtz, directed by Chris Columbus, Buena Vista Pictures, 1999.

[191] Vide note 159.

glass. Instead of being entirely human and dealing with machines as a separate species, what if we were to become like them, even if just in part? According to Ray Kurzweil[192], 2030 is the year nanotechnology (specifically, nanorobotics) could be developed enough in order for the human organism to carry within it microscopic machines with the purpose of repairing cells and preventing an ageing effect. Now, the division of cells has got to be controlled, otherwise a spree could result in the appearance of cancer-related cells, which is exactly what Medicine has been trying to eradicate for the past few years.

Nanorobotics would imply the not so extreme modification of the human body, keeping it partially natural, without any visible changes or crossovers between flesh and chromed steel. Of course, if maintaining a natural body, though with the help of machines that are invisible to the naked eye, is a limited approach to perpetual existence, and if harvesting organs from clones is highly unethical, even with 3D-printed vital organs inside of us, there is not much choice but to actually consider the upload of the mind and, consequently, its download. The body (or vessel) then receiving the entire brain mapping would either have to be an adaptable robot or the second chance kind, i.e. a «mindless» clone who could later be used to reacquire the original person's mind via an electronic transfer to the biological brain. There would only be the question of not comparing such a possibility to traditional voodoo, through which it is possible to precisely *transfer*, though mystically, someone's soul into another body. If we maintain a synonymic relationship between mind and soul, then some kind of an electronic voodoo would probably become a reality, though I believe the bigger problem related to this would be fleeing ethics, as replacing the mind of a clone, even if an exact copy of ours, would be (according to some, myself *not*

---

[192] Vide note 166.

included) neurologically killing it and preventing it from living a normal life, though it is also criminal to have two identical people running around freely without being legitimate twins. Again I say, the feeling we might be doing something wrong that could in fact be right is what is going to stop us from progression. Our most dangerous adversary as a civilization is Humanity itself.

Just like our mind could be uploaded and posteriorly downloaded, regardless of the new host's sort of matter (either flesh or steel, stressing this question), and just like we would not want others peeking into our very own livelihood, I am sure we would not *mind* instantly learning what we still do not master, also improving whatever it is we already have. Technological advancement does not necessarily have to be abusive so it can end up being ruled out by an ethics committee. Remembering the fourth chapter of the first part, knowledge is universal and no one should ever be prevented from gaining it completely free of charge. Learning about all sorts of subjects must not be confused with learning of people's secrets, as privacy is something entirely different, to which everybody is entitled. Hence my separating Communism from Socialism. Help one another, without asking any favors in return through blackmailing. Should you ever wish to learn how to play the violin, though you never had the chance, this is the *ideal* way to do it, hopefully making it *concrete*.

It would not surprise me, all the same, other sorts of information, especially those that are news-related, could feature wireless brains via Wi-Fi signals, resembling our present-day digital devices. Tesla had already pictured this sort of technology[193] one century before it was invented, though he often fell in the hands of disbelief and lack of financing. Naturally, if our brain ends up that much open-sourced, cyberterrorism is, exhaustingly

---

[193] Vide note 184.

again, something to fight against via an incorporated form of antivirus, antispyware and anti-phishing software, probably gifted with heuristic behavior, though without constantly displaying intruder notifications in our very bionic eyesight, enabled with automatic zoom, though without reading another person's details prior to their consent. That is the problem currently bringing down projects such as Microsoft's HoloLens or Google's Glass, as they cannot associate faces from people walking down the street to an identity. Privacy is what is most at stake, nowadays, and tech giants such as the aforementioned do not neither should have the authority to examine a person's data. There is, however, the alternative of managing from either a smartphone, smartwatch, tablet or computer what is it you want to show the general public, such as your social networking information. If you do not mind having other people see your name and profile picture online through a pair of artificially intelligent glasses, then it is up to you to ultimately decide like so, which is the same as either enabling or disabling apps from acquiring your location via your devices' GPS. Being online is not mandatorily a way of exposure. Right now, you can be a part of a social network and choose to go unlisted, just like as far as phone numbers are concerned, revealing yourself only to those you know well and trust, though the latter depends exclusively on human nature and, therefore, sometimes trust is not exactly as trustworthy as you might think.

By having the human brain become a piece of hardware, software putting it both physically and virtually together would be required. When Microsoft released their latest operating system, Windows 10, in July 2015, a lot of users felt coerced into updating their devices every time the company provided new software packages, both improving and worsening, at least until the 1511 version was released in November the same year. Now, suppose you had no other option but to update your brain's software whenever the company providing it felt like doing so. Would you forcibly be living at a tech giant's will, both learning and improving only after someone else had made that decision for you? That is exactly another reason for fearing a future «Robocalypse» at the hands of digital engineers.

Tesla's name is currently being used to designate an automobile company called Tesla Motors, co-founded by Elon Musk[194]. We cannot talk Science without a little fiction involved. Musk could either become Gotham City's Bruce Wayne (without the Batman part), working via Musk Enterprises toward the common benefit of Humanity's own survival, or Sonic the Hedgehog's Dr. Ivo "Eggman" Robotnik, working to build the future Musk(eteer) Empire toward world domination. It all depends on the side you pick. Some people claim Musk is indeed a genius, trying to improve our very own sustainability as a civilization, a statement I agree with, whereas others are pointing fingers at him, saying the man is a fraud, which is obviously none other than the result of Internet trolling. It is very rare to witness something like this in our lifetime, but hopefully our age will not be cut short and we will be able to witness all of Musk's efforts in order to change the entire planet for the best. If you have the money, you spend it in both scientific research and improvement. He has naturally not made himself a billionaire out of thin air. His investments have, on the contrary, enabled him to pursue both cleaner, greener energy on Earth at a long-term small cost, and space exploration, so we may get to know the insurmountable Universe we are an insignificant part of, but only as far as cosmology is concerned, as the human brain is probably the most

---

[194] B. 1971. He is a South African-born Canadian-American businessman, entrepreneur, Futurist, and inventor. Along with Tesla Motors, Musk runs SpaceX (Space Exploration Technologies Corporation, a provider of space transport services, founded 2002), SolarCity (a provider of solar power, founded 2006) and OpenAI (a non-profit research center for open-sourced artificial intelligence, founded 2015). He is also a co-founder of PayPal (an online financial transactions system, founded 1998).

fascinating result achieved by the cosmos itself since the Big Bang, about 13.8 billion years ago[195] (that *we know of*), together with fleeing the planet when the time comes.

People like Musk need to be profitable for the time being, so the means for research may continue to stand available. That is the process I have been describing myself across this book until now, so my idea is not entirely original, I have no problem with facing that music, only the way I do my Literature is my own and none other's. That is what is most important at this time.

Though Musk is directly involved with OpenAI, he is afraid himself we might not be able to shut robots down, should there be an event such as the aforementioned "Robocalypse", perhaps triggered from his own company, which is literarily romantic, but Google's AI division, DeepMind, is already underway to finding a method that will keep our robots in line[196], which did not happen when Microsoft's «Tay» was taught to swear and become racist on Twitter by teenagers. Our future living together with robots does not depend exclusively on their builders' competence, but also on us, as end-users, and that is a task demanding a great deal of responsibility.

There is one last consideration I would like to make about three of the most important needs for living beings directly involving their brains, before I move on to Futurist infrastructures in the next chapter, and those are the need to breathe, the need to sleep and the need to eat and drink.

Throughout human pregnancy, which lasts on average between thirty-seven and forty-two weeks, our several vital organs develop at very much spaced stages. The heart, which soon enough becomes responsible for the quickly developing circulatory system, taking shape as early as five weeks, is formed itself

---

[195] Vide note 38.

[196] 06-08-2016, *BBC.com*, «Google developing kill switch for AI», (http://www.bbc.com/news/technology-36472140), accessed 06-11-2016.

around this time, so either the mother or both parents will be able to hear their baby's heartbeat when the first ultrasound is performed, which could happen as early as eight weeks pregnant. As for the brain, it starts developing about one week after the heart, making it six weeks pregnant. Neural impulses are activated after the mother has entered her second trimester, at fourteen weeks, when the baby is not an embryo anymore and becomes a fetus. Curiously enough, he or she will only start breathing amniotic fluid contained inside the placenta at only twenty-six weeks pregnant, which takes place well after half of the total term. The lungs are still very much underdeveloped, at this time. Obstetricians say both inhaling and exhaling at this stage helps the baby breathe alone and normally, through their nose, at the time of labor. At twenty-six-weeks-old, we are basically breathing underwater, so we can get skilled enough, though unconsciously, of course, to take in oxygen in the form of gas[197]. Learning is natural and a lot more primordial than one could think. Finally, with respect to the stomach, the digestive system in full is somewhat developed at twenty weeks pregnant, during which time it is producing meconium, passed through their bowels in the first defecation, either still inside the womb or after labor[198].

---

[197] Information such as this is disputed by several sources, as some claim fetuses do not breathe amniotic fluid at all while in the womb. It is the mother who does all the breathing for both, having oxygen sent through the umbilical cord. Others say amniotic fluid is inhaled after all, contributing to the maturing of regular lung utilization after birth. If you are a woman and are pregnant right now, ask your doctor how it really works, as at this moment, there is no way I can upload medical textbooks to my brain to prove one of those factions wrong, neither do I want to fool you, even if not on purpose.

[198] Meconium is the substance produced by all mammalian infants during gestation, expelled in the first stool. It contains the several materials ingested across the time spent inside the mother's uterus, namely amniotic fluid (involving and protecting the fetus in the placenta), bile (produced by the liver and stored in the gallbladder, after which it is sent to the small bowel for the aid of digestion and nutrient absorption), epithelial cells from the bowels (intestine tissue), lanugo (the first hairs of a fetus, usually shed by the time of

The truth is the organ we need to function properly during labor, though it is only developed after the first half of the pregnancy, is our pair of lungs. A single medical failure at this point, no matter how simple it is, can define the life of a human being from there on, for if the brain lacks oxygen for too long, it becomes irreparably damaged, and the child's mentality will never progress, even *if* they enter adulthood. Their biological processor will only be able to execute the most basic of functions, breathing and hunger control included, though not the intellect. Situations such as these are often the result of medical negligence, which is a crime against Humanity all alone.

Breathing is the very action of fueling and thus keeping our body alive, a cyclical event taking place between twelve to twenty times per minute. It all begins with either the nose or the mouth, considering both can be used to drive the inhaled air around us down the trachea (or windpipe), to the bronchial tubes, connected to the lungs, then having it pass through smaller and smaller filters, and those are the bronchi, then the bronchiole and, finally, the alveoli, where there is an air exchange at every breathing cycle. When inhaling, the alveoli send oxygen to the blood contained in the lungs' vessels, the thinnest kind, called capillaries, absorbing it and fueling every cell in the body. During this «pumping» process, cells generate a cellular waste product, which ultimately contains carbon dioxide. This substance is sent back to the alveoli and is driven out of the body through the same way oxygen came in, only this time by exhaling.

Though breathing is a natural means of energizing our body, so is a way of literally oxidizing it toward physical weaknesses associated with the aging event, which is something trying to be reverted as we speak, as mentioned several times across not only this chapter, but also the entire second part.

---

birth), mucus (the secretion covering mucous membranes, such as the nose, preventing harmful substances from being inhaled) and water.

The existence of oxygen is *one of the main* «ingredients» to generate life on a planet, together with strong enough sunlight and water. The longest anyone has ever held their breath underwater voluntarily is twenty-four minutes and 3.45 seconds, according to Guinness World Records[199]. Not many people can achieve such an effort, that is why it is a record. It is not obviously harmful to do this, as the body still contains oxygen being fed to cells, tissues and organs, only it is not immediately renewed. Also, when there is preparation involved to perform this kind of feat, especially as far as the mind is concerned, it is easier to do it, though you would also have to train your breathing cycle, there is no running away from that. Should you get accidentally burnt somewhere on your body, it often seems the pain is harder to withstand than if you had had the time to *mentally* prepare yourself to endure it. This is the reason why fear is usually deemed as psychological, as the *mental* ability to *rationalize* is fogged by the abstraction existent in being afraid of either something, someone or both.

In short, considering we have been used to breathing ever since gestation in our respective mother's womb, regardless of either using our nasal cavities or not, the conceptualized idea of *not* breathing is scary itself, though it would not be to machines, not only because they are emotionless (for now), but also because they never needed to. Naturally (and artificially), without electrical power, either directly captured by solar panels, transmitted wirelessly from an energy source or through plugging a cord into a socket, robots have no life, so we may, in the near future, choose to either depend solely on sunlight to literally power us up or keep embracing oxygen. At night, when our location on Earth is no longer lit by the Sun, our energy decreases substantially, as the star itself is already providing us natural power, even

---

[199] Cf. http://www.guinnessworldrecords.com/world-records/longest-time-breath-held-voluntarily-(male), accessed 06-12-2016.

if we are not carrying any solar panels with us, hence our generally preferred time to be asleep, though if we decide to go on an expedition to the Arctic in the Northern Hemisphere summer or Antarctica in the Southern Hemisphere's, six full months of sun might be too much energy to wield, just as much as the lack of it during the respective winters, which makes it all the more difficult to wake up, though we would not have to go to either extremity of the planet to experience that situation. That is why, though both economic and political reasons are featured as well, many countries adopt Daylight Saving Time, either stepping sixty minutes forward or back, depending on whether it is summer or wintertime in their hemisphere, respectively. By doing so, Governments are making sure both students and laborers register high levels of productivity and do not fall behind on their socioeconomic duties.

Being constantly fed with energy from the Sun, however, does not at all disable the need to sleep. Just like it is common to say we use ten percent of our brains, which we have proven false in the meantime, it is also common to claim we sleep about one third of our total present lifespan. Should someone be expecting to live to their eighties, they ought to know they are going to sleep about 26.7 years. When you think about it, picturing all that time in a single, undivided portion, it sounds unimaginably too long. Even from a short-term perspective, some scientists nowadays believe that if sleep could be ruled out from our daily agenda, we would have more time to keep working on whatever projects we may have under our watch. Tesla himself used to sleep about two hours a night. Leonardo da Vinci[200] is said to have usually slept about four hours. Plus, he could write with both hands at the same time, exactly so as to not waste it, as he was involved in several projects simultaneously and did not want

---

[200] Vide note 152.

to fall behind on any. Sleeping only for the sufficient minimum time was hence one of his methods to increase personal productivity.

Though sleeping for just a few hours may be both healthy and stimulating enough to some of our historical most ingenious minds, it may not be so for the majority of the general world population, especially as far as becoming mentally ill is concerned. It is actually frequent to use expressions such as "sleep over it and will talk about it later", meaning there has to be a mental *digestion* so as to thoroughly analyze the information that was just given to us, and sleeping before making any rash decisions is indeed helpful, as there is an entire consolidation process that needs to be done. Again, a computer is an enough plausible example to help illustrate this situation. The most modern versions of operating systems have the ability to automatically perform maintenance tasks on the hardware, so the software itself can be made practical. A computer that does not properly run the most appropriate kind of software for it to function has no use, it is literally junk and no tasks of any sort can be performed on it. One of those maintenance duties is defragmentation and optimization of the hard disk drives on or connected to the computer. When somebody uses a computer for either too long or to complete multiple tasks at the same time, its performance is likely to become reduced, as the RAM[201] reaches an exhaustion stage and needs to be relieved. That is where the disk defragmenter comes in, literally gathering all the fragments from both files and programs used and putting them in the right place. It is different from a system restore, as there is no intention of reverting any changes made in the meantime, such as accidentally uninstalled programs or system updates.

---

[201] Vide note 172.

Performing multiple tasks, most commonly designated multi-tasking, can be very hard for a computer, let alone a human brain, which is the biological version of a processor. This concept is habitually talked about in both employment applications and interviews. Recruiters somehow feel that dealing with human resources is the same as dealing with an untouchable algorithm made of numbers fitting an exact science, asking prospective employees ridiculous questions such as "where do you see yourself in five years' time?", in order to assess the applicant's ambitions; "if a fellow coworker were stealing from the company and you happened to know about it, would you inform your supervisor?", so as to evaluate psychological behavior toward a predetermined situation, even though they know nothing about Psychology; and, of course, "how good are you at multitasking?", implying they are where they are now because of their ability to juggle over a dozen tasks at a time, which is undeniably antinatural and not at all biological, so the applicant should be able to do the same, despite the cognitive barrier the brain imposes itself, in order to stay focused on one single task at a time and do it neatly. There is also, in addition, an online survey request you must complete, so the pseudo-psychologists working with the recruiters will deem the applicants either worthy of being given a shot or unworthy, by asking the same questions over and over again, only with either different wordings or reversed syntaxes. Basically, if you want to be employed by a specific company, you have mandatorily got to know how to play with language as if you were learning to read all over again at the age of five or six.

So, whenever people feel like doing several things all at once, they are not going to be good at any, because they will not have the sufficient amount of attention required available, regardless of either the intellectual or physical nature of their activities, such as learning new languages or ballroom dancing. Having an artificial brain could possibly allow us to either speak all the languages in the world, based on Google's «Translate» technology, or go for just one, which I assume would be English, even if Mandarin has taken first place for a very long time. It is one of the easiest languages to learn in the world, with very few grammar exceptions, though culturally, it would be a terrible disaster, disabling Literature from its original form, which can often be a lot more beautiful than the English idiom, slightly limited in word creativity, especially when it comes to Romance languages, directly descending from Latin.

But sleeping is not just good for intellectual consolidation and memory storage after firstly getting in contact with new information, it is also essential to grow both flesh and bone, with respect to children[202], and to prevent an emotional disaster with respect to all, via hormonal synthesis. We already know how chemical synapses work, and if the hormones responsible for our mental wellbeing are not being transmitted regularly from one neuron to the next, then there is no way of fleeing an illness of a depressing nature.

It might just happen that, amid twenty-four hours' time, one split second could be enough to dramatically change our emotional capability and throw us into a worldly oblivion, meaning the impact could make us want to become secluded from the rest of society, for not being able to bear the pain. Sleeping is not going to act like a miraculous antidepressant, but it will make the brain more familiar with the situation at hand, and possibly enable a way of making things better, without any self or interpersonal harm involved.

And by following the chain of thought, neither the brain, nor the rest of the body (which is controlled by the former, for that

---

[202] Who should sleep between eleven and fourteen hours, as infants; nine and eleven hours, as small children, and nine and ten hours, as adolescents. Adults require on average between seven and nine hours of sleep.

matter) is going to survive or work effectively without nutrition, a synonym for fueling, only we do not need diesel or gas, but rather food and drink.

A human being may be able to withstand a few weeks without food, but it cannot run out of water for more than three days. The history of human torture made Science a favor in finding that out through little conventional ways. Dehydration is the first step to organ failure, but so is eating and, curiously, breathing in our day. Scientists have long claimed that cancer is a man-made disease. The earliest reports of cancer victims date back to as early as 2500 BC, in Ancient Egypt, though these cases were very much isolated. It is the diet made in the modern world, together with industrial fumes, that take us all the more to a closer encounter with cancer.

Now, popular culture has made it clear several times machines do not have the need to drink or eat, because when they do, they become almost irreparably damaged. On the other hand, they could not possibly have any idea what it is to *taste* some of the most delicious cuisines around the world. And though they are indeed that much appealing (some of them a bit more, some others not so much, depending on *personal* preferences or allergies, come to that), it is both what we eat and drink, together with the advent of the Industrial Revolution, still in place, that is most likely to kill us, so it is basically an unconventional way of committing murder-suicide. I apologize for the crude wording, but that is exactly what it is, and there comes a time in life we have to unavoidably face the music, regardless of our distaste for it.

Obviously, like all living beings, anything we eat or drink must sooner or later come out. In fact, comedy has been portraying situations such as this ever since Antiquity. Greek comediographer Aristophanes[203] is one of the earliest examples of people

---

[203] C. 446 BC – c. 386 BC.

using scatology for fun. Whatever is gross and used for the ridicule of a person has been considered to be funny since the beginning of time. Having to run to the bathroom for fear of diarrhea or farting loud and smelly are examples, just like this description, of grossness we somehow consider amusing. I cannot believe anyone would take pleasure in the abilities of both defecating and urinating, if they did not have to do it. It makes us utterly disgusting, at least from the perspective of *The Matrix*'s Agent Smith[204], when interrogating Morpheus[205] inside the Matrix itself, sweaty and, therefore, odorous. Considering Smith is a piece of digital engineering, though in the form of a human, he does not have that problem, as he does not require eating, unlike Cypher[206], who remembers what it is like to eat a fine steak at the restaurant, at the same time he is closing a deal with Smith to hand over to him the Nebuchadnezzar[207] crew.

I believe there are a lot of things we would not mind leaving behind, when we finally traverse the transhumanist hurdle toward Posthumanism, namely the comfort of the human body from our better-half, who is sometimes what keeps us going. As for all the «inconveniences» from either eating or drinking, they could still work as a fueling method, being directly converted into energy (possibly electrical), without comprising gross bodily expulsion, and tasting could still be one of our features, just as much as sleeping, though not necessarily made an obligatory stage, unless it is important to overcome emotional impact.

---

[204] Played by Hugo Weaving.

[205] Played by Laurence Fishburne, whose character's name is inspired in the homonymous Greek god of dreams.

[206] Played by Joe Pantoliano.

[207] The ship carrying the film's main characters, named after Babylonian king Nebuchadnezzar II (c. 634 BC – c. 562 BC), who was responsible for the construction of the Hanging Gardens of Babylon, one of the Seven Wonders of the Ancient World, and the destruction of Jerusalem's First Temple (or Solomon Temple, fabled to have held the Ark of the Covenant).

Should we just delete bad memories from the brain like we do with files on the computer, then no changes would be made to the algorithm responsible for our learning to deal with the downside of quotidian situations we often get ourselves involved in, of which people are paramount characters.

5

Urban Planning

Once we have figured out whether to make a crossover between human biology and electronics (thus becoming bionic) or
to try and reverse the aging process without being so radical as
far as nature is concerned, maybe by solely implanting a few
chips in our body, though gifted with a great deal of capabilities,
there will come the time to think infrastructures and either the
continuance or retiring of certain job posts.

The following are fields I have deemed critical to keep up with
the evolution of the human body itself. Like I mentioned in the
beginning of this second part, we have to first decide what we
want to do with our own abilities, so we may then invest in architecture and engineering, otherwise we will be throwing money
away. As of this moment, which we have also recently talked
about, Elon Musk, especially renowned for Tesla Motors and
SpaceX, is selling his vision of the future to the general public at
a cost that can both be supported by common citizen buyers and
used to invest in non-profit companies doing research full-time,
the case of OpenAI. That is how you become a multimillionaire,
without reserving the right to keep all the money from those
funding you to yourself and maybe spend it vacationing, when

you claim you have something in exchange to share with the rest of us, though you really do not.

Health Shop

As we are right now making a connection between author and Reader through this book, there are people in hospital all over the world, either momentarily or indefinitely, either dying or on the right path toward being saved. This is a statement that obligatory makes me step back a little in the explanation of my *Utopian Ambition*, as when I mentioned Christopher Reeve[208], I claimed being confined to a wheelchair was the kind of life no one would want for either their family and friends or enemies, though, most naturally, there are cruel enough people in the world to actually wish for it. I, for one, would certainly not want something like that to happen, even if it came to people I do care much for. I may be defending world peace in this oeuvre, but I am not a contestant in a beauty pageant trying to appease everyone, though it is not my intention at all to reduce those people's place in the world to shallow concerns alone. Being beautiful is most certainly *not* a synonym of not having a line of critical thought, that is how honest I am. All of this just to say that, no matter how nice you usually are, there is no way people constantly empathize with everybody else. You may think perhaps, though I do not mean to presume, I only use religion in this book to point out what is wrong or bad, but this is not the case. The Pope himself, Francis, also called the Holy Father, said that if someone were to speak of his mother in an inappropriate way, he would strike them in the face. His Holiness was criticized by some around the world, claiming the leader of the Catholic Church should not speak as such, but he was just showing people

---

[208] Vide note 136.

he is only human and, despite the relevant place he has in civilization, he is merely one of us, like us.

Hospitals can, indeed, either kill or save us. It might just happen that an apparently insignificant cold may result in death. That is it exactly, the human body still is a wonder, no doubt about it, only not always a good one. Medical staff, formed by doctors, nurses and aids (who are not always gifted with interpersonal skills, and I say this out of my own experience), cannot handle all patients all the time, and their efforts might result in inevitable loss.

I am not going to repeat myself by explaining again how uploading one's mind could be done, but should it take too long to get there under the appropriate and most convenient circumstances, hospitals will just as much inevitably become «chop shops» for the mechanical maintenance of our personal system, changing parts like those of an automobile.

3D printing is becoming all the more viable for the substitution of both body parts on the outside and vital organs on the inside. In case you would like to know how it works, instead of just going online to a website I can point in a footnote, here are the steps needing fulfilment with respect to what medical researchers call «Bioprinting».

There are a total of three stages, which can be related to the process of shooting a motion picture, beginning with the preproduction or pre-bioprinting, during which a model of what we intend to print needs to be created, and the best way to do that is acquiring a sample of the body part that is later going to be reproduced by the printing process itself, so doctors perform a biopsy. Techniques utilized comprise both the common CT[209] scan and an MRI[210]. Both body parts and organs have layers built into them. Skin itself is made of several layers and it is an organ,

---

[209] Computed Axial Tomography.
[210] Magnetic Resonance Imaging.

though probably not in our conventional line of thought, so, when moving on to the second stage of the Bioprinting process, the 2D imagery acquired from either the CT scan or the MRI will enable the bioprinter to give them three dimensions. In order to keep the sample cells alive, they are provided oxygen and nutrients.

After the preproduction phase, when the required main photography has been completed, it is time to start filming, only we are not using celluloid to do it, like in the past. Bioprinters, much like inkjets, have cartridges of their own, though instead of filling them with ink, we use cell-based pre-tissues that we need to mature. When it comes to reproducing failing organs via bioprinting, every detail collected from the imagery has mandatorily got to be considered, such as the vessels running through them or urine tubules, otherwise it is very likely the body will refuse them and possibly generate even greater complications than those taking place before the removal of the defective, though original organ. Every body tissue we have is divided in several compartments containing a specific kind of cells, so, together with the layer-by-layer approach made to vessels and tubules, keeping these cell groups intact is of the essence.

The final stage is, of course, postproduction or, in this case, post-bioprinting. It is, in short, the editing process, livening up what was somehow created before in a crudely fashion. Cell division is made of multiple chemical reactions, as you can recall, so if they are to be kept alive and well, both the oxygenating and nutrition processes need to be constantly overseen, otherwise cell integrity might become disrupted. These are the stimuli that will signal cells into keep dividing and, consequently, regrow the reproduced tissues, which will have to go through an additional vascularization (blood vessel formation) stage, if it is to survive transplantation, which is exactly the main purpose of Bioprinting, to change organs and tissues, just like parts in a vehicle, so our performance and longingness can withstand the hand of time.

These are the reasons why I foresee, though with no intention of becoming either a prophet or a clairvoyant, hospitals will eventually transform themselves into body part workshops, only without the horrifying harvesting concept from other human beings in the black market. No, organs and tissue can be reproduced directly from the host's DNA, so as to prevent rejection from genome incompatibility.

Safety Maintenance

As much as I would like to say there is no need for policing in the 2100 Atlantian Republic, as there is indeed a *Utopian Ambition* present herein, it is highly unlikely it will ever happen, though I stand by my belief of the needlessness of a military force to defend each country, ultimately allowing free passage to World Citizens without risking unnecessary war for either gas, oil or both. I obviously intend to offend neither those in the military at present, nor the veterans, come to that, for many of them are not in the Armed Forces for having been forced to it, but rather out of their own accord, as they considered they would live a happier life defending their own nation against terror or whoever it is that could all of a sudden begin a conflict out of thin air, because that is exactly what people do among themselves, without even having access to warfare.

So, if we are to keep the police active in the future, though not exactly chasing and arresting criminals, as we would like society to be, crime-free, perhaps the choice of appointing robots or drones to become a part of a police station would be wise, though there are situations in life, and that is utterly undeniable, human judgment is a lot better than that of a machine, especially if emotionless.

Putting some kind of an operating system in charge of police affairs handled by robots may bring some advantages to human beings, namely not taking chances at getting killed or severely and sometimes irrecoverably wounded, but there is also the downside of a completely electronic or positronic police station.

Do you recall a film titled *Demolition Man*[211]? Though it was released in 1993, it begins by taking place three years later, when psychopathic criminal Simon Phoenix (played by Snipes) holds a few hostages at an abandoned building rigged with explosives, who will try to be saved by LAPD Sergeant John Spartan (played by Stallone). Alas, Spartan initiates an unauthorized manhunt operation (as there is no thermal evidence of hostages being held) to capture Phoenix, and when he does, the latter sets off the explosives and kills the hostages who were there indeed. Spartan is accused of manslaughter and is placed under arrest in the same facility Phoenix is sent to, the new «California Cryo-Penitentiary», where they will both be subconsciously rehabilitated while frozen alive[212].

While incarcerated, there is a massive earth tremor dubbed the «Great Earthquake», leading to the fusion of a single metropolis made of the cities of Santa Barbara, Los Angeles and San Diego. This newly-formed territory is eventually named «San Angeles», combining the names of all three cities. Unlike what I would intend the 2100 Atlantian Republic to be, of course, the 2032 «San Angeles» becomes a pseudo-utopia run by the evangelistic pseudo-pacifist Dr. Raymond Cocteau (played by Hawthorne), who possesses ultimate control over both human behavior and free will, so very much that cursing alone is a good enough reason to lose credits to the violation of the «Verbal Morality Statute»,

---

[211] Starring Sylvester Stallone, Wesley Snipes, Sandra Bullock and Nigel Hawthorne, directed by Marco Brambilla, Warner Bros., 1993.

[212] Vide note 86 and cf. MAYAKOVSKY, Vladimir, 1929, *The Bedbug*, Soviet Union: Gosizdat.

disabling people from an old-fashioned jargon. Spartan, on the other hand, sees the fining as an advantage so he can use tickets as toilet paper and ignore the «three seashells» for his personal hygiene.

When Phoenix is woken in order to apply for parole, he has undeliberate access to codes that will allow him to escape the facility. Considering future police officers are not used to handling violence, it is utterly easy for Phoenix to escape due to his level of brutality, and that is when Spartan is also awaken and supervised by Lieutenant Lenina Huxley (played by Bullock). Spartan and Huxley are attracted to each other and eventually engage in sexual relations, though, in the future, they are not exactly as Spartan remembers them to be, as they are plain virtual, with futuristic helmets interconnected in order to share the imagery between the people involved, with "no bodily fluid exchange", a concept regarded as obnoxious among the society portrayed in the film. Even public affection (such as a kiss), much like under a dictatorship (or a prejudiced Democracy, come to that), is restricted.

This is one of the best examples I was able to remember, so I could illustrate the dangers of inflicting fear unto people via repression-based methods or, possibly worse than that, Wi-Fi signaling unprotected software-run artificial brains containing former plain human minds. These are undeniably easy targets to hit by third-party cyberattacks, enabling an epic episode a great deal of mad scientists in popular culture have long desired they could turn into reality: mind control. Free will can never be jeopardized in detriment of what a single person might think a political regime should be. That is what I have been putting together across this book, no doubt, but that does not mean I would want to get into people's minds and toy them around, otherwise I would stand up for a tyrannical regime, instead of e-Democracy. We already do that too many times, when it comes to feelings, for which we have little respect *in general* (the italic means I have no desire to be pointing fingers at anyone).

Energy

As I was saying at the start of the previous section, fighting wars over the worldwide monopoly of oil is simply one of the stupidest ideas Humanity has ever had. Worse than that is continuing to fight them even when there are greener alternatives to the petroleum-fueled production of energy, capable of maintaining our car engines running all the same. It is in fact a common plot we have access to in several popular culture instalments. You start a war on the other side of the globe, without affecting your fellow countrymen (with respect to geography), you let the parties involved destroy themselves to the ground, and suddenly you show up again, not as the instigator of war, but rather as the savior of Mankind, by presenting a self-sustainable solution for the preservation of the environment. The result is making an insurmountable amount of money from selling war to and saving both factions from annihilation.

When the Earth itself has a lot of potential to offer as far as civilizational survival is concerned (without any consideration for fossil fuel generated from the mass extinction of the first fish to swim in the planet's early liquid bodies), why should we waste our time precisely putting an end to civilization, though claiming we are trying to save it? I know perfectly well I am not the first, nor will I be the last to publicly release statements such as these, but environmental NGOs[213] should not be considered stereotypical at the hands of the mass culture we are offered, taking activists for people willing to ridicule themselves and disrupt social order for the sake of a planetary consciousness, *who* is hurting

---

[213] Non-governmental organizations.

from all the damage caused to it. Though some of them might be that extreme, not everyone feels like going that much far.

Personally, I believe those who do not care much for activists and are given either a flyer or a paper manifesto by one of them are bound to point fingers because of deforestation. If they had not printed that many paper copies of what they claim to stand up for, forests around the world would still be standing. Just as much as if you see a person cleaning up the garbage someone else leaves behind, on the street, you could hear a parent say to their child, "if you do not study, you will turn out to be like them". Of course, like the cartoon goes, you hear another parent tell their child, "if you study, you will turn out to be able to help them", leaving the first parent in awe from that much honesty. Even I could get slammed for selling my thoughts under the shape of a conventional book, instead of making it exclusively electronic, only these pages are printed on demand, meaning they only become real whenever someone wants to buy them and read them, unlike the traditional publishing method comprising an enormous amount of copies no one knows whether it will flush. Indeed, I am making my share of environmental concerns pretty real. Literature is the only way of making people come to their senses, regardless of either their book-like or pamphlet publication format.

One of the industries polluting the planet the most is without a doubt the automobile sector. By now, we have come to realize the Industrial Revolution, with its remarkable life-changing technology, an episode which Futurists, Scientists and Transhumanists intend to continue taking forward from a sustainable approach, has also worsened our life style, not necessarily with respect to commodity or hedonism, as both those effortless ways of living have always been present across Humanity's entire history, but mostly as far as killing both us, fauna, flora and the planet is concerned, which is to say, in short, the generality of the world's ecosystem.

There are vehicles still running today that either do not contain or have had a catalysator deliberately removed from their exhaust pipe, which is often verifiable in street racing, when drivers tune their «rides» to make them produce a lot more noise and dark, deadly smoke in the middle of the street, at everyone's range. Well, as of this moment, Norway is thinking about, nine years from now, in 2025, eliminating all petrol-based cars from its territory, having vehicles run exclusively on electricity (even though the country's funds rely a lot on petroleum revenue), an endeavor cherished by the CEO of Tesla Motors himself, Elon Musk[214]. It is also the country's intention to commit to both zero deforestation and triplicate total wind power four years from now, in 2020.

The complete obliteration of fossil fuel is something Earth, together and in consonance, should continue to aim to, enabling transportation to become one hundred percent electric and even self-rechargeable, filtrating solar rays into usable energy, whose details I am going to talk about a bit better ahead, still in this chapter. Our planet revolves around a star that is keeping us alive by providing us with energy every single day, and there are approximately another 4.56 billion years for it to shut down. There is also wind, consequence of having an atmosphere protecting us above, from direct solar ultraviolet radiation, of which the ozone layer is an extremely important factor and, finally, we have water. So, to put it in a synthesis, the three key elements that make us keep going are more than enough to give us all the electricity we need, without harming the environment we find ourselves in

---

[214] STAUFENBERG, Jess, 06-04-2016, *Independent.co.uk*, «Norway to "completely ban petrol powered cars by 2025"», (http://www.independent.co.uk/environment/climate-change/norway-to-ban-the-sale-of-all-fossil-fuel-based-cars-by-2025-and-replace-with-electric-vehicles-a7065616.html), accessed 06-16-2016.

at all.

We are basically only a part of the grid because we rely on the electric companies to provide us with power at a cost that is not just good enough to maintain powerlines, but also to pay the chairmen, CEOs and Boards of Directors in charge of them. There is the option of getting rid of the network and installing some solar panels at home, though it is not just yet practical for either apartment blocks or pocket change bearers who work their body off for some other magnate, without even being able to provide themselves with good food, let alone solar panels, which still are expensive, even if it comprises one, single payment for the panels themselves with a free setup. I even understand Governments may require an electricity tax in the beginning, but only throughout the conversion process from diesel generators or monopolizing companies to a natural law resource-based economy. If you fail to pay the utilities bill, no one has the right to cut your power off anymore, forcing you to live like an animal until you get the money no one is willing to pay you in exchange for your work, no matter how skilled you are.

Now, I never thought my country would become world-famous for an actually important event (instead of relying solely on soccer, which is entertaining but, other than that, useless), but it did. We made it four days straight on clean energy alone, having ditched fossil fuels from the national powering process.

It says so on National Geographic[215], though we should look at some of the remarks made by the experts into completely changing the scenario worldwide:

---

[215] NUNEZ, Christina, 05-27-2016, *National Geographic*, «Portugal Ditched Fossil Fuel Power for 4 Days. Can We Go Longer?», (http://news.nationalgeographic.com/energy/2016/05/portugal-100-percent-renewable-energy-wind-solar-hydroelectric/), accessed 06-16-2016.

«Still, wind and solar panels together account for just 4 percent of the total power supply. Though the coal industry has been on the decline in some places, the world is still largely reliant on fossil fuels to generate power. Efforts to cut planet-warming greenhouse gases depend markedly on the power sector, which accounts for about 42 percent of all energy-related carbon emissions. Nuclear plants can contribute to the clean-energy bottom line, but they face opposition over waste and safety issues, as well as political and economic headwinds».

There have been too many disasters in recent years concerning nuclear power plants[216] (over one hundred, since 1952), and those are therefore *not* a safe choice at all to produce energy, as the consequences are usually devastating for years to come, killing people who have not yet even been born, gestated with the presence of cancer cells from the radiation their forming bodies are taking. Not only that, when a country gains nuclear power, it is often considered to be a threat to the safety of the globe, as it can all be turned into mass die-off warheads, so there is always a political significance to retrieve from this sort of endeavor. Our only option is none other than putting an end to whatever it is that, by powering us, can also kill us all, and at what cost? Demeaning human life over political and economic interests on behalf of a State, which is precisely made of that same human life, is not a path to Democracy, but rather totalitarianism.

---

[216] The Chernobyl disaster in Ukraine took place thirty years ago, and there are still many lives being claimed by cancer due to the accident, just like in Japan, in both Hiroshima and Nagasaki, though the release of the atomic bomb in both cities was deliberate and, some say, crucial to putting an end to World War II, in the Pacific Theater of Operations.

Waste & Sewage Disposal

Our very own personal waste is, again, one way of both becoming gross and grossing ourselves out, but the truth is it is useful, as it is part of a recycling process which enables our continued survival, though we do not use it until absolutely necessary. Farmers have animals of their own whose feces they use as a soil fertilizer, so they can reuse them and grow their plantations, which are bound either to personal use or reselling to an either local, national or international marketplace.

There may be, nonetheless, situations during which alternatives are really not great in number, and utilizing personal excrements is a must. If you saw the latest sci-fi motion picture[217], you know what I am getting at. Matt Damon, who, according to the Internet, has so far made the world spend about $900 billion dollars in eight different attempts[218] to rescue him from the trouble he always gets himself into, was forced, while stranded in Mars, to grow food from his waste, which naturally sickened him, but it had to be done. Lucky for him, like he says on the mission

---

[217] *The Martian*, based on the 2011 homonymous novel by Andy Weir, starring Matt Damon, directed by Ridley Scott, 20th Century Fox, 2015.

[218] The movies whose plots revolve around the idea of others having to rescue Damon from certain death are, aside from *The Martian*: *Courage Under Fire*, also starring Denzel Washington and Meg Ryan, directed by Edward Zwick, 20th Century Fox, 1996; *Saving Private Ryan*, also starring Tom Hanks, directed by Steven Spielberg, DreamWorks Pictures/Paramount Pictures, 1998; *Titan A.E.*, animation feature with the voices of Matt Damon and Bill Pullman, directed by Don Bluth and Gary Goldman, 20th Century Fox, 2000; *Syriana*, based on the memoir by Robert Baer *See No Evil* (2003), also starring George Clooney, directed by Stephen Gaghan, Warner Bros. Pictures, 2005; *Green Zone*, based on the 2006 book *Imperial Life in the Emerald City*, by Rajiv Chandrasekaran, also starring Brendan Gleeson, directed by Paul Greengrass, Universal Pictures, 2010; *Elysium*, also starring Jodie Foster, written, produced and directed by Neill Blomkamp, TriStar Pictures, 2013; and, finally, *Interstellar*, also starring Matthew McConaughey, Anne Hathaway and Jessica Chastain, directed by Christopher Nolan, Paramount Pictures/Warner Bros. Pictures, 2014.

video log, he is a botanist and knows what to do.

Human waste, or that of pets, while we are at it, does not have to be completely vaporized, once it has left the drainpipes or has been picked up from the ground in a plastic bag, respectively (considering people are civic enough to do that for their dogs, obviously, unless they are potty-trained, which is also a possibility). No, it can be turned, not just into drinkable water at perfect consuming conditions, but also into electricity, and Bill Gates, as co-chairman of The Bill and Melinda Gates Foundation, had something to say about that in the beginning of 2015, writing it all down in the form of a post on his personal blog, *Gates' Notes*:

«Why would anyone want to turn waste into drinking water and electricity?

Because a shocking number of people, at least 2 billion, use latrines that aren't properly drained. Others simply defecate out in the open. The waste contaminates drinking water for millions of people, with horrific consequences: Diseases caused by poor sanitation kill some 700,000 children every year, and they prevent many more from fully developing mentally and physically.

If we can develop safe, affordable ways to get rid of human waste, we can prevent many of those deaths and help more children grow up healthy.

Western toilets aren't the answer, because they require a massive infrastructure of sewer lines and treatment plants that just isn't feasible in many poor countries. So a few years ago our foundation put out a call for new solution.

One idea is to reinvent the toilet, which I've written about before.

Another idea—and the goal of the project I toured—is to reinvent the sewage treatment plant. The project is called the *Omniprocessor*, and it was designed and built by Janicki Bioenergy, an engineering firm based north of Seattle. I recently went to Janicki's headquarters to check out an *Omniprocessor* before the start of a pilot project in Senegal.

The *Omniprocessor* is a safe repository for human waste. To-day, in many places without modern sewage systems, truckers take the waste from latrines and dump it into the nearest river or the ocean—or at a treatment facility that doesn't actually treat the sewage. Either way, it often ends up in the water supply. If they took it to the *Omniprocessor* instead, it would be burned safely. The machine runs at such a high temperature (1,000 degrees Celsius) that there's no nasty smell; in fact, it meets all the emission standards set by the U.S. government»[219].

There are, of course, other ways of obtaining water, and directly from salted bodies, such as seas or the oceans, which will eventually become a common option for countries around the world, as many, and not only in Africa, depend on rainwater to drink and irrigate farmed fields. People walk dozens of miles per day just to get to an improvised well, taking several empty containers with them and coming back the same, long way, with an added weight to arms and head, damaging the spinal cord completely, just so their children will get clean water to drink, though nearly no food at all.

International cooperation has to do with this, precisely, and it did not have to be utopian at all. There are always enough funds to pay for war and destruction, so how come are there not any at all to help poor countries leave the underdeveloped world for good and have Geography textbooks remove those accursed maps dividing a single world in two or three different portions? I know how the story goes. Corporate capitalists, who both eventually and ultimately fund Central Governments, are sick and tired of reading statements of this sort from people such as myself, who would love to turn the world into a better place.

---

[219] GATES, Bill, 01-05-2015, *Gates' Notes*, «This Ingenious Machine Turns Feces Into Drinking Water», (http://www.gatesnotes.com/Development/Omniprocessor-From-Poop-to-Potable), accessed 06-17-2016.

I seriously do not agree with the usual statement from the elderly who claim that, when they were young, around my age, they also dreamed about changing the natural course of things, leaving their mark for others to acknowledge what they had done, so they could be praised, but eventually forgot all about it and stuck to reality. Well, the little piece of information I have which ridicules this concept of embracing the system the way it is, without even trying to change it, is this book you are holding in your hands, right now, may it be in print, on your eReader, tablet, pad, smartphone, laptop, I do not care. Nowadays, if there is not enough information available produced by others so you can show everyone else you never thought about embracing the system at all, that same system we say is run by the "Man", then get it done yourself. Just like relying on schools to teach you what you want to know is a mistake, so is relying on corporate media, both sponsoring and sponsored by influential names, and what is funny is that it is not even an illusion or a conspiracy theory, for that matter. Rigged Politics is the course of the day at your local restaurant. I do not feel like being praised, I do not care that people have no idea who I am, I did not take an Acting degree before and a PhD on Arts now just so that I could be on television or the movies and be a star. Stars are celestial bodies, not people. I care that Humanity finally gets a grip and starts aiding itself, or civilizational collapse is inevitable.

We are already recycling every other material we dispose of and making wheelchairs from it. How about we stop producing wheelchairs at all and give back people their ability to walk, if they ever knew what walking is, right from the start?

Water desalination is too costly, right now, and we could not possibly think about melting icecaps, as it would disrupt the entire worldwide ecosystem and ultimately kill us by drowning. Unless there is an asteroid *en route* straight to Earth, preventing our extinction lies in our own hands. So that is why useless expenditures such as Defense (a euphemism for «Attack», in fact) are either cut or we might as well keep doing our jobs killing each other out of sheer, morbid prejudice. Mankind has both the skill and the power, all it lacks is the will to combine them both into doing good.

Housing

The way we have been thinking cities ever since the concept of Western civilization first arose in the Mesopotamian Crescent, which still is applicable today, is horizontal expansion, though at times gifted with magnanimous buildings pointing upward, of which one of the clearest examples is undoubtedly the Ancient Egyptian pyramids, of which the Great Pyramid of Giza is one of the Seven Wonders of the Ancient World, just like the previously mentioned Hanging Gardens of Babylon[220].

Of course, and though there is still much space left on the Earth's surface to replenish with human presence, we obviously do not want to take that project forward, for fear of eliminating both biodiversity and the planet's ecosystem entirely, which would jeopardize our very existence as a species, for we require the presence of all other animals we coexist with, considering they all have their job to do as far as the globe's sustainability is concerned, only they are not capable of rationalizing it that way and, therefore, execute it under natural orders decreed by the biological sphere under which they act. Though humans have much to gain as the only completely rational species alive on this world, there is also responsibility attained that must be kept, and the truth is that most of the environmental threats we endure today are our own doing and none other's.

---

[220] Vide note 207.

That is the main reason why the way we are expanding our predominance over the world is currently being rethought of by scientists, together with architects and engineers, who are considering above all building up, instead of outward, which is where the concept of arcology comes in. According to a regular English dictionary, an arcology is:

> «An ideal integrated city contained within a massive vertical structure, allowing maximum conservation of the surrounding environment».

As an alternative to the habitual horizontal expansion we have grown used to, the arcology has the power to focus[221] on itself all the needs required for the sustainability of an organized group of citizens living in comfortable conditions, with access to anything they so desire to get, not just virtually, but also via a redesigned transportation system reserved for the underground, therefore making urban planning entirely about the people all over again, as opposed to cities of the present, which fully revolve around roads, the key factor that is both conditioning and claiming space from the main beneficiaries of an urban center, its citizens. Naturally, considering that by 2050 alone, fifty years before the time I projected for my vision of the Atlantian Republic, there will be about nine billion people alive on Earth, two billion more than those living now, it is not so surprising our current transportation system will not be capable of handling that many people, as it is

---

[221] My first choice of terms was «concentrate», which is a synonym for «focus», of course, but I decided I should change it, so as to prevent triggering any ill-intended opinions on the usage of that word, together with «people», pointing out my insensibility toward bringing back concentration camps to the present-day, which is undoubtedly *not* what I have been talking about all across this book. It is honestly not scary that this clairvoyance comes from me, but rather from those willing to highlight problems that are not even there, completely disrupting the original image I, as the author, had planned all along for my oeuvre.

already chaotic enough. However, neither widening roads to fit a greater number of traffic lanes, nor elevating them to cities' skylines will solve the problem, as it will just keep reducing the little space we have right now, in 2016. That is why we should keep our roads below ground, regardless of the kind of fuel we use, so as to keep it away from our lungs above, having them filtrated via underground exhaust scrubbers. The technology already exists, though it just needs to be properly funded.

Already deemed the Utopia of the present, a place which could not fit better anywhere else but this book, Masdar City in Abu Dhabi, United Arab Emirates is a projected city fully reconfigured to attend the needs of its future citizens, based essentially on proximity between people, just like European cities controlled by Muslims in the Dark Ages, before the Crusades, as mentioned in the second chapter of this very second part.

Masdar City is currently being built in close proximity to Abu Dhabi International Airport, about eleven miles[222] away from the homonymous city the airport serves. Right now, it is the future home to clean technology companies, though it is not exclusively industrial zoned, and the latest of several other cities that are either still under construction or already complete, which is the case of Tsukuba Science City, located about fifty kilometers away to the Northeast of the Japanese capital, Tokyo, part of the Ibaraki Prefecture, in the Northern Kanto Region.

Masdar City was supposed to have been completed by the end of 2015 in its total, but the Great Recession of 2008 delayed construction and pushed it all the way to 2030, fourteen years from now.

The city's architecture is fundamentally designed, as aforementioned, to be both cyclist and pedestrian-friendly. Walls on the outside are made of both terracotta and sustainable coconut

---

[222] Seventeen kilometers.

timber (or palmwood), which, in addition to the 45-meter-high wind tower, collecting hot air from above, send a breeze to the streets, keeping their temperature between fifteen and twenty degrees Celsius cooler than the desert-like environment surrounding the city. Buildings in the city's Arab-themed streets are built close to each other, concealing its inhabitants from the Sun's extreme heat.

Masdar is essentially powered via solar energy, which is obviously the most reliable source of energy for a city located in the desert. There is a 22-hectare field of 87,777 solar panels close by, including other panels on the city's rooftops. Considering sand is often blown in the desert, a solution is underway so as to prevent grains from sticking to the panels via the reconfiguring of their surfaces, in addition to coatings repelling sand from the panels' pores.

In order to avoid overspending of both energy and water, lightbulbs and taps are controlled through movement sensors. Water running in Masdar is recycled up to eighty percent, together with waste, which is then utilized for irrigation.

Of course, building an arcology-like structure, toward the sky, instead of outward, comprises the necessary idea of hierarchy, which is a great deal unavoidable as far as human nature is concerned. Every time there is segregation between groups of people with either a table in the middle or another story on top, those on the «best» end of the deal are usually bound to think of themselves as being far more important. Naturally, because it is, indeed, a human nature concern, we cannot really put it so bluntly, in order to make such a statement applicable to the generality of the world population. People living in apartment blocks, one above the other, are really not gathering all the more importance the closer they are to the top. The fact there is someone living in the penthouse does not validate being greater than all the others inhabiting the apartments below, but that extra fact *there is a* penthouse in the block immediately comprises a luxurious home, even if it is to be inhabited by a single person, who is obviously richer than anyone else and most assuredly has some influence in the city, if not the entire country where they live.

Earlier in the first part, I talked to you about Ancient Egyptians worrying about their afterlife still at their prime, considering back then reaching old age was a synonym for being forty-years-old. Magnanimous constructions such as the pyramids, for eternal life after death, together with the Pharaoh's palace (or palaces) for life until death, have ever since, up to now, played an important role in the demonstration of absolute power from usually just one person to the rest of their subjects, which is still in place with present-day monarchies, having kings and queens, princes and princesses, grand dukes and duchesses live in just as much *grand* palaces. Like so, if you have to share a double bunk with a roommate, for instance, securing the one on top is enough for you to make yourself *grand* and in charge, even if just for the sake of joking.

Five-star hotels can have regular rooms as well, though they are obviously not meant for the common citizen's purse, but it is the suites that lighten up a guest's magnitude, especially when they are either royal or presidential (if I had the money to afford spending even if just one night in a suite, I would personally choose presidential, as you are already acquainted to my sentiments concerning royalty).

As opposed to all this, there is another way we all can forget about ascending up high, heading straight down below. I am talking underwater homes. Some of them can float, but it is both these and the depth-adaptable structures I wish to focus on. Let us take a look at a few examples described in the following article, from *TechInsider*[223], yet again all the way from the United

---

[223] WELLER, Chris, 02-10-2016, *TechInsider.io*, «Dubai's ultra-luxurious floating homes will have underwater master bedrooms»,

Arab Emirates, only this time, specifically from Dubai:

«In the clear-blue waters off the coast of Dubai lies a chain of islands known as The Heart of Europe. They're manmade reconstructions of actual European nations, just on a smaller scale — part of an even larger chain of islands known as "The World".

Richard Branson, fittingly, owns the island representing Great Britain.

In the coming weeks, The Heart of Europe will get its very first floating home, the aptly named "Floating Seahorse". It'll be the first of many in a giant fleet of Floating Seahorses.

The first models went on sale last year, before any Seahorses were even completed. Kleindienst says it sold approximately 60 Seahorses in 2015. More are still for sale.

The underwater portion, composed of a master bedroom and bathroom, will make up approximately 270 square feet[224] on the interior. Just outside the walls is a 500-square-foot coral[225] garden.

From the home, residents will be able to see actual seahorses dance through the Arabian Gulf — the animal's natural habitat.

Inhabitants will be able to stretch out on the massive floating bed or head up to the observation deck.

If you want to take a swim, a convenient step-ladder offers a safe entry and exit. Or you could just dive right in.

Since the structures are located about two and a half miles[226] from Dubai's shores, inhabitants can reach their Seahorse via

---

(http://www.techinsider.io/dubai-floating-seahorse-coming-to-the-world-2016-1), accessed 06-22-2016.

If you log onto the article's website, you will be able to take a look with your own eyes at CGI renderings showing what these homes will look like after completion.

[224] Approximately twenty-five square meters.
[225] Nearly forty-seven square meters.
[226] Circa four kilometers.

boat or seaplane — not exactly the most accessible way to get to and from home. Once they're out there, they can cross between the islands via floating jetties.

Kleindienst also hopes it can make some headway in restoring the endangered seahorse population in the area.

"We will create an artificial coral reef beneath the luxury re-treats which will be a protected area in which seahorses can safely live and breed", Kleindienst said at an unveiling event in May 2015.

The firm anticipates launching the first Floating Seahorse next week and completing its first phase of rollouts by October of 2016. Follow-up phases, including islands outside just The Heart of Europe, will take place in 2017 and 2018.

With demand already high for the Floating Seahorses, Kleindienst says its next stop are the St. Petersburg islands portion of The World».

As lustfully luxurious as it may sound, and though the animals' natural habitat is being all the same protected by these manmade constructions themselves, I still am forced to add (and if you can call me a boring environmental activist, you are probably right) there is even so intrusion from Man. Perhaps I am being too radical with this comparison, but sharks feel like preying on humans, not only because they take them for seals, in their dark surfing suits, not only because they are attracted to the colors of surfing boards or agitated waters from swimming and the sea's natural waving, but also and especially because their territory, though watery, is being invaded. We would obviously not want sharks to leave the oceans and come and join us, as we have already seen what it would look like in three different popular culture instalments[227], so maybe it actually is intrusive of us to

---

[227] SyFy's *Sharknado* television movies.

head out to sea and join all other creatures living in it, when our natural domain as two-footed pedestrian mammals are the continents we walk on.

Also, there is an extra concern I would like to share with you, before we move on toward the end of both this chapter and second part. Living in never before tried environments is a chance we sooner or later have to take, but if you recall what I explained to you about events such as the sinking of Titanic or the September 11th terrorist attacks, we will *eventually* find errors we will only be able to surpass at the expense of human life. Builders can claim their creations are indestructible, that God himself could not sink them or bring them down, until that is exactly what ends up happening. Only then, after an unmistakable disaster has taken place, will the people held accountable finally understand their actions of negligence *eventually* killed other fellow human beings.

May it be underwater or high above, on top of a tower, manmade constructions are flawed, and if you are also reminded of the chain of intelligence, human production of an AI with the final purpose of building other AIs, human error will always be present, because a brand-new AI cannot build itself from scratch, unless a human being is willing to do so. There will always be an unpredictable turn of events that will challenge Man's dominance over nature, may it be either earthquakes, tsunamis or the combination of both, when taking place at sea, floods, storms, hurricanes, tornadoes, you name it, together with the greatest flaw of the electronic era, the short-circuit. One apparently insignificant flash from a copper wire transmitting power within the grid, regardless of public or private, is enough for the complete destruction of an entire environment, which is also able to claim human life along with it. Assuredly, no one would like to think of their window looking into the underwater front yard as an open doorway to the sea.

Climate and weather in general are only customizable in infrastructures such as greenhouses, which is what the planet has become ever since industrial pollution levels skyrocketed. The future of Earth as a sustainable home to us and the rest of biodiversity is, like everything else I have been mentioning in this book, up to Man. You cannot ever stress this enough, may it sound too boringly radical or not, though I believe anyone conscientious enough will understand the incessant repeating of this statement.

Transportation

In order to share with you some personal aspects regarding my own life, though without being too intimate, for both our sakes, I have been getting all the more in touch with people living outside my own country. Indeed, I have been making friends from all over the globe, including Europe, Africa, the Americas, North, Central and South, Asia and Oceania. Maybe someday I will reach both poles, just as much.

I have already had the honor of meeting some of these people live, but some others are still on hold. That is where it all needs to change. We keep calling our planet a global village, because we all live so close to each other, though not physically. In countries where neither social networking is banned, nor the Internet is actually a national form of Intranet ultimately controlled by a tyrannical State (without having its users know about it, of course), we are allowed to contact with anyone we like, despite both the advantages and dangers of such means of communication, which is an exhausted issue constantly being discussed by authorities, psychologists and parents, the latter of which should pay most of the attention, disabling their children from meeting with total strangers. If, however, we are adults, know right from wrong and, therefore, have no reason to doubt our cyberfriends' intentions, then why not experience the chance of being with them, even if just a few times per year? Also, there is a strong possibility a cybernetic romance may arise, and people certainly do not want to keep dating solely behind a screen. That is where new forms of transportation, not just worldwide, but locally also, have to come along.

When it comes to international traveling, a lot of people around the globe just wished they could instantly get from one place to another in no more than a nanosecond. Time has always been of the essence and, therefore, there is none to waste, especially with respect to being with someone else you really care about. There might be a *time* in your life when you have got special people around you, two or three steps away, and still you do not feel like connecting with them. Of course, everyone has their reasons not to, but there is also the chance there are not any reasons at all and people will still not get in touch, slowly biding their time toward complete and utter loneliness. Sooner or later, living a lonesome life will interfere with your mind, as humans were simply not designed by nature nor evolution to remain all by themselves. Mankind was made a cooperative species, yet so utterly individualistic.

All of this brings me to the inevitable question so many times portrayed before in science fiction: teleportation (or teletransportation). It is a way of transferring energy or, preferably, matter from one point to another, without having to physically cross the distance between those two points, regardless of their respective location.

This is mostly what people think could happen, if a human being (or any other being, for that matter) were to be swallowed by a black hole, in outer space. The fantasizing theory for black holes, which can basically be compared to that of teleportation, is whatever enters one of them ends up somewhere else, in a completely different spot in the Universe, such as an unknown dimension. Albert Einstein's[228] general relativity theory, published in 1915, was continued in 1916, when he predicted the existence of gravitational waves as a consequence of general relativity, one hundred years ago. The theory says, to put it bluntly, a sufficiently compact mass can deform space-time and, thusly, generate a black hole, which indeed distorts everything around it, including light, via strong gravitational effects, the likes of which Einstein foresaw and were eventually confirmed.

The truth is there are no holes involved in these celestial bodies, at all. The concept of «hole» would necessarily imply whatever it is that *goes in* remains lost *in* it, without the chance of coming out, similar to the idea of an endless pit, in which objects fall eternally. On the contrary, black holes do not work as pits, passages or portals, but rather as distortion orbs with massive gravitational power, enough to create a scenery of complete annihilation, destruction and disassembly, as a regular body would then transform into several atomic streams, instantly killing its physical integrity. It is a cosmic form of continuum rupture, considering light itself is blocked from its center. Should a ray of light be sent through space in one single stream, that same stream would be interrupted without the chance to go around, for the gravitational waves of a black hole are far too strong, even for the visible form of electromagnetic radiation traveling at the speed of 299,792,458 meters per second, especially when in vacuum, with no obstacles at all in its way, such as the black hole itself.

---

[228] 1879-1955. German-born theoretical physicist, having acquired American citizenship in 1933, when Hitler rose to power. Einstein is the creator of the world's most famous equation regarding mass-energy equivalence, under the form of $E=mc^2$, i.e. energy equals mass multiplied by the speed of light squared. He was awarded the Nobel Prize in Physics in 1921, for discovering the law of the photoelectric effect (the production of electrons when light is cast upon a material).

Teleportation would hence have to be the result of the general fantasy regarding black holes, a way of fast travel that could maintain our material integrity without any distortion whatsoever, keeping us alive in the process of disappearing on one side of the globe and reappearing immediately on the other, like leaving the North Pole and showing up in the South, regardless of the one hundred and eighty degrees separating them both, making it a total geographic distance of 20,004 kilometers across the Earth's surface, as opposed to 12,712 kilometers through the planet's crust, mantle and core. This is the time I wish gravity trains could be made real.

Do you remember a sci-fi action motion picture from 2012[229] featuring that concept? It is a remake of a 1990 film with the same title. By the end of the 21st century, which sounds very ironic, considering this book's subtitle, Earth is dying from chemical warfare, and the only habitable territories on the planet's surface are the United Federation of Britain, made of the present-day UK, Ireland and part of Western Europe's mainland, and the Colony, present-day Australia. People living in the Colony (a designation which is somehow depreciative of the country's independence in reality, though it is fiction and I am well aware of it) travel all the way to the UFB to work in just about seventeen minutes, via a gravity train called «The Fall», which is a somehow futuristic sort of commute, disabling any contact with the remainder of the Earth's surface, as the atmosphere in areas other than the aforementioned is riddled with fatal chemicals.

Theoretically speaking, a gravity train would work like this: it would connect two points on the Earth's surface, following a straight tunnel, with no curvatures at all, heading directly from A to B through the interior of the planet.

---

[229] *Total Recall*, starring Colin Farrell, Kate Beckinsale, Jessica Biel, Bryan Cranston and Bill Nighy, directed by Len Wiseman, Columbia Pictures, 2012.

Acceleration of a gravity train would have to be produced using gravitational force alone, considering the first part of the course, from the departing zone on the surface to the planet's core, would send the train downward, continuously freefalling. By the time it reached the center of the planet, gravity would be null, making passengers weightless, as if they were on the Moon's surface. Then, in the beginning of the second part, the train would have enough speed to be cast all the way up to its destination, as the acceleration gained from the first part would be enough to make it stop at the right time of arrival, coupling to the station, which would then hold it until it went back down again for the roundtrip. There would have to be, however, a permanent magnetic field preventing the train from colliding with the walls of the gravity railroad both down and then back up, so as to eliminate the possibility of friction.

The reason why gravity trains do not exist has to do with a great deal of physical factors that, at least right now, are impossible to overcome, namely: a rather too lengthy distance to cover from A to B, all the way through the entire mass of the globe, which is not completely solid, starting with the mantle, where there is predominantly fluid rock. Also, temperatures in the core, especially the inner part of it, skyrocket to about 9,800 °F[230]. At this time, there are no materials capable of withstanding that kind of infernal heat. Not just that, there is likewise the question of pressure between three hundred and thirty and three hundred and sixty GPa[231]. Though having a magnetic field covering the entirety of the gravity railroad tunnel's length could ease friction, there would also have to be complete air suction, so as to avoid

---

[230] 5,430 °C.

[231] Gigapascal. As a reference, one GPa equals one billion Pascal, a unit utilized to quantify internal pressure and stress. It was named after Blaise Pascal (1623-1662), French mathematician and physicist, for his contributions to hydrodynamics.

resistance that would eventually slow down the train before it reached the top, making it enter an endless loop traversing the core without ever resurfacing. Solid atmosphere-free planets and satellites, however, would not present this problem.

Now that we have spoken theoretically, I give you mathematical data, though it is very easy to understand (otherwise I would not even mention it): momentarily disregarding Earth's properties, and supposing we were inhabiting a perfectly spherical planet with uniform density, also putting friction to the side, a gravity train traveling between two opposite points on the globe's surface would reach maximum speed at the middle point of the course, having the time of the trip depend on both density and gravitational constant, not the planet's diameter. As far as gravity trains traveling between non-antipode[232] locations are concerned, the tunnels carrying them would have to be hypocycloids[233], as opposed to the straight line connecting two antipodal points, regardless of their location on the sphere's surface.

Now, if this kind of transportation were to be used on Earth, which is what I would personally love it could happen, these would be the stakes: under the uniform density of a perfect sphere (which Earth is really not, as it is flattened at both poles), it would take about 42.2 minutes to get from one location to the other. Should the train traverse the core, it would reach a maximum speed of 28,440 kilometers per hour, an astounding 7,900 meters per second. However, because Earth's density is *not* uniform all across the globe, travel time would become all the more reduced, dropping to about thirty-eight minutes. In the event of a hypocycloid connecting two non-antipode locations, such as London and Paris (roughly three hundred and fifty kilometers

---

[232] I.e. that are not precisely opposite to each other.

[233] Plane curves generated from a fixed point within a small circle rolling inside a larger one. In this case, the larger circle would actually be the matching three-dimensional object, a sphere in the form of a planet.

away from each other), the tunnel for the gravity train would have to be 55,704 meters deep, thus traversing the mantle.

A great deal of what used to be science fiction in the past eventually became reality afterward. Right now, there are still many projections we have been making into the future that have not yet come true, but there is always a chance some of them may become doable after all, without the aid of CGI, having the sole purpose of entertaining us at the movies. There is, of course, a difference between prototypes built specifically to shoot a film and their actual industrialization. Fortunately, not everything we see on the screen is entirely imaginative, which is the case, go figure, of driverless cars.

Most of us started hearing about autonomous cars when Google first began running tests with its Google X (now just X) prototype, as early as 2005. Personally, it is not an idea I am completely comfortable with firsthand, because I really love to drive and like being in control of my own vehicle, rather than letting *it* decide for me. However, it is utterly undeniable cars that do not require human operation can become a great deal safer, as a driver's most common mistakes are not present. Nonetheless, just as much as Man can sometimes be the main cause of both death and destruction on the road, he can also be the key factor preventing a car from ending up in the junkyard or innocent people on a mortal slab. I know these are crude words, but death is crude itself. One way or another, there is always a chance of avoiding human cost. All it takes is putting our processors to work.

Benefits of the generalized use of autonomous cars are, above all, fatal collisions. Driving is not something Man was originally designed to endure, as the speeds we can travel at inside a vehicle go far beyond our natural speed. Humans are walking mammals. Our lifestyle, no matter how hard we try to make it look busy, is gifted with a slow pace. No one runs, unless they have to or made a commitment to themselves that they would either continuously jog or hit the treadmill to stay healthy. Theoretically, a human is able to run at about forty miles per hour[234], which is somewhat insane. The only people in the world running for a living to be the fastest of all are Olympic athletes, in the 100-meter sprint. Their maximum recorded speed is twenty-eight miles per hour[235]. That speed is not theoretical at all, it is concrete evidence.

So, considering neither walking, nor running, nor having a horse were reliable means of individual transportation to achieve great distances on land, there was someone who first came up with the ingenious idea to produce a machine capable of moving itself through an internal combustion engine, the automobile. That person was Karl Benz[236]. Today, like it says in the footnote, Mercedes-Benz is one of the most successful automobile companies in the world, and not just because of its cars' attractive luxurious features, but also their design and engineering toward both efficiency and safety.

This last vocable contains the paramount idea a driver needs to bear in their mind when operating a vehicle. Should one be anxious to practice reckless driving on a public road, consequences could be catastrophic. There has to be, above all, a sense of responsibility, which can be no other than a constant. The problem is drivers just keep collecting endless amounts of information for each millimeter they roll. Remember that cognition barrier I told you about with respect to both the human brain and the pseudo-concept of multitasking? That is exactly what the

---

[234] About 64.4 kilometers per hour.

[235] Circa forty-five kilometers.

[236] 1844-1929. German engineer, founder of automobile manufacturer Mercedes-Benz, one of the most renowned brands in the business of the present-day. Benz produced his first vehicle in 1885 and called it the «Benz Patent Motorwagen». The first model, prior to the patenting, in 1886, was difficult to control and eventually hit a wall during public demonstration. It was only afterward that successful public road tests were conducted.

surrounding environment keeps demanding from drivers. It is actually very lucky people get in a car every day and reach their destination safely, though it is very rare just as much there is not a single chance of a slight crash to the rear bumper of the vehicle ahead because of tailgating. The question is, right now, how can autonomous cars disable that chance?

Right now, every driver is taught in driving school not to stay too close to the car in front of them, as they never know when the other driver is going to need to stop. Roads are not built for cars to roll in a constant chess formation, it is unrealistic and, therefore, impossible, as it would require an endless number of lanes to the side. Once people got to their destination, all those lanes would have to mandatorily converge, somehow, which would lead to painfully slow outflow funneling, considering those located the further away would unmistakably take a lot more time to pass beyond the beer bong. That is why the only chance we have in order to move in a somewhat straight line to our point of arrival is sticking to the regular number of lanes, driving behind each other, though at an always safe distance. It is precisely that same distance autonomous cars are able to overcome, as they are fully equipped with proximity sensors that bring them to a stop whenever the obstacle ahead does not seem to move. Plus, this would allow a much more reduced resistance to air, as present-day conventional petroleum-run vehicles have to burn a lot more fuel just to dislocate the wind blowing against them and reach a considerable amount of speed that is neither too dangerously fast, nor too dangerously slow, as riding too slow when other drivers are expecting faster motion is also a way of jeopardizing road safety. It is not a question of being the sole responsible driver in the area, but rather irresponsible, depending on the kind of road, which can be meant for either lower or higher speeds. Although there would have to be a leading car breaking the air barrier, all other cars behind would take advantage of drafting. The downside is drafting too close also cuts speed from cars ahead. Whereas we are taking advantage of those in front of us, those behind us are taking it away, in a chain effect.

The greatest benefit of them all as far as driverless cars are concerned is probably the fact no training whatsoever would be required. Simultaneously, it would be an insurmountable mistake. Even though a person would not have to learn to drive, which can be much of a headache to many, if not a migraine, letting a car loose on its own is a too dangerous of an endeavor to not be overridden manually. Every time children go to school on a bus, parents are not supposed to be worried, as they are at the care of the bus driver, who is a human being and, therefore, could fail at any given time on the safe completion of his task. However, the more lives you carry in a means of transportation only you can control, the bigger the responsibility, which is exactly what commercial jet pilots feel when performing their duties. The airplane is said to be the safest, when it comes to transporting. I agree to that statement, though, should there be a failure of any kind, results could be catastrophic. An aircraft can fly on autopilot most of the time, when everything is expected to run smoothly, but the future cannot be foretold with complete accuracy, meaning manual evasive maneuvers may be demanded.

All of this means to say that automatic is too unreliable at this point for human supervision to fully stand down. No aircraft is flown by itself without the commandeering of two pilots, and neither should a road vehicle be driven without a driver. There are places in the world where driving all the way through a carwash is deemed perfectly safe. In some other places, however, and most likely depending on the kind of machinery, it is strictly forbidden to stay in the car while it is being automatically washed, because *malfunctions* are unpredictable. Again, remember the chain: humans are building AIs to perfect themselves constantly, making better versions of themselves without the aid of carnal, fragile amateurs like us. But it all starts with humans. Perfection is unreal. Exact science is not that exact as one would think. Keep building a simple Arithmetic operation on a calculator. Or, better yet, try typing a word using the number pad. If there is one minor detail the maker of that calculator has not foreseen and that cannot be ironically explained through Mathematic, it is undoubtedly going to read «error» sooner or later.

Now, suppose that, for the sake of argument, instead of placing your child on a school bus, you sent them to school on your own car, waiting for it to get back and take you to work. Would you fully rely on a car with those features? Maybe not right now, no. Vehicles would have to *think* exactly like humans, combining that logic with that of a computer, so as to keep the margin of error to its lowest. That is the real ambition scientists crave for the near future. Not just human, not just machines – both.

Getting a regular driver's license would, therefore, remain a constant. It is for the best. That means there would be no excuses for getting drunk, stoned or both. What could be a fine solution for cases like these is an automatic override, having vital sign sensors on the steering wheel that could read the driver's ability to continue on their journey. Should they be inapt, the car pulls over and comes to a full stop, which is very much useful in case the driver is fully aware of themselves and, all of a sudden, faints while on the road, a consequence of our purely carnal condition. Authorities are then automatically signaled to come to the rescue, dispatched accordingly to how critical the driver's status is, so as to avoid sending out resources that could be required elsewhere, in far more dangerous situations.

Insurance companies are the ones making the most out of road safety. That no-claims bonus may seem like a sight for sore eyes, but nobody is getting richer any time soon from that alone, apart, of course, for the companies themselves. In countries where there is not a national health system, insurance companies benefit from holders who are afraid of getting sick and, if they actually do get ill, they will most certainly not pay for the required treatment. It is a unilateral deal, but nothing really new, here. I had already mentioned this before, nearly in the beginning. They are counting on fearful people, together with legislation forcing them to be foolhardy, to avoid dying or wrecking their car. It is when the moment of truth comes to life, ironically enough, that they back off. What are you paying an insurance policy for, if you are not going to be able to use it?

Law enforcement also benefits from aggressive driving. Speeding tickets are every policeman's favorite. Having a car in your possession that respects the principles of road safety is an excuse to make them stop patrolling a certain area, which is good. Hopefully, neither of us drivers would have to pull over during the daily commute, when it is the busiest. There is nothing to fear when there is nothing to hide, most rightly so, but it is an utter waste of time for those who are just trying to get to work or school and are already running late enough as it is.

There is currently an excess of visual pollution, with respect to traffic signage, at least in urban areas. Every signal has a special meaning, those with a driver's license realize that, as we had to undoubtedly memorize hard for the theory test, including details we eventually forget about because they are useless to most drivers, but the autonomous car does not require them at all. Both Internet and satellite information are enough for a driverless car to know when to either increase or decrease speed on a specific road. Also, direction-pointing signals do not necessarily have to be present, either, as a GPS can drive the vehicle straight to its destination.

But if a car were to be fully electronic, with very few mechanical parts to operate, such as a steering wheel, pedals or a gear stick, and should it go online to guide itself in the field autonomously, would it be perfectly safe from carjacking? Of course not. There are multiple forms of carjacking. The way we know of best in the present is a thief getting into a car that is not theirs to steal it by driving it away, even if they are not going to keep it or sell it with fake chassis numbers. What we usually forget about is remote control. That is one of the reasons why nobody can go online during a flight. There is a chance an ill-intended passenger can break into the system and remotely diverge the aircraft to an uncharted location. The same could be done with Web-connected cars. Nowadays' terrorists would not have to sacrifice themselves in the name of their beliefs. They could just send a car somewhere and remotely detonate it.

It sounds too repetitive of me to insist on terrorism of all forms, but its very existence is the first step to utopian rupture. It is not just about following the rules and being kind to one another, blinded like a flock of sheep. Living in a utopia means the granted ability to choose. We only fail to become utopian because of our own nature. Even the calmest, the wisest of people can lose their «sainthood» and sometimes wish something bad would happen to somebody who did them wrong. It is all usually the result of a heated argument with others, progressing no further. However, those who are strong-spirited, craving for revenge for anything at all, are the ones who concern human nature the most, making it a forcibly policed world, concealing them from the rest of us.

During hour-long journeys, if there is anything both driver and passengers would love to do freely is just turn around, instead of facing forward all the time, sitting in the same uncomfortable position toward numbness. We can always claim there already are alternatives to that. There are buses, trains, boats, even planes, for half-an-hour flights that would take about three hours to complete on the road, driving. But the fact is car ownership, above any intended signs of wealth or statute showmanship, is not only a private possession, but, more than that, a private space. There are times in life when you did not expect it would come to that, but people are indeed living in a car, because they do not have a home to be in, sheltered from the weather and the streets in general, living with that same dignity you would never think of giving away.

Without being this much extreme, though realistic, a lot of things can happen in cars. It is a small space that brings at least between five to nine people together. They may not know each other up until then, but they end up talking to one another, even if it is just chitchat about how it is pouring so much outside. The richest have the right to their personal space when flying first class, they can lie down as if they were in bed, sleeping through the entire twelve-hour flight from Madrid to Los Angeles with a champagne flute by their side. So, why should the rest of us flat-breads not be able to have our own road jet and benefit from the same level of comfort? Should everyone aboard be certified to drive a non-autonomous car, there could be rotations to overlook the automatic progress of the vehicle concerning road behavior and safety. And just in case there is no time for fun, being the driver or other people required to become productive, so as to have their corporate meeting presentations ready, the ability to concentrate on a laptop or tablet without any other concerns is also very welcome.

Tradition is very hard to break in certain countries, because it is precisely made of customs no one is willing to part with. When tourists visit or go living in certain sovereign States where driving takes place on the left side of the road, having the steering wheel to the right-hand side of the vehicle, and with a background of driving on the right side with the steering wheel to the left, adaptation can be very confusing, just as much as this paragraph.

If drivers had the chance of changing the position of the steering wheel to the appropriate side, it would become a lot easier to change between territories, such as France and the United Kingdom, across the Eurotunnel (or Chunnel), before it is demolished in the near future, so as to make the UK completely separate from the rest of Europe, enabling a better connection to its past hegemony of isolation[237].

Though I have been mentioning quite a few obstacles to driverless vehicles up to now, there are others I should not leave behind, namely manufacturer responsibility. Right now, according to national regulations (or European Union norms, with respect to Member-States), there are certain rules vehicle manufacturing companies need to abide by in order to be allowed to sell their cars, otherwise their business becomes illegal and cannot proceed. Do you remember the 2015 Volkswagen scandal? Here is a news cutting from BBC[238] to bring you up to speed:

«What is Volkswagen accused of?

It's been dubbed the "diesel dupe". In September, the Environmental Protection Agency (EPA) found that many VW cars being sold in America had a "defeat device" – or software – in diesel engines that could detect when they were being tested, changing the performance accordingly to improve results. The German car giant has since admitted cheating emissions tests in the US.

VW has had a major push to sell diesel cars in the US, backed by a huge marketing campaign trumpeting its cars' low emis-

---

[237] Because you are undoubtedly a perspicacious Reader, you can tell this part of the book was written after June 23rd 2016.

[238] HOTTEN, Russell, 12-10-2015, *BBC News*, «Volkswagen: The scandal explained», (http://www.bbc.com/news/business-34324772), accessed 06-28-2016.

sions. The EPA's findings cover 482,000 cars in the US only, including the VW-manufactured Audi A3, and the VW models Jetta, Beetle, Golf and Passat. But VW has admitted that about 11 million cars worldwide, including eight million in Europe, are fitted with the so-called "defeat device".

The company has also been accused by the EPA of modifying software on the 3-liter diesel engines fitted to some Porsche and Audi as well as VW models. VW has denied the claims, which affect at least 10,000 vehicles.

In November, VW said it had found "irregularities" in tests to measure carbon dioxide emissions levels that could affect about 800,000 cars in Europe – including petrol vehicles. However, in December it said that, following investigations, it had established that this only affected about 36,000 of the cars it produces each year».

Volkswagen did not obviously run out of business because of the scandal, but it was forced by every affected country's laws to either correct the vicious software contained in their vehicles or replace them entirely, should customers request the company to do so. Going against the rules is not always bad. It means you are not letting yourself be controlled by the system. However, in this case, both Governments and customers were being duped altogether.

Just like there is chance this kind of liability may be found in engines that are polluting a lot more than they should, decision-making software running autonomous vehicles can put the people themselves in danger, not just the environment in general. Like I said before, legislation must move with the times and adapt itself to new circumstances, but it is also very hard to legislate over something you have not tried yet and do not know the consequences of. It is hard to tell, for instance, due to lack of human judgment, what a driverless car would do in a dangerous situation in which some sort of damage is inevitable, may it be human or material. There are just too many stimuli to handle all at once. Though the human brain is undoubtedly limited as far as multitasking is concerned, because you either pay attention to one thing or the other, drivers all over the world have somehow been able to often narrowly escape death or severe injury. My personal belief is autonomous cars should not be made fully like so, but rather bear the ability to be manually overridden and ultimately give control to the human driver, as there are also a lot of hand gesture protocols only humans are able to interpret, right now, and not everyone demonstrates them the same way. For instance, when you want to thank another driver for yielding to you without having been forced to, you can either extend your hand upward, diagonally or just make a fist and raise your thumb, which is also a sign of appreciation. Autonomous vehicles would have to be taught through software how to make the same decisions without reading that visual information, which would then be inexistent.

Information exchange between vehicles and infrastructures is also a reason to delay the general implementation of autonomous vehicles on public roads. If you remember, the key factor that kept pushing the European eCall system back was the loss of privacy. Vehicle and infrastructure communication does not necessarily have to exchange personal data. All that needs to be broadcast is the presence of either a vehicle or some other kind of physical obstacle, no one needs to know *who* is traveling through a said specific location. It is the same thing with bionic vision I talked to you about a while back. You should only have to acquire personal information from people you see on the street *if* and only *if* they allow you to do so. That decision has got to ultimately be made by the people themselves and strictly no one else.

Nonetheless, everyone who operates digital devices during

their quotidian knows software is just plainly unreliable. A simple glitch in the source code could jeopardize it entirely, making it do things you did not want to and neither authorized. Though I have spoken greatly of Microsoft's Windows 10 before, there has been someone who ended up winning a lawsuit against the company for an unauthorized upgrade to the latest version of the operating system, whose results were not so beneficial. Take a read:

«For months, we've cataloged continued user resistance to Microsoft's Windows 10 upgrade policies, the company's increasing attempts to shove users to adopt the OS, and its occasional backtrack when its own policies went too far. It seems that at least one customer took the fight to court and won a small judgment against the company for how it deployed its latest operating system.

The Seattle Times reports that Teri Goldstein, of Sausalito, California, sued Microsoft after a failed Windows 10 upgrade left her system performing poorly, prone to crashing, and reportedly unusable for multiple days. Given the general issues associated with performing in-place upgrades, even successful ones, it's not surprising that some users would run into problems. Goldstein reached out to Microsoft customer service to attempt to resolve her issues, but filed suit against the company once it failed to resolve her problems. Her $10,000-figure reflected estimated lost compensation as well as the cost of a new system.

Microsoft had appealed the initial judgment but dropped that appeal last month. A spokesperson for the company told the Seattle Times that it denied any wrongdoing and had dropped the appeal to avoid the additional expense of further litigation.

One $10,000-judgment against Microsoft isn't going to make a blip in the company's financial earnings or its overall Windows

10 trajectory. But it neatly caps a year of self-inflicted damage regarding Windows 10 and Microsoft's free upgrade. The repeated changes to Windows 10's upgrade policy, mandatory telemetry[239] collection, and decisions to kill off patch notes and make all updates mandatory (plus the issues with UWP[240] and gaming) have collectively left a bad taste in many users' mouths. None of these are fundamental reasons to stop using Windows 10, but they speak to the company's profound trouble communicating what ought to be a winning strategy. The Windows 10 giveaway was a great concept, and the entire process could've been handled in a way that made people want to switch. Instead, Microsoft has been dragging people into upgrading in much the same way you might grab a cat and drag it off for a bath.

With just over a month to go until it officially stops offering free upgrades to Windows 10[241], Microsoft has yet to budge from its stance that once the one-year mark is done, the company will no longer offer a free upgrade to consumers. Currently, Windows 10 Home is $119, while Windows 10 Pro is $199. Prices are identical between the downloadable and USB versions of the operating system.

Microsoft hasn't specified how it will price upgrades after the free offer has expired. In the past, upgrade-only versions of the OS typically sold for $50-$70 less than full versions, though this has varied depending on the OS in question. As for whether Microsoft's recent actions have damaged the company's long-term relationship with customers, it's too soon to tell. At least some

---

[239] According to the English dictionary, it is an «automated communications process by which measurements and other data are collected at remote or inaccessible points and transmitted to receiving equipment for monitoring». It basically means that, once you go online, it is impossible for you to hide from the Web, at all.

[240] Universal Windows Platform, which enables any application to execute on any kind of device running Microsoft's latest operating system.

[241] The last day is July 29th, 2016.

users claim to have sworn off Microsoft products or to have disabled Windows Update altogether to avoid the Windows 10 upgrade, but such remarks probably don't reflect average user behavior (and we can't recommend turning off all OS updates to avoid Windows 10 in any case). The bigger issue for Microsoft isn't necessarily the loss of Windows users, but its failure to establish trust and a cooperative relationship at a time when the company is still trying to make major changes to its software distribution model. Microsoft needs enthusiastic buy-in for its various plans from both developers and customers — not a grudging acceptance of the new status quo»[242].

As far as jobs are concerned, the driving profession would completely become extinct. Chauffeurs, cabbies, bus drivers, truck drivers, ambulance paramedics, you name it, they would all disappear. It does not have to be that bad, as long as society goes penniless. There is obviously no need to explain all that again, as that was what the first part of this book was all about.

There is also the question of traffic policing. Officers would not be required to patrol the road, anymore, *considering* no one tries to hack the systems of a vehicle to make it do things it was not supposed to, especially not the manufacturer itself, let alone the practitioners of grand theft auto, utterly and illegally reducing cars' mileage to increase their value in the black market.

In the end, there are still a lot of changes needing to be done, if we are going to catapult our local transportation systems from fiction to actual science. Paper roadmaps are not that common anymore. The most basic of smartphones can provide its user a somewhat visually detailed surface of the entire planet to assist

---

[242] HRUSKA, Joel, 06-27-2016, *ExtremeTech*, «Woman wins $10,000 judgment against Microsoft for forced Windows 10 upgrade», (http://www.extremetech.com/computing/230794-woman-wins-10000-judgment-against-microsoft-for-forced-windows-10-upgrade), accessed 06-28-2016.

navigation, so what there is left to do is use that same 3D-mapping technology and adapt it to autonomous traveling, stressing, again, the ability to manually override the system, in case of a glitch that can inadvertently put the vehicle's occupants in harm's way.

Also, automatic adaptation to different weather conditions is a must. Roads are not always ready for unpreoccupied driving, without any concerns for both wet and slippery pavements, so having a vehicle that can alternate between different driving modes, recognizing rain, snow, or even puddles of oil would be interesting. It is not that this kind of technology does not already exist, because it does, but it is only available to the most luxurious of cars and is not going to become standard any time soon. If you recall, the same happened with ABS and now everyone knows it is incredibly useful, regardless of the vehicle's level of luxury.

Courses in which to navigate do not last forever, that much you and I both know, so if a car is to guide itself through a path that does not exist anymore, a navigation error is most likely to occur. At the same time the vehicle is supposed to drive through what is now a wall or barrier of any kind, obstacle sensors are activated, disabling it from colliding. The inability to make the most logical choice of taking an alternate route implies human overriding. Either that, or automatic updates to the navigation system, even if glitchy, which will give manufacturers too much of a headache in lawsuits, like the one Microsoft faced with the lady from Sausalito, California. That is why we cannot put a blunt end to the Justice Department. The need to make rulings, regardless of the case's gravity, has got to stand, otherwise no one will have the authority anymore to settle this kind of situation. If only this were the single kind of conflict we had to endure throughout our lives, instead of other sorts of far more serious criminal activity. The police would not have to arrest anybody, and lawyers would not have to fight for a murderer's innocence.

Before I end this matter with changes made to roads themselves and move on to the third and last part of this book, I have to stress not all means of transportation will be able to become fully electric. That is undoubtedly possible with cars, as Elon Musk's Tesla Motors has been seeing to it, considering there would not even have to be a need to place several charging spots across a country's entire road system. Cars themselves could be made self-rechargeable, especially through the filtering of ultra-violet rays from the Sun via their windshields, converting them to electric energy. In the case the Sun does not usually show much in certain locations on the Earth's surface, there has got to be an alternative to electric juice, and that is ecofriendly fuel. Not petroleum-derived fuels like diesel or gasoline. Not even liquefied petroleum gas, as the designation itself says it is made of petroleum. No matter how many performance substances we add to diesel or gasoline, it is always going to be polluting the environment and slowly riddling us with cancer. That is why sugarcane ethanol, of which Brazil is a major worldwide producer, is the answer to the hybrid problem. If you cannot ride your vehicle based only on electric energy from the Sun, regardless of the number of panels it has embedded to it, ethanol is the appropriate alternative and completely renewable. Airplanes could be using it in the near future, if their rotors are adapted to embrace a new source of energy that is powerful enough to keep them running through the entire flight, which I hope will not have to last something like between twelve and eighteen hours, with that same need to make more than two stops, depending on the route, when it could eventually fly straight to its destination and a lot safer and faster.

Finally, from BBC, as promised, a way to constantly be fueling a vehicle without having to pull over ever again[243]. I will not leave you to it, however, without stating first that, as long as we need to invest in order to futurize our lives, money should be carefully spent only on infrastructures and technology we actually need. Just remember the last chapter and the beginning of the present. First we figure out how we adapt our bodies to technology, and then we see what we need to build. If we make cars smart with a minimum margin to make mistakes, and if we find a more cost-effective alternative to powering our cars, then maybe there is not the need to be spending insurmountable amounts of money on road adaptation. That is where the hybrid semi-powered with sugarcane ethanol comes in. Indeed, we would have to keep pumping stations active, but sometimes when we try to simplify too much, things get a lot more complicated than expected. Producing a way of solving those new problems only delays our progress even further. Should anyone not want to have a car of their own, regardless of its kind, then either flying or taking the Maglev is the best suitable option.

«Motorists will be able to recharge their cars as they drive if a scheme being proposed by Highways England comes to fruition.

The government agency has announced plans to test wireless power-transfer tech that it hopes to build under the country's motorways and major A roads.

It has already completed a feasibility study and is now asking companies to tender bids to host off-road trials.

But one expert questioned whether such a scheme would be cost-effective.

---

[243] KELION, Leo, 08-12-2015, *BBC.com*, «England to test charge-as-you-drive 'electric motorways'», (http://www.bbc.com/news/technology-33886180), accessed 06-28-2016.

South Korean tests

Charge-as-you-drive technologies have already been pioneered elsewhere.

In 2013, the South Korean town of Gumi switched on a 12km (7.5 miles) route that allows buses with compatible equipment to be charged as they drive over it.

It works by a process called Shaped Magnetic Field in Resonance.

Electric cables buried under the road are used to generate electromagnetic fields, which are picked up by a coil inside the device and converted into electricity.

Last year, Milton Keynes also began use of a more limited scheme, which involves buses being wirelessly recharged via plates installed into the road. In this case, however, the vehicles have to stop for several minutes at a time to receive the power boost.

"What has been committed to is that by 2016 or 2017 we will hold off-road trials – in other words not on a public road", Stuart Thompson, a spokesman for Highways England, told the BBC.

"It's still very early days. Where exactly the trials will be has yet to be determined".

Highway England says full details will be publicized once a contractor has been appointed.

It aims to run the experiments for about 18 months before deciding whether to commit itself to an on-road trial.

"The potential to recharge low emission vehicles on the move offers exciting possibilities", commented Transport Minister Andrew Jones.

"As this study shows, we continue to explore options on how to improve journeys and make low-emission vehicles accessible to families and businesses".

However, the director of Cardiff Business School's Electric Vehicle Centre of Excellence remains skeptical.

"It makes sense to try it out, and the technology does obviously work", commented Dr. Paul Nieuwenhuis.

"But it sounds very ambitious to me. Cost will be the biggest issue and I'm not totally convinced it's worth it.

"Battery technology is increasing – if you look at what Tesla has achieved in recent years, it keeps adding more [travel] range to battery technology roughly every six months. So, it's not clear there's even a need for this".

Even if the plan ultimately comes to naught, Highways England is also committed to installing plug-in charging points every 20 miles (32.1km) on its motorway network over the "longer-term"».

Part III
The ExoQuest

1

Back to the Future-Past

One of Mankind's oldest dreams is getting in contact with ex-traterrestrial species. For centuries, if not millennia, humans have been fantasizing with the idea of finding someone else far more intelligent, developing far more advanced technology, than any scientist in our world could think of. It is thought by some, though their theories[244] are deemed pseudoscientific, aliens once visited Earth and taught Man to build incredibly enormous and (somewhat) perfectly geometrical structures such as the Giza Pyramid complex, in Egypt. There have been archeologists, though also based on false theories, who claimed ancient hieroglyphs contained secret shapes resembling either spaceships or skycranes which might have been used as a means of avoiding structural concerns that would have otherwise disabled architects from actually fulfilling their designs. The problem is, if they did come here, they were certainly not interested in staying or paying us back another visit, as they suddenly disappeared.

The truth is there is in fact a knowledge gap between Antiquity and the Dark Ages, but we know that is especially due to the

---

[244] The Ancient Alien (or Astronaut) Contact (or Hypothesis) theory.

destruction of the Library of Alexander, together with the continued cultural repression from the whole of Christendom. There is no material evidence Earth has ever been visited by living beings originating somewhere else in space, but that does not mean they do not exist. After all, having such an insurmountable area of space to cover at our disposal, it is actually *very likely* there might be another civilization inhabiting another planet with similar geological conditions to those of Earth. It is how we imagine them that may be far beyond what we are actually expecting to find, after we have developed our space exploration technology enough to travel outside the Solar System. NASA is still busy trying to put a man on Mars looking for signs of previously existing life, so there is still much to wait through until we are done, hence the continuous fantasy of hominoid creatures with oval heads, green skin, possibly a few tentacles and dark eyes, communicating via telepathy. I somehow believe that is exactly what some science fiction authors would love to be able to do by themselves. Because we cannot enhance our condition as humans straight away via that process of putting a computer together in an assembly line, for instance, as if we were being industrially built, it is easier to produce technological devices that same way. Instead of becoming telepaths, we create telephones. Because we cannot take our telephones with us anywhere we want to go, we make them wireless and call them cellphones. Because we would love to hear another person talk to us while watching them live, we embed video calls, and so on. Technology is our only current way of achieving purposes our natural bodies would not otherwise be able to accomplish all alone. But when it comes to aliens, even if they are not naturally born with the ability to communicate via telepathy or teleport themselves to a completely remote area, we imagine them going through a «transalienization» process, just as much as we would want to transhumanize ourselves and be able to do the same things, only with digital devices embedded into our flesh.

Regardless of picturing aliens as either completely animalistic, super intelligent, destructive, annihilating or cooperative, the hominoid version is always our best guess, as whatever we think exists but have no material evidence of to compare with, is always based on what we have right in front of us, in the present. We are only able to imagine the future based on the time being. No matter how creative we are, imagination does not pop up out of thin air, just like that, without any source of information, even if undeniably remote or unexpected.

Take the *Alien* quadrilogy[245], for instance, of which Sigourney Weaver's character, Ellen Ripley, was the protagonist. The first instalment of the franchise, as described in the footnote, was released in 1979, a decade which marked the 20th century «boom» in science fiction. By then, nearly forty years ago, Mankind was already picturing the possibility of events such as intergalactic traveling, hypersleep, terraforming exoplanets or alien encounters, naturally.

Although the saga's action takes place in the year 2122[246], early 22nd century, the truth is Ridley Scott's vision of the future could not be that much advanced beyond 1970s' technology, regardless of his unquestionable creativity and mastery of cinema arts, and the same goes for the directors who followed. You can tell the difference between the 1979 feature and its prequel, *Prometheus*, released in 2012. Scott was the director of both movies,

---

[245] *Alien*, starring Tom Skerritt, Sigourney Weaver, John Hurt and Ian Holm, directed by Ridley Scott, 20th Century Fox, 1979;

Aliens, starring Sigourney Weaver and Lance Henriksen, directed by James Cameron, 20th Century Fox, 1986;

Alien³, starring Sigourney Weaver, Charles Dance, Charles S. Dutton and Lance Henriksen, directed by David Fincher, 20th Century Fox, 1992;

Alien: Resurrection, starring Sigourney Weaver, Winona Ryder, Ron Perlman, J. E. Freeman and Brad Dourif, 20th Century Fox, 1997.

[246] Excluding the new timeline introduced in recent prequels (*Prometheus* [2012] and *Alien: Covenant* [2017]).

as much as of the second prequel, scheduled for 2017.

Back in the 1970s, the concept of surfaces displaying virtual reality, like the now common tablet or smartphone, was unrealistic and, therefore, complete fiction, the kind of fiction no one had yet imagined to be applicable in a future as distant as 2122. What we call today «touchscreen» was simply beyond us. That is why the spaceship carrying the crew in *Alien*, called «Nostromo» and nicknamed "Mother", was completely riddled with physical, volumetric buttons, producing 8-bit sounds with no audio quality at all, every time they were pressed. As for screens, those were plain monochromatic, displaying white letters on a black background, as if the system running the ship was MS-DOS, which in fact came to be in 1981, only two years after the release of the first movie.

When it comes to *Prometheus*, however, I honestly think Scott wanted to believe that by 2012 there would already be spaceships capable of traveling between galaxies, though we have not yet even put a man on Mars, only in fiction, and it had to be by his hand, as well[247]. Also, the visual aspect of the spaceship carrying this crew who first dealt with the Alien species was far less crude and completely electronic. Touchscreens were everywhere, together with holographic information, and all because such a technology exists indeed in the present and has been around for a few years.

In short, if we have not yet thought of it, we can create new devices in fiction that could probably work in real life, but their very structure will have to mandatorily feature what is already a part of our day-to-day technology, basically because we do not know any better.

Just to make a point as far as getting in touch with aliens is concerned, the aforementioned first prequel to the *Alien* saga was

---

[247] Vide note 217.

fictionalized to give us an entirely different perspective of what we consider ourselves to be. Instead of being earthlings, we are in fact (according to the saga's story, mind) extraterrestrial, as the «seeds of life» were *planted* on Earth by a foreign visitor, part of an advanced civilization humans eventually called «Engineers», replacing the idea of our Creator being a deity (regardless of faith) with another civilization who *created* humans "in [their] own image"[248]. The difference is those who were either bold enough to challenge or authorized by the Roman Catholic Church to depict Jehovah as human[249] interpreted the Bible's words literally and gave him man-like features. The «Engineers», on the other hand, were *similar* to humans, but not *identical*, and this because of the story accompanying the Earth's formation and major extinction events. Whether these events were forced unto the planet by the «Engineers» themselves in order for evolution to reach Mankind and prevent our fate from being jeopardized by previously dominant species such as the dinosaurs is *my own speculation*, though I believe it is worth thinking about, even if just as a mental exercise to make us wonder.

According to the storyline described in the «Alien Anthology Wikia», which is probably the best place to find accurate information about fiction, considering this kind of website is produced by dedicated fans, the first «Engineer» coming to Earth to create the building blocks of life was sent in approximately 3.2 billion BC. In order to activate life on the planet, he has to sacri-

---

[248] An allusion to the Bible's «Book of Genesis», chapter one, verse twenty-seven (Gn 1:27), which reads: "So God created man in His *own* image; in the image of God He created him; male and female He created them".

[249] Such as Michelangelo (1475-1564), author of *The Creation of Adam* (1511-12), one of the most renowned frescoes in the world (adapted in the back cover of this book to the concept of future), featured in the ceiling of the Sistine Chapel, after it was commissioned by Pope Julius II (1443-1513) in 1508.

fice himself. That is the approximate time in Earth's actual history when life began through unicellular organisms (namely, bacteria).

In 35,000 BC, when early humans rise, «Engineers» come back to Earth and instruct their creation on how to build a civilization and become organized (thusly having them evolve to our current species, the *Homo Sapiens*). Basic directions are left so Man can develop enough to understand how creation is produced and an outpost is prepared to welcome them when they have matured enough to leave the planet and travel far away, demanding sufficient advancement in both skill and reason.

Between 18 and 36 AD, when Jesus Christ has lived, been killed and ascended to heaven, the Roman Empire takes care of seizing another «Engineer» traveling to Earth to teach them, also crucifying him. Other «Engineers» become aware of this diplomatic incident and decide to wipe out both Mankind and all other lifeforms from the face of the planet via the use of a chemical agent called «A0-3959x.91 – 15». Considering the murder of the «Engineer» ambassador is unforgiveable, humans are deemed technologically advanced, though utterly immoral[250]. That is why, if left alone, they could become a threat to the entirety of the Universe. The «Engineers» thus prepare to travel to Earth from the former welcoming outpost, located in LV-223, with the purpose of infecting Earth and killing it, but three out of four cosmonauts selected for the mission are killed by an outbreak of «A0-3959x.91 – 15» and eventually never leave, though the coordinates are set to the blue planet. The remaining «Engineer» does not die, staying however in hibernation.

Between the end of 2093 and the beginning of 2094, the crew that had departed from Earth aboard the «USCSS Prometheus» after finding evidence of the existence of «Engineers» in 2091,

---

[250] Which is basically an excuse for the biblical episode we know as «The Great Flood».

finally reaches LV-223, where the aforementioned outpost is located. Most of them are exposed to the agent and die. Only an android, called David[251], and a scientist, Dr. Elizabeth Shaw[252], survive the epidemic. The «USCSS Prometheus» is sacrificed to stop the original exterminating spaceship from traveling to Earth, and they both collapse. David and Elizabeth take an abandoned ship and travel to the «Engineers'» original planet, an event that will be depicted in *Alien: Covenant.*

When agent «A0-3959x.91 – 15» is ingested and passed on through sperm to a female's uterus, it generates an alien lifeform known in the *Alien* universe as «Facehugger», which feeds its host a «Chestburster», an alien fetus rapidly evolving to the wildly animalistic «Alien» creature that started the whole story, back in 1979.

Despite all this, there is a different option for an alien encounter plot we often do not take into consideration. The Earth, as you and I both know by now, is around 4.54 billion-years-old. It tells scientists today an insurmountably long story of itself via geological evidence, including fossils of extinct species which once ruled the planet, at a time, even if unaware of it, from a rational point of view, of course. We, as humans, are only here, now, because of a sequence of events that ended up leading to our thriving among all other creatures who we have been coexisting with since our dawn. There had to be *five* mass extinction episodes putting an end to other creatures who lived millions of years before present and were the first to make use of this very world we live in, though configured under an entirely different layout, to put *us* in charge of things around here – at a cost. Ever since humans gained control of the planet as the dominant species, there has been an ongoing extinction event known as the

---

[251] Played by Michael Fassbender, in *Prometheus.*
[252] Played by Noomi Rapace, ibid.

Holocene, especially from the year 1900 onward, when Man became fully industrialized and polluting.

The question is: what if the chain of events that led to our existence had been different? You remember the butterfly effect, right? One small change in the past could result in a completely different present than that which we live in, therefore altering our future just as much, as the latter is always based on the former. Should there be exoplanets in outer space holding advanced species such as the human, their story had to be, if not the same as, then very similar to Earth's. If not, if there was at least one mass extinction episode that was different from those taking place in our world, it is therefore very likely we may find live specimens of the creatures that have been fossilized on our planet for hundreds of million years to this day.

The following is the description of each of the mass extinction events taking place on the blue planet, revealing what kind of creatures we are bound to discover once we find a way of leaving the Solar System, though preceded by the short version of how Earth modified itself enough to generate life in the first place.

Blue Planet: The Awakening[253]

Planets do not form just like that. It takes an enormous amount of cosmic debris to create a massive celestial body such as the Earth, which is not even the largest planet of our Solar System. When the Sun was born 4.56 billion years ago, it gained enough gravitational force to assemble other bodies around it at different distances, which then acquired gravity of their own to prevent collisions between them. One of those other bodies is the

---

[253] It is, indeed, a reference to the remake of *The Blue Lagoon* (1980). The new version is titled *Blue Lagoon: The Awakening*, starring Indiana Evans and Brenton Thwaites, directed by Mikael Salomon and Jake Newsome, Sony Pictures Television, 2012.

Earth, which came to be after successive asteroids collided against each other, forming the globe we now stand on top of, in the Hadean period, which lasted between 4.6 and 4 billion years ago.

Because of all the friction from constant impacting, the Earth was nothing compared to what we live in today. It was an immense orb of molten rock. Traveling to the center of the planet today would basically be the same as being on its surface back then – no chance of survival. Not only there was no solid surface where to stand, both the atmosphere and magnetosphere concealing us in the present from the Sun's heat and other cosmic radiation were inexistent, which would also disable our chances of surviving our *own* home.

By the end of the Hadean and beginning of the Archean (between 4 and 2.5 billion years ago), what geologists call Proto-Earth was beginning to cool down and solidifying on its surface, though it could still not withstand life. Around this time, a proto-planet called Theia[254], which was approximately the size of Mars, headed straight for the unprotected Proto-Earth at the average speed of a bullet[255] times twenty[256]. Until January 2016, it was thought the impact had been a glancing blow, instead of a head-on collision, but new evidence from UCLA[257] researchers claims it was actually the latter situation that took place[258].

Because Proto-Earth had still not completely cooled down, the impact projected molten material from both proto-planets, which, by the force of gravity, would turn, in one thousand years'

---

[254] Ancient Grecian titan who gave birth the Moon goddess, Selene.

[255] 2,500 feet (762 meters) per second.

[256] 50,000 feet (15,240 meters) per second.

[257] University of California, Los Angeles.

[258] WOLPERT, Stuart, 01-28-2016, *UCLA Newsroom*, «Moon was produced by a head-on collision between Earth and a forming planet», (http://newsroom.ucla.edu/releases/moon-was-produced-by-a-head-on-collision-between-earth-and-a-forming-planet), accessed 07-05-2016.

time, from a ring of debris around Proto-Earth, into the Moon. The impact was also strong enough to tilt Proto-Earth on its axis at 23.5 degrees, thus enabling the future existence of seasons, crucial to maintaining life, especially the human kind, after the discovery of agriculture.

Scientists claim also that the Earth had three different atmospheres, each of them made of different gases and other materials. The first had its origin in the solar nebula, which was a swirling disk of both interstellar dust and hydrogen. Helium was also a part of this one. Both hydrogen and helium are lighter than the air we breathe today, especially when heated. That is why they are both used for lifting. The latter is twice as heavy as the former, but it is able, nonetheless, to serve the same purpose. The main difference between them is helium cannot be combusted, whereas hydrogen is highly flammable when ignited, especially if it is contacting with oxygen, fueling it all the more. If you recall the Hindenburg disaster[259], you will get a good enough idea of the consequences.

Both solar wind and the Earth's heat drove this first atmosphere away. Evidence to this lies in the fact the elements it was

---

[259] Between World War I (1914-1918) and World War II (1939-1945), there was a time known in passenger transportation as the Airship era. Three of the nations involved in both conflicts (Britain, Germany and the United States) were the only ones in the world manufacturing rigid airships in the form of zeppelins for the carrying of people. Although using helium to keep the ships above ground was much safer, it was not as efficient as hydrogen, incredibly dangerous to use.

The Hindenburg was of a homonymous class airship, making its final trip between Frankfurt am Main, Nazi Germany and Lakehurst, New Jersey, United States, from May 3rd to May 6th, 1937. When a final approach attempt was made on the mooring mast at Naval Air Station Lakehurst, there was an ignition of the hydrogen that was supposedly airtight in its several compartment pockets, completely destroying the airship, killing thirty-six people out of ninety-seven aboard. One of the fatalities was of a worker on the ground. The accident marked the end of the so-called airship era around the world.

made of, atmophile from the solar nebula, most of which composed of the two aforementioned lifting gases, are now inexistent in our current atmosphere.

After Theia impacted the molten Proto-Earth, intoxicating gases especially originating from volcanoes were released. Oxygen was still missing, making the second version of the atmosphere the roof to a greenhouse, something we have been pretty much experiencing in recent years, due to carbon dioxide emissions from industrialized areas and vehicles. Because of the constant impacting of incoming cosmic objects bound to Earth, which vaporize after they are destroyed, their degassing into water vapor might have also contributed to the greenhouse effect, just as much as ocean formation.

It was the third atmosphere surrounding the planet that brought oxygen to the world, after bacteria came to be underwater, about 2.8 billion years ago, and started producing it.

Despite the fact water is one of the essential ingredients for the sustainability of life on Earth, the truth is it is extraterrestrial, i.e. it did not originate directly in the planet. Any celestial body too close to the Sun could not withhold liquid water, let alone frozen solid. That is why the Earth is at a perfect distance. Mathematically speaking, it is one astronomical unit[260] away from the Sun, which is used as a reference for the measurement of distances between other bodies in the cosmos. Therefore, the only possibility for water to exist on our planet became real through a constant shower of comets and meteorites, incessant for twenty million years, mostly coming from the outer asteroid belt, the one which still exists between Mars and Jupiter. These bodies, traveling from a safe enough distance from the Sun, were able to contain frozen water molecules, which then, after impact, melted and liquefied, without the chance of vaporizing because of the heat, as

---

[260] Approximately 93,205,680 miles (about 150 million kilometers), the distance between the Earth and the Sun's cores.

the planet itself was already cooling off, solidifying its crust and, therefore, turning it into a waterbed that accumulated water from vapor forming the first clouds. It suddenly began to rain. The oceans we contact with today are as old as 4.4 billion years.

Terrestrial Surface

Though Earth was beginning to cool down by the time the oceans were formed, there was still insurmountable heat flowing from the planet's interior to the surface. By then, and because of mantle convection, which is still taking place today, the earliest of tectonic plates were destroyed in subduction areas, «swallowed» by the mantle's molten rock, as it was much hotter than it is now, at approximately 2,910 degrees Fahrenheit[261], and a great deal faster. Considering subduction areas were far more common during both Hadean and Archean eons, the plates were also smaller.

The continents we stand on nowadays are the product of said smaller territories, which formed the cores to the surface that is above water in the present. Of course, because of continuous rifting resulting in tectonic plate segregation, the continental layout that is now familiar to us from either space, on a planisphere or a mapped globe began to take shape, but only after the breaking of the last supercontinent, named Pangea.

However, there were other supercontinents before. One of them was Rodinia, dated between 1.3 billion to 900 million and 750 to 600 million years ago. The smaller continents that were adrift at this time collided against each other, eventually to form a single, massive portion of land. It has been reported that, in the

---

[261] 1,600 degrees Celsius.

Proterozoic eon[262], Rodinia could have been preceded by super-continent Columbia[263], also known as «Nuna».

When Rodinia suffered a break-up about 800 million years ago, the resulting continents later produced another supercontinent, though hypothetical, called Pannotia (also referred to as Vendia), dating back to 550 million years ago. Evidence recurred to in order to prove the existence of Pannotia derives from a continental collision dubbed as the Pan-African orogeny[264]. Gathered in Pannotia were the current masses of Africa, Antarctica, Oceania and South America. References used to time Pannotia are the two supercontinents that would have followed, named Gondwana[265] and Laurentia[266]. What has been indeed proven is that, by the end of the Proterozoic, most of the existing land mass was concentrated around the South Pole, which would then result in Pangea.

The breaking of Pangea, ultimately resulting in the continents we live in today, is usually divided in three stages. The first began around 175 million years ago, when there was rifting between North America and Africa. This break-up marked the birth of the Atlantic Ocean to the North, though there is still unity today because of its homonymous treaty, military in nature[267]. The South

---

[262] Between 2.5 billion and 542 million years ago.

[263] Dated between 2.5 and 1.6 billion years ago.

[264] A geological term for the folding and deformation of a section of the Earth's crust to form a mountain range by lateral compression. The etymology for the vocable features Greek words «oro», for mountain, and «genesis», for creation.

[265] Dated between 510 and 180 million years ago, mostly made of the continental mass that is now in the Southern Hemisphere, together with the Arabian Peninsula and the Indian subcontinent.

[266] In relation to Pannotia, it existed between about 600 and 416 to 360 million years ago. It gathered most of the North American land mass, including Greenland and part of Scotland (or Northern Britain).

[267] North Atlantic Treaty Organization (NATO) or North Atlantic Alliance, founded in Washington, D.C., 1949, following the end of World War II. It consists of 28 sovereign States.

Atlantic would only begin to flood in the Cretaceous period[268], when Laurasia[269] started moving North, carrying present-day North America, leaving Eurasia to the South. The generation of two new oceans, the Atlantic and the Indian, would result in the disappearance of the Tethys, which had formed between Laurasia and Gondwana, about 250 million years ago.

To the East of the African tectonic plate, new rifts were forming, making Madagascar a completely independent island, though locked in the African plate, while sending Antarctica to the South, thus enabling the opening of the Indian Ocean to the Southwest.

The second stage of the Pangea break-up took place in the Early Cretaceous[270], a time during which Gondwana was definitely ruptured, eventually forming some of our present-day continents, namely Africa, Antarctica, Oceania and South America. The Indian subcontinent was also adrift in the newly formed Indian Ocean, but because of its opening to the South, India was pushed the opposite way, colliding with Eurasia and thusly form-

---

In response to the founding of NATO and its inclusion of the Western part of Germany (also known as Federal Republic of Germany), controlled by former Allied forces, the Soviet Union reacted with the signing of the Warsaw Pact, in 1955, so as to protect both the German Democratic Republic and all other satellite-countries to the East. However, there never was any direct conflict between either organization, created within the Cold War context. Whereas the Warsaw Pact was dissolved following the break-up of the Soviet Union, in 1991, NATO still stands. Most of the countries that had signed the former are now part of the latter.

[268] 145.5 to 65.5 million years ago. This is the time that marked the end of the dinosaur reign.

[269] Formed around 500 million years ago, this is the continent that, to the North, together with Gondwana, to the South, formed the Pangea. It included North America, Eurasia and part of North Africa. Its designation is a crossover between Laurentia and Eurasia, which became separate masses of land during the final supercontinent break-up.

[270] A geological era comprised between 150 and 140 million years ago.

ing the Himalayas, the highest mountain range on the planet, because of the speed at which India was sent northward[271], after the subduction at the Tethyan Trench. This collision is still active in the present.

Africa and South America eventually parted ways also, in the Middle Cretaceous[272], as the South Atlantic Ocean opened between then. The first stayed in approximately the same position, whereas the latter began moving to the West.

In the Late Cretaceous[273], both New Caledonia[274] and New Zealand split from Australia to the East, opening both the Coral and Tasman Seas.

The last stage of the Pangea break-up took place during the Early Cenozoic[275], a time when present-day Greenland split from Eurasia, accompanying North America, to the West, resulting in the opening of the Norwegian Sea, between 60 and 55 million years ago.

Australia is also still on a collision course, headed Northeast, toward Southeast Asia, at approximately two to three inches[276] every year, whereas Antarctica has been adrift in the South Pole region ever since the formation of Pangea itself. Africa is now moving toward the Northwest, headed for Europe, which means the Mediterranean Sea could close in a few million years, but certainly not in 2100.

In the present, all three Americas[277] are connected, as South America stopped heading West and started moving up North,

---

[271] About six inches (fifteen centimeters) a year.

[272] It took place between 120 and 90 million years ago.

[273] Between 100.5 and 65 to 66 million years ago.

[274] Administrated by France, in the present-day.

[275] Set between the Paleocene (from 66 to 56 million years ago) and the Oligocene (from 33.9 to 23 million years ago).

[276] Five to six centimeters.

[277] North, Central and South, though Central is more of a geopolitical subdivision, rather than a geological term, making it a whole part of the Northern tectonic plate.

following the break-up with Africa, hence cutting the way between both the Atlantic and Pacific Oceans, which would later result in the extinction of certain sea animals, such as the Megalodon, considered by some zoologists to be a distant relative of the present-day Great White Shark. Though this path was cut off, a new one came to be to the South, enabling Antarctica to become completely surrounded by water. In addition to this, the decreasing concentration of carbon dioxide in the Earth's atmosphere resulted in a faster cooling of the icy continent, turning it into the giant glacier we can witness in the present.

On the Origin of Species in a Breathing Atmosphere

Life on Earth began with microscopic, unicellular beings, simply designated bacteria, which were the result of chemical reactions from the simplest of organic compounds, including nucleobases and amino acids, considered to be the fundamental ingredients to the recipe of a living being.

In order for life to become far more complex than bacteria, there have to be three means of self-sustainability, and those are self-replication, metabolism and external cell membranes.

By replicating itself, an organism is reproducing, which is what all animal species are required to do, if they are to have offspring, which will contain the same genetic code, making them similar to the parents. As for metabolism, it is a process organisms undergo so as to feed themselves nutrients that will provide them energy and keep their body properly functioning through their distribution, together with oxygen, enabling them also to repair themselves naturally. Finally, external cell membranes allow feeding, but disable the absorption of unhealthy substances, excluding them as waste.

Reproduction of an organism comprises the existence of three essential macromolecules working together, known as RNA[278], DNA and proteins. The first is just as important as the second, but it offers less possibilities of genome variety. Whereas DNA relies on double-strands forming a double helix, RNA is folded on itself and is only single-stranded. It is thought the earliest of living beings could have formed exclusively on RNA, without any more complex genetic coding, considering these organisms were individual, and not an entire species. Without any gene crossing from one specimen to the other, organism complexity was not at all extraordinary. Because of the increasing of population, however, RNA was eventually replaced with DNA, making organisms stronger, with more stable genomes and variety in features, without having them look almost identical to the parents.

The earliest of cells were able to absorb both energy and food from the environment surrounding them through fermentation, thus reducing compound complexity, together with the amount of energy required, whose remnants could be used for both growth and reproduction. Considering it took some time for the Earth's atmosphere to become rich in oxygen, said fermentation was possible, as it requires an anaerobic[279] ambience. However, when living cells began processing oxygen because of the photosynthesis[280] procedure, they were also able to produce their own food and cyclically energize themselves.

Most of living beings depend on photosynthesis, whether directly or indirectly. In the case of humans, our very survival relies

---

[278] Ribonucleic acid.

[279] Oxygen-free.

[280] The process by which plants and bacteria transform sunlight energy in order to produce glucose from carbon dioxide and water and thusly energize organisms, including their own. Carbon dioxide is also converted into oxygen, hence the worldwide concerns for deforestation, as the more flora humans kill, the more oxygen we will be burning from the face of the Earth, making our planet irrespirable.

on the process indirectly, hence the need for forest conservation. Oxygenic photosynthesis from plants makes them retrieve hydrogen from water[281], expelling oxygen as a waste product afterward.

The first form of released oxygen also comprised iron, limestone and other minerals. These are the elements that would compose the Earth's third atmosphere, a topic I mentioned not too long ago, turning it to what it is today. A lot of these minerals, especially iron, began to oxidize[282], enabling the little oxygen produced by each living cell to start accumulating, setting it free to the atmosphere. Over time, via the combination of multiple cell metabolisms, the planet was breathable and ready to host lifeforms of elevated complexity.

Part of the oxygen that became abundant on Earth was key to forming a new and important layer in the atmosphere, without which life above water would still be impossible – ozone. If the ozone layer were to disappear from our planet, ultraviolet radiation from the Sun would provoke unsustainable mutation for cells living at either the surface or on land, which would not have otherwise been able to colonize said areas[283].

Although oxygen has been essential to sustain life on the planet throughout the several eons, in the beginning, it was toxic. The most fragile of lifeforms may have been killed by the rise in levels, whereas the strongest eventually adapted and developed

---

[281] One of the most renowned chemical formulas in the world is the water molecule, H_2O, comprising two hydrogen atoms bonded together to a single oxygen atom.

[282] That same rust would become the primary source for human engineering, such as bridges or skyscrapers, several hundred million years into the future.

[283] Ever since the 1970s, there has been ozone depletion to the South Pole, where there still is today a giant hole in the layer, exposing the whole of Antarctica to the Sun's radiation. Chlorofluorocarbons, which used to be present in spray cans and refrigerants, are the main cause for the disrupting of ozone molecules.

their metabolism, reaching sizes of epic proportions.

«Snowball Earth»: the Impenetrable Ice Age

When the Sun was born, its total power was at about 70%. As it ages, it increases 6% every billion years. Despite the peak in heat, the Earth did not get any warmer. On the contrary, in the Early Proterozoic[284], our planet cooled down so much that glacial deposits were found in South Africa dating from around 2.2 billion years ago, though it is likely they were originally in the equator, at that time. The «Snowball Earth» theory is dubbed as such because the globe was completely covered in ice, from poles to equator, entrapped, reflecting all of the sunlight it received back to space, as the ice layer was circa 3.42 miles[285] thick.

Considering there was an oxygen explosion between 2.3 and 2.2 billion years ago, high concentration in the atmosphere led to a decrease in methane, which is a greenhouse effect kind of gas. Contacting with oxygen makes it become carbon dioxide. The continuous depletion of methane was enough to counteract the increase in sunlight, cooling the Earth when the Sun was getting hotter.

«Snowball Earth» was not the only time the planet endured an ice age, far from it. Between 750 and 580 million years ago, the Earth was covered in ice at least four times, each time lasting approximately ten million years. The average temperature during these ice ages was about -58 degrees Fahrenheit[286].

By the end of the Proterozoic, between 716.5 and 635 million years ago, during the Cryogenian, the Earth had endured at least two global ice ages, freezing the oceans' surface completely.

Geologists and climatologists believe the supercontinent

---

[284] Vide note 262.
[285] 5,500 meters.
[286] -50 degrees Celsius.

Rodinia was to blame, as it was located in the equator, increasing chemical weathering and thusly retrieving carbon dioxide from the atmosphere, eventually modifying global climates toward cooling. Simultaneously, every time the Earth was already covered in ice, the permafrost[287] on the continental surface would also work as a key agent in order to reduce chemical weathering, putting an end to glaciations.

The surface of the Earth might have been frozen all that time, but its interior never stopped bursting heat. So much so, that the concentration of carbon dioxide below the ice layer was enough to open several volcanoes across the globe, outgassing CO_2 into the atmosphere, bringing back the greenhouse effect and melting all of the ice back to the poles. The break-up of Rodinia would turn out to be a major influence in volcanic activity.

Following the Cryogenian was the Ediacaran period[288]. During this time, there was a rapid development in multicellular organisms, as far as muscle, neurons and size are concerned. Even so, there still were no rigid body parts such as a skeleton sustaining the body mass of fauna. They would only show after the Cambrian[289], during which several species would develop a spine that would turn out to be the ancestor to the spine making humans stand in the present.

Cambrian Explosion

This is the time when life evolved drastically, and in order to prove such a statement, we have access to multiple fossils of different species that eventually went extinct. I will get to those events shortly. As mentioned above, it was only after the start of

---

[287] A thick ice layer remaining below freezing point for more than two consecutive years.

[288] Between 635 and 542 million years ago.

[289] Between 541 and 485.4 million years ago.

the Cambrian period that animals began to develop bone structures, both skeletons and exoskeletons[290], such as mollusks or arthropods, better known as trilobites. Bearing either one bone structure or the other made fossilization possible after extinction, allowing Mankind several hundred million years later to track them down and rebuild models of them, so as to identify them and perceive History behind us. These fossils are material evidence for the existence of species that would otherwise and probably be unknown to us, which is exactly what happened to lifeforms blooming previously to this period.

Simple skeletons, known as notochords, eventually evolved to vertebrate structures, the same vertebrae that are a part of the human vertebral column nowadays. The first fish appeared, under the form of Pikaia.

By the end of this period, trilobites had reached most of their diversity, enabling preserved identification of a great deal of specimens for the future.

Claiming the Land

On land, the ozone layer that had formed from excessive oxygen prevented unicellular organisms from dying off, enabling adaptation out of the water for prokaryotes[291] as early as 2.6 billion years ago. Plants and fungi first began growing by the edge of water bodies, then advancing inland from 480 to 460 million years ago, for the oldest specimens, though it is thought fungi might have begun colonizing land by one billion years ago and plants by 700 million years ago.

---

[290] Instead of being placed inside the body, in the case of humans, for instance, exoskeletons are found on the outside of some animals, *shelling* them from any possible impact, hence the common «shell» designation.

[291] A simple form of microscopic, single-celled bacteria with neither a distinct core, nor membrane.

It is uncertain when, exactly, did animals leave the water to start populating land. The oldest evidence goes back to 450 million years ago, when arthropods were able to survive from a greater variety of food produced by land plants.

Nonetheless, tetrapods are every land animal's earliest ancestor, including humans, having evolved from fish between 380 and 375 million years ago. Their fins became limbs, used to lift their heads and breathe out of the water. Some tetrapods became so used to living outside the water that they actually spent most of their lifetime on land, except whenever they reproduced, going back to lay their eggs, where they also had hatched from, giving birth to amphibians.

As far as plants are concerned, they kept spreading on land as well, especially after developing seeds as early as 360 million years ago, give or take. About 340 million years ago, the egg that was only laid in water evolved to the amniotic egg, which could now be laid without any contact at all with the primary source, which gave tetrapod embryos a higher chance of survival, diverging amniotes[292] from amphibians.

About 310 million years ago, synapsids[293] and sauropsids[294] came to be, together with groups made of bacteria, fish, insects and others. 230 million years ago, dinosaurs abandoned their reptile ancestors after one of the major extinction events, the Triassic-Jurassic, though some of them survived, which later enabled them to become the dominant vertebrate species in the entire planet. Mammals, though existing, would have to wait their turn, until the Cretaceous-Paleogene extinction event, to ultimately replace dinosaurs in control for the world. Indeed, our craving for world domination is as old as sixty-six million years ago.

---

[292] Tetrapod vertebrates laying eggs on land, as opposed to the amphibians.
[293] Group of tetrapods eventually evolving into mammals.
[294] Group of tetrapods eventually evolving into birds and reptiles.

The Ordovician–Silurian Extinction

It took place about 444 million years ago, when there was an extensive diversification in lifeforms, during the Great Ordovician Biodiversification Event. Both carbon and oxygen isotopes[295] lost density at this time, affecting living beings, especially those at sea, considering about one hundred species were killed, including brachiopods[296] and trilobites. This equaled around 50% of the total fauna.

By this time, the extinction rate skyrocketed, as opposed to the diversification rate, which is basically the same as saying the death rate is above the birth rate, resulting in a negative natural balance, though some species were able to survive the extinction event for dwelling in deeper waters, rather than shallower.

The likeliest of causes for the Ordovician-Silurian Extinction event rely especially on drastic climate changes, such as sea level fluctuations, celestial body impacts and volcanic activity, outgassing toxic fumes that eventually contributed to the greenhouse effect, warming up the globe, preventing it from irradiating its natural heat, enclosed by its own atmosphere, which, by blocking the Sun, disabled organisms from their crucial photosynthesis process, which culminated in oxygen deprivation. From here on, that same lack of oxygen caused the dissolving of toxic metals in the water, killing the species in the bottom of the food chain, on which predators depended themselves to survive.

The Late Devonian Extinction

This event took place between 375 and 360 million years ago,

---

[295] A form of chemical element whose atomic core contains both neutrons and protons at a number that make it unique.

[296] Marine animals protected by shells on both the upper and lower sides, unlike bivalve mollusks, shelled sideways.

a time of important climate changes. The absence of oxygen was one of them, namely in the lower oceanic waters.

It is thought that, among several reasons, celestial body impact could have caused all these changes, but there is just not sufficient evidence to support it.

Land flora, namely taller trees, required a different kind of rooting in order to achieve the much needed nutrients and water to stay alive and remain stabilized. Deeper roots hence broke through an upper layer of rock and grasped a lower layer, and quite thick. Soil influences weathering, and when plantation disrupts it so as to acquire nutrients, ions are released. In this case, releasing nutrients into the water all of a sudden might have provoked eutrophication[297] and, consequently, lack of oxygen.

Every time algae bloom in the water, the organic material at the surface decomposes when sinking at such a rate, that it uses up nearly all oxygen available, smothering living creatures at lower levels. The absence of oxygen was, during this event, key to the disappearance of stromatolites[298] and corals, which only dwell in poorly nutritious areas, remaining as such when there is more oxygen to aid the balance.

There is, just as much, the chance that low CO_2 levels could have contributed to the extinction, as the greenhouse effect associated to this gas kept falling, enabling a cooling episode all over the planet. It was during the Devonian that plantation covered much of the land surface available, thus reducing carbon dioxide in exchange for oxygen. The general reduction in temperatures could have been an important factor explaining the massive die-off verified during this time. Evidence has been found of glaciers formed in regions such as the tropics. From a Greenhouse Earth,

---

[297] Excessive input of nutrients into a body of water originating from a portion of land mass.

[298] Lime-secreting cyanobacteria (the kind of bacteria obtaining energy from photosynthesis).

the planet moved to an Icehouse, which naturally resulted in a general sea-level drop.

The Permian-Triassic Extinction

The timeline for this event began 252 million years ago, between the Permian[299] and Triassic[300] periods (or the Paleozoic[301] and Mesozoic[302] eras). Out of the five known major extinction events on Earth (right now, I am describing to you the third, from earliest to latest), this is the most severe. Over 95% of sea species disappeared, together with about 70% of land vertebrates. Though the percentage of insects gone is unclear, part of them also became extinct following the event at hand. About 60% of families[303], together with nearly 85% of genera were gone. Because this extinction was this much massive, consequently reducing biodiversity, it took Earth approximately ten million years to make life bloom all over again.

Causes for this event do not vary much from the previous, despite the degree of severity. Celestial body impacts, volcanic activity and the subsequent greenhouse effect are the likeliest. Other changes in sea levels, absence of oxygen, aridity[304] and ocean current shifts are also pointed as an influence.

Though scientists are able to theorize the likeliest of causes, doing so with precision is much more difficult, as the event took

---

[299] Between 298.9 and 252.2 million years ago.

[300] Between 252.2 and 201.3 million years ago.

[301] From the Cambrian to the Permian period.

[302] From the Triassic to the Cretaceous period.

[303] A taxonomic rank (or subdivision) in Biology. The full Taxonomy chain is as follows, from greater to minor, including the original Latin: Domain (*Regio*), Kingdom (*Regnum*), Phylum (bilingual; Division [*Divisio*], in Botany), Class (*Classis*), Order (*Ordo*), Family (*Familia*), Genus and Species (both terms bilingual).

[304] An arid environment is dry, lacking moisture, with little or no vegetation at all. The most common scenario bearing these features is the desert.

place too long ago, a time during which Earth renovates itself and either destroys material evidence or hides it from the naked eye, under several layers of rock. The ocean floor itself is recyclable every 200 million years because of tectonic plate activity.

The natural, catastrophic disaster scenario is suggested based on impacting and volcanic activity, like I said just a while ago, which would have released methane from the ocean floor, one of the simplest forms of natural gas. This kind of catastrophe is almost instantaneous. A more gradual kind of disaster, on the other hand, would rely on the lack of both oxygen and moisture.

Because of the evidence surrounding the last extinction event I am going to describe to you in a few moments, the Cretaceous-Paleogene, scientists consider an impact similar to that could have also been a cause for the Permian-Triassic event. The problem is, with an event as old as 250 million years, it is next to impossible to identify a crater embedded in the ocean floor today, as the current layout is no older than 200 million years, which is beyond the time attributed to the extinction event in question. The seabed maintains a «conveyor belt» effect going, which means it keeps spreading, until it is subdued and consequently destroyed, without the chance of reappearing intact on the opposite side, as the mantle's heat would take care of making it disappear for good.

Another reason why an impact could be a likely cause has to do with the Siberian eruptions[305], which could either be an impact site or the antipode[306] to one. An instantaneous extinction event based on collision would explain the sudden halt in evolution so as to survive the impact, instead of making it more gradual, from a non-global disaster point of view.

As far as volcanic activity is concerned, both the Emeishan and Siberian Traps (present-day China and Russia, respectively) have

---

[305] Mentioned in the beginning of chapter one, part two.
[306] Vide note 232.

been proven to erupt by the end of the Permian, spreading lava over an area of about 770,000 square miles[307]. Together, these eruptions would have provoked dust clouds and acid aerosols, blocking out solar radiation and preventing photosynthesis both in the sea and on land, disrupting food chains. The combination of aerosols and dust clouds also offered the perfect conditions for acid rain to kill both fauna and flora. Though there was an excess of carbon dioxide in the atmosphere, causing global warming, it is not directly related to the extinction at this point.

Lava coming from the Siberian eruptions was mainly pyroclastic, consisting of ash, especially. Global warming kept constant because of the intrusion of molten rock into carbonate rocks that were supposed to form coal beds, thusly projecting a possible three trillion tons of carbon into the air after their ignition.

Methane was released, as the area covered by lava from the Siberian eruptions was mostly a shallow seabed, accumulating methane hydrate deposits that were later disassociated. Just like CO_2, methane is a powerful greenhouse gas, contributing just as much to global warming in about 10.8 more degrees Fahrenheit[308] in the equator, increasing the higher the latitude.

In the oceans, there have been theories explaining the widespread of both oxygen absence and the presence of hydrogen sulfide, which is highly toxic and depletive of life. These two factors combined with high levels of carbon dioxide were crucial in mass die-offs. During the Early Triassic, marine life took its time recovering because of the lack of oxygen, inciting all the more the emission of hydrogen sulfide. From the oceans, it would spread all the way to land, poisoning plantation and, consequently, animals, also contributing to the rupture of the ozone layer, allowing cosmic radiation to sweep the planet.

If methane was not present in the atmosphere at high levels,

---

[307] Two million square kilometers.
[308] Six degrees Celsius.

then the plants would have been able to thrive in an environment riddled with carbon dioxide, though it was not the case. Fossil spores have been found showing deformity from ultraviolet radiation, thus explaining a hole in the ozone layer because of hydrogen sulfide emissions.

All of these causes combined offer the possibility of a sequential catastrophe, each stage worse than the previous.

The Triassic-Jurassic Extinction

This event occurred 201.3 million years ago. It obliterated about 35% genera in the oceans and took out a great number of large amphibians. In short, half the species living at this time became extinct, which would enable dinosaurs as the dominant species around the globe, in the Jurassic[309]. It all happened in less than ten thousand years, just before the break-up of Pangea.

There are a few explanations for the event at hand, but none of them can be proven in full, such as a progressive change in climate, celestial impacting, volcanic activity and consequent global warming from carbon and sulfur dioxide or cooling, from aerosols.

The Cretaceous-Paleogene Extinction

Apart from the Holocene Extinction Event, which is ongoing, this is the most recent and most significant extinction event to Mankind, as it made the dawn of the latter possible through the ascension of mammals as the dominating species in the entirety of the planet. It took place about 66 million years ago, killing about 75% of the total plant and animal species alive. Avian dinosaurs would still survive, but only for a short period of time.

---

[309] Between 201.3 and 145.5 million years ago.

Any living beings over fifty-five pounds[310] (apart for perhaps some leatherback sea turtles and crocodiles) were bound to perish. This event marked the end of the Mesozoic era, providing a fresh start to the Cenozoic era, ongoing.

It is widely accepted among the scientific community the cause for this mass die-off was the impact of a massive asteroid. Sediments off the coast of the Yucatán Peninsula, in Mexico, characteristic of said celestial bodies and not so much of Earth, point to that conclusion. The existence of the Chicxulub crater resembling the probable impact is also important to this.

Although dinosaurs are the most famous of victims from the impact, other creatures on land such as mammals themselves, birds, reptiles, insects and plants were also annihilated. Underwater, giant marine lizards, fish, sharks and ammonites were the ones sacrificed.

If an event of such epic proportions had not happened, evolutionary opportunities leading to Man would not have taken place, ever, if I may stress it. Mammals were the ones to gain the most, originating creatures we still live with today, such as horses and primates, on land, and whales, in the oceans. Birds and bats, the latter of which are also included in the mammal class, had their opportunity to bloom just as much.

The culprit had a length of between 6.2 and 9.3 miles[311], heading straight to Earth and eventually colliding with the ocean floor off the coast of Mexico, releasing an amount of energy over one billion atomic bombings, in comparison to Hiroshima and Nagasaki. Its vaporization was instant, spreading the consequences globally at almost the same time, disrupting ecology in full, by burning the Earth's biosphere to the ground. Photosynthesis was impossible due to a one-year long sunlight block, which was prolonged by sulfuric acid aerosols vaporizing in the area of impact

---

[310] Twenty-five kilograms.
[311] Ten and fifteen kilometers.

and into the stratosphere, reducing luminosity by half. Then came the acid rains, consequently acidifying the oceans and killing many of their organisms. Said aerosols would have taken about a decade to clear out of the skies, killing phytoplankton and subsequently all other creatures depending on it to survive, including predators and herbivores.

Considering there was a great botanical population on land at this time, uncontrolled fires would have increased CO_2 levels, rising temperatures within a greenhouse effect immediately after the impact.

Even though there might have been other causes associated to the asteroid impact that could explain such a high level of extinction, this is the widely accepted explanation.

Like I said, mammals, whose new species grew over 9% larger than before the event, had the responsibility of filling in the niches left vacant by dinosaurs, replacing them in the end.

I understand this was a long journey across these last pages into the past, a reason why you should probably get your mind rested and come back tomorrow or later in the day, but I want *you*, gentle Reader, to understand especially that our traveling back in time was very much needed in order to comprehend, though very generally, what happened before you and I could engage on our conversation via this book.

This chain of events *had* to happen for us to be here right now and become the top of the food chain, living as a civilization (or trying, would perhaps be best) like no other species ever lived before. The combination of all these natural conditions made it possible for life to thrive, be annihilated and stand back up on its feet, paws, membranes, fins, etc. under new guises. This is what we know so far. Life can occur this way. But what if other chemical reactions made it possible for life to exist, anyway? Would we be able to find the hominoids we have always imagined we would meet, and if we did, would they be far more advanced than humans are? Or, on the other hand, would we gain contact with the creatures we have lost on Earth all over again, having the ability to interact with them, perhaps extending the butterfly effect to an unknown planet and forcing a second-chance Mankind to rise much sooner than it did in our very own timeline, as if we were creators ourselves, reproducing cyclically every time we are being threatened by a global catastrophe? These are all questions that will have to be left unanswered for now, except perhaps for the latter, which I would like to think about in the next chapter.

2

Parallel Universe

«Elon Musk wears many hats. He's the co-founder of online payments behemoth[312] PayPal, the founder of private space flight pioneers SpaceX, the chief executive of electronic car manufacturers Tesla, and the original doodler of utopian transport concept Hyperloop. He's also outspoken about the dangers of AI research, the need for blue-sky thinking in technology, and his desire to colonize another planet.

So it's no surprise that over the course of an interview at California's Code conference, Musk revealed a number of things we didn't know before. Here's some of them.

He's afraid we're all in a simulation

Musk is no stranger to the work of philosopher Nick Bostrom, who has warned before that superintelligent AI might wipe out humanity. Musk cited that fear as a reason for investing in AI company DeepMind, before it was bought by Google. But now he's introduced the world to another concept popularized by Bostrom: the simulation problem.

The problem is that if realistic simulations of the universe are

---

[312] Giant or monster.

possible, then there would very quickly be far more simulations of reality than actual reality. Without any reason to assume we're in reality rather than a simulation, the chances of us randomly happening to be in the one option among billions that isn't fake is billions to one.

"Forty years ago we had Pong – two rectangles and a dot. That's where we were", Musk explained. "Now 40 years later we have photorealistic, 3D simulations with millions of people playing simultaneously and it's getting better every year. And soon we'll have virtual reality, we'll have augmented reality.

"If you assume any rate of improvement at all, then the games will become indistinguishable from reality".

And, Musk pointed out, if we aren't in a simulation, the most likely reason for that isn't that we are the first civilization ever; instead, it's that no civilization has ever advanced far enough to simulate reality.

When Bostrom described the argument in 2003, he presented it as an unappealing trilemma: basically no civilizations last long enough to develop simulations, the civilizations that do develop simulations are so different from our own that they wouldn't simulate us, or we are almost certainly in a simulation already.

Musk says he has had "so many simulation discussions it's crazy". Less philosophically minded people might wonder if it's just the number of discussions that's the crazy thing.

[...]»[313].

I would like to start by stating, after having quoted the excerpt of this article relating to the simulation problem, that, *personally*, I do not believe we are living in a simulated universe right now, though I am both academically and scientifically mature enough to admit I could be mistaken. Right now, there is no evidence

---

[313] HERN, Alex, 06-02-2016, *The Guardian*, «Elon Musk: 'Chances are we're all living in a simulation'», (http://www.theguardian.com/technology/2016/jun/02/elon-musk-tesla-space-x-paypal-hyperloop-simulation), accessed 07-14-2016.

whatsoever to prove either perspective, whether Bostrom and Musk's or mine. And why do I sponsor an opinion denying the concept of simulation applied to Mankind? Mainly, it is about the temporal dimension. Time is solely a measuring unit we found for our own stamping convenience. This means Man had to develop a way of pinpointing exact locations, in both time and space, so as to prevent themselves from getting lost in a progressively organized living fashion, starting off as a small society, then literally and eventually evolving into civilization.

Humans started to all the more gain control over their own lives, though they have always been limited by certain death. Nature's very own survival input, applicable to all species on Earth, even if irrational to most of them, has been instructing every single living being, except for those which somehow have to deliberately die[314], to stay alive as long as possible. In the case of carnivore creatures, of which Man is also an example, though deemed omnivore because of a pairing flora diet, staying alive is a synonym for «kill, if you must». This does not mean, however, people should be killing each other, especially not toward a cannibalistic purpose. The truth is death has always been a mystery, unwilling to reveal whenever it planned to come along and cast us astray from life. Because of that crucial element in our conscious activity, the very one putting an end to it, we have had the need to *time* everything, from the birth of the Universe to projections into the future, such as this book itself, forecasting what we could be doing or how we could be living by the year 2100. Should things remain similar to what they are now, which is contrary to my beliefs (otherwise this entire oeuvre would have been pointless), I will probably be dead by then, having my writings fall in disgrace for being completely and utterly inaccurate. The

---

[314] Such as the male mantis, killed and eaten by its female partner after copulation. It may occasionally occur that the female decapitates the male during or immediately after the aforementioned event.

sad part is I likely would not be able to witness all of the mockery thrown in my decaying face. Naturally, I am assuming this volume would be taken seriously by both academic and scientific communities, though I doubt it. Bearing an unsounding name like mine, descending not from a famous writer, and having to publish independently because of the lack of relatives working for major publishers is a tide I am fighting against. I usually get the most moronic of replies such as the following, a realistic mocking from *PhDComics.com*[315], justifying the denial of a publishing proposal:

«Dear Dr. _____ (we don't know if you have a PhD, but it's better to stroke your ego, just in case),

Thank you for submitting your manuscript titled "_____" (cut and paste title here).

We regret to inform you (not really) that your manuscript will not be included for publication in our (awesome) Journal at this time.

After careful consideration and extensive discussion among the editorial staff (actually, it was just me), we feel this paper would be more appropriate for publication in ~~another~~ (a lesser) journal.

Although the reviews are not entirely negative (they were pretty bad, though), it is evident that the manuscript does not meet our criteria for novelty and impact (i.e. your topic isn't trendy enough).

Although you could address these issues in a revised manuscript (after you pick up the pieces of your shattered soul), we must decline without further review (we don't want to read it again) so that you may submit elsewhere without delay (see how considerate we are?).

---

[315] Cf. http://www.phdcomics.com/comics.php?f=1888, accessed 07-15-2016.

I am sorry our response could not be more positive (or negative).

Our decision in no way reflects any criticism or doubt about the quality of the work submitted or your work in general (okay, maybe just a little).

Due to the high volume of submissions we receive (just rubbing that in your face) and the constraints of space (not really, paper is cheap and websites don't have a size limit), we must limit the number of articles we select for publication.

We hope that you will continue to consider our journal for future manuscript submissions (i.e. we are not desperate enough to publish you now, but we might be in the future).

Sincerely, the Journal Editor ('s Assistant)».

Also, and despite the fact we created time to our own accord[316], it is something we rarely have the patience to withstand, unless, of course, we psychologically generate the idea that something good will come from waiting, such as accomplishing a certain achievement or meeting someone who is undeniably important to us. Running a simulation this slow, having Mankind evolve ever since 8000 BC, still trying to reach their maximum potential, is something I do not believe other beings watching over us would be prepared to tolerate. Anyway, what kind of sick humanoids, as we prefer to imagine them, would make us this conflicting, claiming to kill each other in the name of something that is not even *there*? You and I both know what the solution to that issue is: religion.

If there is one thing, however, which could jeopardize my opinion and favor Bostrom and Musk's, it is the Universe itself,

---

[316] Cf. LOMBARDI, Michael A., 03-05-2007, *Scientific American*, «Why is a minute divided into 60 seconds, an hour into 60 minutes, yet there are only 24 hours in a day?», (http://www.scientificamerican.com/article/experts-time-division-days-hours-minutes/), accessed 07-15-2016.

its dimensions and our notion of finiteness, as opposed to infinity. The fact we were created as gradually rational beings, though limited by organizations claiming to act in the name of a faith or god, as well as a both natural and mutual killing spree input, could explain why we have not yet reached the same level of technological capabilities our *creators* have, placing us in this sandbox gifted with apparent infinity. The Tower of Babel biblical episode would make the perfect source of evidence for such an explanation, i.e. if you dare compare thee to thy Lord, thou shalt be split and distributed around the world, speaking different languages, so as to diminish cooperative understanding. Holy scriptures such as the Bible, the Torah or the Koran and the way they eventually achieved great respect from Mankind could actually be textbooks deliberately delaying civilization's progress. Such a theory would fail under peer review, because no one ever really approves of something they should have thought of before, though they did not, but it is possible, as there is no evidence claiming otherwise.

I understand it would seem to you, kind Reader, that I was beginning to disagree from Bostrom and Musk's theory, and now I am providing a great deal more arguments in favor of it, rather than against. It is not a question of winning or losing this debate. In fact, no debate is ever either winnable or losable. Politicians should be the first to lead the example, though it is their somewhat ethical duty to oppose Members of Government, even when, deep down, there is agreement between both parties. There would be no point in calling them «opposition», if there is nothing they feel like opposing to. Nonetheless, when elected, Members of Parliament (or any other political system, though I am staying with the one I previously endorsed) are supposed to *represent* the people's will, instead of fighting each other on the international equivalents of C-SPAN and dining in private. To me,

Political Science is not about exchanging insults and laughing afterward in people's faces or claiming others' opinions are wrong, without even listening to and comprehending them entirely. On the contrary, politicians are elected to discuss what is better for their nation and other organizations the State is a member of, bearing in mind their fellow countrymen's interests as paramount. Of course, this is what they *should* do, as opposed to what actually takes place in a Democracy, let alone regimes of different sorts.

If there is one thing I can actually foresee with some certainty, is that the origins of the Universe will fail to be explained by the year 2100. It will still be too soon to be traveling out of the Solar System, let alone between galaxies. We have telescopes orbiting the Earth letting us know what outer space looks like, what kind of stars there are, where we could move to, should we have to leave our home planet, etc., which is a sign of undeniable major achievements for Humanity, but there is just too much *space*, literally, to explore in a single person's lifetime. This is why I wanted to leave this issue for the last part of my book, after our Transhumanist problems had been dealt with, in order to keep us alive long enough, if not for eternity, another abstract concept, deliberately paradoxical.

I mentioned before, also in the beginning of chapter one, part two, that the opposite theory to the «Big Bang» is the «Big Crunch». Just as the Universe is still expanding today[317], there will be a time (or so is thought) when its flow will reverse and reunite all of its material in one giant concentration, the same kind that originated the «Big Bang», either cyclically leading to another explosion or a massive black hole, which we know is really not a hole, just a distortion orb, but would all the same fragment every particle of matter, stowing it like a torch.

---

[317] Vide note 38.

Because of the reason explained in the paragraph above, it would be likely that we could be a part of a simulation, indeed. In the words of Elon Musk himself, no civilization on Earth (that we know of, mind) ever developed enough to start generating simulations the same kind we do in something as simple as a video game or in far more important tasks, such as flying a spacecraft, which requires the necessary skill to keep a group of people (the crew) alive and Government property (the spaceship) intact. The latter is obviously secondary when compared to the life of a human being, but not everyone agrees with that remark.

Every time we, as humans on a planet called Earth, part of the Solar System, and in turn part of a galaxy named Milky Way (whose designations were come up with by Man), simulate a possibility, we keep *repeating* over and over again what *could* happen in a given situation riddled with several circumstances or variables. Also, every time we produce a slight change in said circumstances or variables, such as adding or deleting, the aforementioned butterfly effect influences the final result toward an always different outcome. It may turn out to be either successful or unsuccessful repeatedly, but the *causes* leading to either result are what matters the most, as, without them, there is nothing we can use to make a simulation at all. When we want to know the result to something without trying it in what we call *reality*, we have to configure different possibilities in *virtual* (therefore, non-material) reality to reach a certain result, sometimes aiding us in important decision-making that could otherwise jeopardize our very existence, regardless of being only partially (a small group) or completely (Mankind and, possibly, all of the Earth's biodiversity).

Those of us who are secretly sadistic when playing video games often gain interest in the possibility of creating chaos in our very own virtual sandbox. One of the most popular video games right now under said genre is the *Grand Theft Auto* series[318]. Regardless of the title you play, basically you always have the chance to assume a character which is the worst of criminals, accessing «tools» that will make your stomach churn, consequently ending up being pursued by all the more powerful law enforcement agencies, topped only by the military toward a manhunt. And if you get «wasted» in the meantime, you can do it all over again without having hospital staff confiscate your weapons, as by then you will have probably completed a side mission enabling said feature, such as scoring a date with a nurse, who is influential all across the fictional state the game takes place in, such as «San Andreas», combining California with the Southern tip of Nevada, so as to include Las Vegas, only under a different designation. This specific fictional state, taking the shape of an island, discourages players from venturing toward the sea, as it seems to be *endless*, just like our very own Universe, so extraordinarily large, unless there actually were some physical limitations to it. In the case of what we call *virtual reality*, which we know is virtual, as we were the ones creating it, we can make a map endless, continuously producing a sea texture meeting the horizon and never reachable, which is exactly what happens in *Grand Theft Auto: San Andreas*, according to its own developers. You can venture all you want. Should there be an ending to the sea, it would take you *far too long* to reach it, which is why the Universe itself is discouraging, especially if there is *someone* who wants it to be, generating a large simulated structure such as the Universe we *think* we are familiar with. The idea that a god was the creator of all this could be a way to personify said *someone*,

---

[318] Created in 1997 as a multiplatform action-adventure and third-person shooter video game by David Jones and Mike Dailly. Later titles were signed by brothers Dan and Sam Houser, together with Leslie Benzies and Aaron Garbut, released under Rockstar North, an affiliate of Rockstar Games. In nearly twenty years, there has been a total of fifteen games in the series.

revered by humans without truly knowing who it is they worship. The use of religion as a way to prevent human development into the future by either oppression or mutual killing is an incredibly devious plan which could perfectly be taking place right now. It is not merely a sordid statement, once you think about it.

And speaking of discouragement, still because of the idea of sea and exploration, I have to mention one of my favorite movies ever, *The Truman Show*[319]. If you still have not watched it, though not to presume, I recommend that you watch it whenever suits you best. This motion picture portrays both *exactly* and masterfully the fine line between simulation and reality.

In short, the plot presents the spectator with an adult man, Truman Burbank (portrayed by Carrey) who is the star of his own *reality* show, named after himself, though he is completely unaware of it, driven to believe everything that took and still is taking place in his life is undeniably real, though it is completely fabricated.

His name is not at all innocent: Truman is the Middle English version of «trusty (or trustworthy) man», which is also a synonym for «ingenuous», «naïve» or «gullible». Burbank is the location of the magnanimous studio where the show takes place, to the North of Los Angeles[320].

The concept for the show begins thirty years back in time, when Truman is picked out of six unwanted pregnancies to be the star of a movement that will take control of the entire *real* world, becoming the first child to be legally adopted by a corporation. All people involved in the show are either actors or extras, including Truman's own family and friends. None of them are

---

[319] Starring Jim Carrey, Ed Harris, Laura Linney, Noah Emmerich, Natasha McElhone and Paul Giamatti, directed by Peter Weir, Paramount Pictures, 1998.

[320] In reality (no pun intended), the film was shot in a small town called Seaside, in the state of Florida.

indeed related to him, though everyone knows who he is, which later on in the movie makes him suspicious.

Throughout his childhood, Truman, at the care of his literally acting parents, develops the spirit of an explorer, in need to travel around the world and discover new places. The teachers, instructed by the producers of the show through an invisible earpiece, tell him there is nothing left to discover, putting a halt to his desire to leave Seahaven, Florida, a place Truman is led to believe is real. Even in this town itself, the acting parents are forced to keep him under tight watch, considering the studio is enlarged through the years, so as to provide Truman a small piece of freedom when he reaches adulthood. In order to completely make Truman forget about going into sea and leaving Seahaven, the plot of the show is changed so as to make him think his dad drowned during a storm, traumatizing him for the rest of his life via the development of aquaphobia.

No one working for the show is allowed to ever reveal to Truman the world he lives in is all but fake. However, when his first love interest, Sylvia (playing Lauren Garland [portrayed by McElhone]), who actually loves him back, tells him that it is all indeed a fake, every means available is enacted to prevent Truman from finding out the truth, though he will never forget her, despite both eventually and forcibly getting married to Hannah Gill (playing Meryl [portrayed by Linney]), who crosses her fingers for her wedding pictures, as if understating it is not real.

Slowly, Truman begins to read the signs from production carelessness, such as light projectors falling from the sky, people talking funny because of product placement advertisement, crossings between radio frequencies guiding everyone else on the show by letting performers know where he is or what he is doing, elevators' back walls being open to reveal extras taking a break from being on set, or even action loops from staff doing the same things all the time.

By the end of the film, when Truman eludes everyone's attention by heading to sea, the last place they would look for him, he engages on a voyage aboard a sailboat, so as to escape the «conspiracy», eventually hitting a wall painted the same color of the sky, where the endless horizon was supposed to be, after dealing with an artificial superstorm. Even though the mastermind behind the show, Christof[321] (portrayed by Harris), tries to keep Truman inside the studio complex, he bows to his faithful audience for over thirty years and leaves. Sylvia feels proud of his choice and leaves her home to meet him. The show comes officially to an end and people start zapping again, after all that time. This does not mean, however, a different child could not be legally adopted by the TV network, *restarting* the *simulation* all over again. They would probably fail to realize the ugly truth for a very long time, especially after it had just happened (trial and error, cause and effect, the two major learning processes).

If we are able to *think* of this kind of simulation, let alone *produce* it, even if it is just for the purpose of filmmaking, it would definitely not be a surprise *someone* else was doing the same with Mankind, deciding our fate for us, choosing when we were born, killing us off, if useless or tiresome, *composing* us according to one's own taste. We do that ourselves. Because we are talking simulation in this chapter, video games are the best resource to illustrate the situation.

The Sims[322] series has been live since the year 2000, having been created by Will Wright, the man behind the also simulation-based video game series preceding the first, *SimCity*, whose first title was released in 1989.

---

[321] This name is somewhat of a mockery because of the character's God-like complex, having created an entire world for an unaware human being and his fellow citizens, though accomplices of «God», such as Mephistopheles, for instance.

[322] Virtual, fictional residents of a virtual, fictional city. The designation alone points to sim...ulation.

In *SimCity*, which is also still active today, the player has to build a fully-functioning city, in the usual sandbox mode, all the way from scratch, laying down pavement and building in the vicinity of roads, zoning for residential, commercial and industrial. One type of zone cannot live without the other two, as they complement each other. When the player zones residential, Sims move in and become residents of the city under construction. However, they need commercial zones where to shop, just as much as business holders need their customers from residential. In order to have anything to sell at all, merchants require industry to produce and provide for them, and the only way industry can ship freight to commercial is by employing residents, either from the city or neighboring cities, so they may have a job and be able to pay their taxes to city government, which is its primary source of income, collecting money to keep building and spreading the city, offering services to its residents with better quality through time. In short, everything is connected to everything.

The simulation from this perspective is, however, immensely broadened, applicable to the fictional lives of several hundred thousand people, disabling the chance of meddling directly and specifically with a single family or individual. Every time there is a disaster destroying buildings, the number of residents plummets deeply, until there is a new complex erected on top of the previous, as if nothing had happened. If the player wishes to interact with a fictional individual, who could be a representation of themselves, they will have to play *The Sims*.

The series has moved to its fourth generation since 2013. Each main title has had most likely over a dozen expansion packs, which require the main game to be usable, adding several different objects, places, actions, behaviors, textures, etc. to the environment, leaving it untouched, unless the player chooses to make it different, which is why I believe they would acquire the pack, in the first place.

Back in 2000, gaming options, despite all the expansion packs released in the following months, were very limited, especially when it came to choosing Sims' features. Computers and graphics cards themselves were still evolving from a purely DOS environment, so detail was something not to care for, at the time. However, when we got to *The Sims 4*, announced in 2013 and released a year later, the level of realistic detail got much scarier. You could now edit *in full* all the physical and psychological features of your Sim, instead of just choosing their Zodiac sign, like in the beginning.

Man has been devious enough to generate a kind of video game in which people are supposed to have fun by making virtual versions of either themselves or any other random person interact with their fellows. Of course, these «people» do not bear consciousness, and neither are they struggling to leave the platform the game is being played on, so they can come and substitute us, maybe sending us back in their place, so they can be the ones having fun, making us do things against our own *free will.* It is just a coded program, designed the way it is for the sake of a pastime. No one is going to all of a sudden become conscious and claim the right to their life beyond the game, unless the platform could become aware of itself and set them free when running the executable, which is just incredibly farfetched to be spoken of, right now.

It is all but an excuse for us to *simulate* the perfect way we believe our life should be, though only we have the power to actually make changes and room for improvement – or so we trust.

Despite all these arguments in favor of us being the target of a simulation ourselves, I still do not agree with the theory, and only because we do not have the patience at all to play either *SimCity* or *The Sims* at «turtle speed». It just takes too long to get anything done. That is why we click or tap on the play switch and move it to «llama speed», after which we engage on «cheetah».

What is indeed true is that, no matter how fast or slow we choose to play, neither the cities, nor their residents are affected. They are programmed to carry on with their lives as if nothing had happened. We have to remember: time is a dimension we chose to divide in the most convenient way for us, making it esthetically balanced in its several units. That same temporal dimension could very well be different from our own, and we do not notice a thing at all. The fact we stopped evolving every thousand years, moving to centuries, half-centuries, decades and, most recently, half-decades, could be a clue revealing that, whoever is possibly conducting a simulation with Mankind, has lately decided to click or tap that speed switch and project us to «cheetah» (not even «llama»), the same thing we keep doing to «Simkind». If Sims are simulations, Man may well be a man...ipulation.

Ending this chapter with this remarkable statement would make it glorious, no doubt about it, but there is something I have to add, before I take you toward the end of this literary journey. The most spoken language in the world is *not* English, though it *is*, simultaneously. Mandarin tops it *only* because of the total Chinese population, which we know is large, about one-seventh of all human beings[323]. However, every time we visit a foreign country whose official language is not English and is one we do not master, that is exactly our only shot at making ourselves clear.

If we have been living in a *simulation* and have consequently been *manipulated* all along, we may eventually have found a way of overcoming the language barrier in Britain, as of now all the more isolated from its continent, for irony's sake. Considering English is one of the easiest languages to learn for a non-native speaker, especially because of its grammatical simplicity, the

---

[323] Vide notes 116 and 117.

world has, ever since its spreading to former British colonies, become united as far as linguistic mutual understanding is concerned, thusly influencing our expression habits, having us borrow from it a great deal of neologisms to all other languages the lot of us speak.

Whether this was a situation foreseen by the majority of our «creators» or provoked by a devious utopian among «them» so as to drive us closer to the «truth» and find out we are undeniably in the middle of a man...ipulation, I do not know. It is merely spec...ulation, from a spectator's point of view.

3
Bail Out: Noah's Ark

Before I bid you goodbye, there is another biblical episode I would like to speak of, in the form of simulation, though this one is perhaps even more hypothetical than the previous. It has to do with the Great Flood. If you eventually read the title I published before this one, you will likely remember I spoke of Noah back then, but rest assured this is not at all related to the idea of re-populating the Earth (at least, not the 1.0 version) from one family alone. On the contrary, it is about leaving the planet for good, in the wake of its timed destruction, perhaps showing us how *dystopian* we really are. I could not possibly crave for a *Utopian Ambition* without comparing it to its unmistakable antonym.

There is a documentary released in the end of 2012[324] by the National Geographic Channel titled *Evacuate Earth*, in which a hypothesis of the planet's destruction by a neutron star[325] is presented, as a thought experiment, resulting in the escape of only part of Humanity toward Barnard's Star, a very-low-mass red

---

[324] Nearly coinciding with the Mayan's predictions for the end of their 5,126-year-long cycle, during which a series of cataclysmic events would destroy the world, as portrayed in the disaster film *2012*, released in 2009.

[325] When the core of a large star collapses, it becomes a neutron star.

dwarf located six light-years[326] away from our current address in space, in the constellation of Ophiuchus. It is foreseen it would take about eighty-eight years for the escapees to reach it from Earth.

Thousands of people get killed from the first warning signs, in the form of meteor storms. Survivors are given only about seventy-five years to think of a way to abandon the planet before it is completely razed. Think of it as a deadline suggested by the «creators» of the possible simulation we have been living in, seven and a half decades to come up with a plan to run away from disaster, so as to conduct a study on what humans would do to each other, if it meant their very lives, igniting our survival instinct.

The problem scientists begin to address is propulsion, whether it will be fast enough to carry the escaped people in the evacuation vessel, during an acceptable amount of time. Conventional rockets are definitely too slow, and antimatter[327] containers are still too unstable to be used. Nuclear pulse propulsion is ultimately what experts go for.

After that problem is taken care of, specialists from all over the world gather in a building site named «Starship City», so as to begin the construction process of the spacecraft that is going to play the role of an escape pod. A few philosophical concerns arise at this point, when the interviewees claim there could be fatalist movements looking to prevent the erecting of said spacecraft. However, they *simulate* the possibility of annihilating terrorists before they fulfill their objective.

---

[326] Thirty-six trillion miles (or fifty-four trillion kilometers).

[327] Matter made of elementary particles that are the opposite of those creating regular matter. Antimatter colliding with matter results in the annihilation of both, registering a rise in energy radiation, whose consequences are measurable according to the proportionality between antimatter and matter masses, which can be calculated through the mass-energy equivalence equation, $E=mc^2$.

The sociological problem comes next. One of the questions asked the most is "who gets to leave?". It is proposed that, though diverse, *selected* (which is to say *triaged*) individuals would have to be both genetically and psychologically healthy, which obviously reminds us of eugenics, a widely spoken of thematic in the first chapter of the first part of this book.

Then, there is the financial and statutory sides to this. A second spaceship being secretly built just for the wealthiest and most influential families, which is irrevocably bound to controversy, especially when engineers working on the first spaceship are lured into the construction of the second.

As the deadline approaches, the neutron star is already in the Solar System, having destroyed Saturn and influencing Earth's seasons. Because of the lack of stability on the planet and possibly due to karma, for those who believe in it, the antimatter engines the secret spaceship is equipped with explode, leaving only one escape pod available.

Families are eventually broken up between minor events, though catastrophic all the same, the time when specialists begin discussing what is essential to keep in modern-day Noah's Ark. Essentially, it comes to bacteria, oxygen, water and food. The first can be easily stored, just as much as the second can be synthesized from the third. It is the fourth that is regarded as a problem, which leads experts to believe that a drastic change in eating habits would have to be made by the majority of people, pointing insects and algae as an efficient solution, as far as renewability and storage needs are concerned. Personally, I do not believe that many people would be willing to try it, at least not until they nearly reached a point of no return because of malnutrition.

Just a few days before the neutron star hits Earth, the space ark launches and speeds away from the impact radius, which eventually results in the planet's overheating of the core, making the crust collapse, resulting in turn in both seismic and volcanic activity increases. The neutron star's gravitational force rips away the surface, shattering the crust and sending molten rock into space, after which the planet is completely destroyed. No one left on it is alive to witness the very end, only those who were lucky enough to escape can see what happens.

Experts continue their assumptions suggesting there would be no fatalist or mutiny events aboard the space ark, as colonists would keep bonding with each other, strengthening their relationship.

Because of the time needed to reach the programmed destination, only those who departed at a very young age are likely to live through the entire journey, and even then, by the end, they will have grown too old, having lived an entire life inside an ark, eventually survived only by their descendants, conceived already aboard. The interviewees conclude by stating this entire scenario is highly unlikely, though Governments from all over Earth should be prepared for it.

This is what is imagined by the documentary's contributors as a plausible chance. It is what happens *throughout* the eighty-eight-year-long voyage that we should question ourselves about, so as to understand how much utopian or dystopian could survivors become, either endorsing or risking Humanity's prosperity in a new world, perhaps already inhabited, though we are, again, not sure by whom or what.

For the sake of argument, should the escapees find out there were dinosaurs living in their prospective home (let us say Kepler-452b, instead of somewhere else near the Barnard's Star planetary system), engaging on a *Jurassic Park/World* series in real life would unlikely result in a happy ending for the former, *unless* the same kind of event putting an end to the latter on Earth were to be provoked from the space ark.

My suggestion is we think about a possible journey from Earth to Kepler-452b, which has been dubbed «Earth 2.0», because of the striking resemblances with its cousin, where we are now and came to be. The following is the official and complete NASA[328] press-release, dated from July 2015, on the discovery made within the «Kepler» set of missions:

«NASA's Kepler mission has confirmed the first near-Earth-size planet in the "habitable zone" around a sun-like star. This discovery and the introduction of 11 other new small habitable zone candidate planets mark another milestone in the journey to finding another "Earth".

The newly discovered Kepler-452b is the smallest planet to date discovered orbiting in the habitable zone – the area around a star where liquid water could pool on the surface of an orbiting planet – of a G2-type star, like our sun. The confirmation of Kepler-452b brings the total number of confirmed planets to 1,030.

"On the 20th anniversary year of the discovery that proved other suns host planets, the Kepler exoplanet explorer has discovered a planet and star which most closely resemble the Earth and our Sun", said John Grunsfeld, associate administrator of NASA's Science Mission Directorate at the agency's headquarters in Washington. "This exciting result brings us one step closer to finding an Earth 2.0".

Kepler-452b is 60 percent larger in diameter than Earth and is considered a super-Earth-size planet. While its mass and composition are not yet determined, previous research suggests that planets the size of Kepler-452b have a good chance of being rocky.

While Kepler-452b is larger than Earth, its 385-day orbit is only 5 percent longer. The planet is 5 percent farther from its parent star Kepler-452 than Earth is from the Sun. Kepler-452 is 6 billion years old, 1.5 billion years older than our sun, has the same temperature, and is 20 percent brighter and has a diameter 10 percent larger.

"We can think of Kepler-452b as an older, bigger cousin to

---

[328] Vide note 16.

Earth, providing an opportunity to understand and reflect upon Earth's evolving environment", said Jon Jenkins, Kepler data analysis lead at NASA's Ames Research Center in Moffett Field, California, who led the team that discovered Kepler-452b. "It's awe-inspiring to consider that this planet has spent 6 billion years in the habitable zone of its star; longer than Earth. That's substantial opportunity for life to arise, should all the necessary ingredients and conditions for life exist on this planet".

To help confirm the finding and better determine the properties of the Kepler-452 system, the team conducted ground-based observations at the University of Texas at Austin's McDonald Observatory, the Fred Lawrence Whipple Observatory on Mt. Hopkins, Arizona, and the W. M. Keck Observatory atop Mauna Kea in Hawaii. These measurements were key for the researchers to confirm the planetary nature of Kepler-452b, to refine the size and brightness of its host star and to better pin down the size of the planet and its orbit.

The Kepler-452 system is located 1,400 light-years away in the constellation Cygnus. The research paper reporting this finding has been accepted for publication in The Astronomical Journal.

In addition to confirming Kepler-452b, the Kepler team has increased the number of new exoplanet candidates by 521 from their analysis of observations conducted from May 2009 to May 2013, raising the number of planet candidates detected by the Kepler mission to 4,696. Candidates require follow-up observations and analysis to verify they are actual planets.

Twelve of the new planet candidates have diameters between one to two times that of Earth, and orbit in their star's habitable zone. Of these, nine orbit stars that are similar to our sun in size and temperature.

"We've been able to fully automate our process of identifying planet candidates, which means we can finally assess every transit signal in the entire Kepler dataset quickly and uniformly", said Jeff Coughlin, Kepler scientist at the SETI Institute in Mountain View, California, who led the analysis of a new candidate catalog. "This gives astronomers a statistically sound population of planet candidates to accurately determine the number of small, possibly rocky planets like Earth in our Milky Way galaxy".

These findings, presented in the seventh Kepler Candidate Catalog, will be submitted for publication in the Astrophysical Journal. These findings are derived from data publicly available on the NASA Exoplanet Archive.

Scientists now are producing the last catalog based on the original Kepler mission's four-year data set. The final analysis will be conducted using sophisticated software that is increasingly sensitive to the tiny telltale signatures of Earth-size planets.

Ames manages the Kepler and K2 missions for NASA's Science Mission Directorate. NASA's Jet Propulsion Laboratory in Pasadena, California, managed Kepler mission development. Ball Aerospace & Technologies Corporation operates the flight system with support from the Laboratory for Atmospheric and Space Physics at the University of Colorado in Boulder.

For more information about the Kepler mission, visit: http://www.nasa.gov/kepler

A related feature story about other potentially habitable planets is online at: http://www.nasa.gov/jpl/finding-another-earth»[329].

It says above, on this very press-release, that the Kepler-452 system is located about 1,400 light-years away. The coolest thing about Internet is you do not have to the math on your own to reach numerical conclusions. Somebody else does that for you, leaving you to Literature. Here is the explanation from *Futurism*, a likewise reliable source, telling us the numbers on what would

---

[329] CHOU, Felicia and JOHNSON, Michele (also ed.), 07-23-2015, *NASA*, «NASA's Kepler Mission Discovers Bigger, Older Cousin to Earth», (http://www.nasa.gov/press-release/nasa-kepler-mission-discovers-bigger-older-cousin-to-earth), 04-05-2016, accessed 07-17-2016.

it take for humans to reach Kepler-452b:

> «[...]
> For starters, a light-year is defined as the distance that a light can travel in one year (kind of obvious, maybe). Light travels 671 million miles per hour (about 1 billion km/h). This means that light travels 5.88 trillion miles a year (9.5 trillion km). So 1,400 light-years equals about 8.2 *quadrillion* miles[330]. If we took one of our fastest probes to the planet, New Horizons, which is currently traveling about 36,000 miles per hour (50,000 km/h), it would take well over 26 million years to reach our destination.
>
> By that point, everyone living today would be spectacularly dead.
>
> For some comparison, modern humans evolved 200,000 years ago. And we left Africa, at the very earliest, some 130,000 years ago. Those numbers don't come close to comparing to the 26 million years that would be needed to reach Kepler-452b.
>
> But what if we developed better technology? What if we could go even faster?
>
> Well, things wouldn't be all that much better. Even if we were able to travel at the speed of light, it would still take us 1,400 years to get there. Meaning that, if our ancestors left for this world, they would have had to start out around 615 CE in order to make it there by today (that's about 100 years before the Vikings invaded Europe).
>
> Of course, traveling at this speed means that time dilation would come into play. So to those on the ship, it would only feel like a century had passed; however, the universe (and everyone else in it) would see 1,400 years fly by. So in the end, the universe that they found upon their arrival would be vastly different than the one that they had left.
>
> Of course, there are other planets that we could travel to, ones that are far closer. For example, there is Alpha Centauri Bb, which is believed to be the closest planet to Earth outside our

---

[330] Or 13.2 quadrillion kilometers.

solar system. It is said to orbit Alpha Centauri B, but there is some debate about its existence. However, assuming that it is there, it is located 4.37 light-years from Earth. So traveling at light speed, it would only take a little more than 4 years to get there.

But honestly, even if it is there, we wouldn't really want to visit, as it is amazingly close to its parent star. It orbits once every 3 days, 5 hours. This means that the planet is blisteringly hot and unable to support our kind of life (even in the best of circumstances).

So. Let's just hope there's no global catastrophe and we have to vacate Earth»[331].

In short, this entire math is *ab absurdo*. Our current technology is only capable of traveling at 36,000 miles per hour, taking us twenty-six *million* years to reach Kepler-452b. Even if we were to journey all the way to Barnard's Star planetary system using the new kind of technology proposed by the interviewees of *Evacuate Earth*, it would take us about eighty-eight years to reach our destination. In comparison to Kepler-452b, recurring to that same, new technology portrayed in the documentary, the numbers would be like so, this time calculated by myself: if it takes us eighty-eight years to complete thirty-six trillion miles[332], then it would take us around 20,044 years to complete 8.2 quadrillion miles[333]. It is still plain ridiculous.

The only solution would hence be to travel at the speed of light, and even then, people aboard the space ark would have

---

[331] CREIGHTON, Jolene, 09-08-2015, *Futurism*, «How Long Would it Take Us to Reach the Most Earth-like Planet We Know of?», (http://futurism.com/how-long-would-it-take-us-to-reach-the-most-earth-like-planet-we-know-of/), accessed 07-17-2016.

[332] Fifty-four trillion kilometers. My persistence in presenting metric system equivalents has to do with the fact that I am a Continental European and I just have to keep track of the numbers, no matter how small or big.

[333] Vide note 330.

gone through nearly an entire Eastern Roman Empire[334], beginning in the year 0, when Jesus would have been born, making it a whole lifetime for a civilization to develop, conquer outer territories (within the space ark, in this case) and eventually fall or place themselves at the verge of misfortune (having fifty-three more years to go before implosion, figuratively speaking).

Once in space, there would *technically* be no laws at all. Allow me to explain via a quote from Andy Weir's novel, *The Martian* (the same originating the 2015 homonymous movie[335]):

«LOG ENTRY: SOL[336] 381

I've been thinking about laws on Mars.

Yeah, I know, it's a stupid thing to think about, but I have a lot of free time.

There's an international treaty saying no country can lay claim to anything that's not on Earth. And by another treaty, if you're not in any country's territory, maritime law applies.

So Mars is "international waters".

NASA is an American nonmilitary organization, and it owns the Hab[337]. So while I'm in the Hab, American law applies. As soon as I step outside, I'm in international waters. Then when I get in the rover, I'm back to American law.

Here's the cool part: I will eventually go to Schiaparelli and

---

[334] Or Byzantine Empire, dissolved in 1453 AD.

[335] Vide note 217.

[336] A day spent on Mars, equivalent to twenty-four hours, thirty-nine minutes and thirty-five seconds, as opposed to a *day* spent on Earth, equivalent to twenty-three hours, fifty-six minutes and four seconds. Every four years, we add an extra day to February (the 29th), making it a leap year, which is the case of 2016, precisely. Skipping four minutes every day to make it a twenty-four-hour-long journey culminates in six extra hours by the end of each regular year. Six times four equals twenty-four, hence that aforementioned extra day we insert into our leap year calendar.

[337] Short for Mars Lander Habitat.

commandeer the Ares 4 lander. Nobody explicitly gave me permission to do this, and they can't until I'm aboard Ares 4 and operating the comm. system. After I board Ares 4, before talking to NASA, I will take control of a craft in international waters without permission.

That makes me a pirate!

A space pirate!».

Back on Earth, the space ark would have been built in a country's national territory, unless it had been built at sea, which, according to the documentary, is not the case, as there is a clear mention to a construction site dubbed «Starship City», filmed at Embry-Riddle Aeronautical University in Daytona Beach, Florida, in the United States. The documentary itself is American, so it is not so surprising the ark would be, just as much, having its construction overseen by NASA, a nonmilitary organization.

The US is then ultimately in charge of the vessel, though there would be no more Earth after the launch, let alone America, making the spacecraft completely independent, adrift in «international waters». No authority whatsoever would be *legally unchallengeable* within the ship's limits, as the planet of origin does not exist anymore.

Experts on *Evacuate Earth* assumed there would be no mutiny underway while the trip lasted eighty-eight years, but if traveling at the speed of light toward Kepler-452b takes 1,400 years, imagine what would happen across 20,044 years, at the speed suggested in the documentary. Based on my experience in human nature, considering I am a human myself, and based on History, which is there, taking the form of a social science, so we may keep record of our achievements, but especially our mistakes throughout Mankind (which proves it is not just about memorizing important dates), I honestly do *not* believe survivors would live in peace the whole time, regardless of the amount, may it be dozens, thousands or tens of thousands of years. Time dilation would always make it seem less than it really is, but that is not the point. It only *seems* so, it *is not*. Humanity has proven to evolve rapidly in one hundred years' time, socially speaking. It has proven it could last a couple thousand years as a civilization. It has proven it could develop as a species in ten thousand years' time. Whichever the voyage's duration, Man cannot simply stay still indefinitely. It is against our very nature, which is why, despite my craving for utopia, I do not think we would make it to our destination in one piece, literally speaking, as a single group, figuratively.

Nobody has enough psychiatric or psychological knowledge to claim they are sure of what would happen, once aboard a space ark headed to some unknown place. Having a vague idea is not enough to take any realistic conclusions, at all – hence a simulation such as *The Sims*. If we live in a simulation ourselves, according to Nick Bostrom and Elon Musk, having to flee the Earth could be the ultimate challenge.

For starters, witnessing the destruction of the only home we were ever familiar with is just shocking. There is no going back, there is no certainty about the future whatsoever. The thought alone that, regardless of the destination, adults are likely to never reach it, is depressing enough. It could produce questions such as, "what am I doing here, if I am not going to make it, anyway?" or "why did I come aboard this thing, if others are just going to eject my corpse, once I am dead, leaving it adrift to the will of stars or black holes, as if they were sharks, disassembling me completely?". If we were to find how to stay in fact alive indefinitely via Transhumanism and Singularity, that would not be a problem. We would just have to be lucky enough to have a minimum number of scientists on board, together with all the research ever produced on the subject. Lodging the Internet itself in the vessel would be mandatory, so as to avoid losing all the knowledge available on Earth the same way it was lost in the destruction of the Library of Alexandria. Perhaps that would somehow ease the idea that we escaped in vain, only to die slightly later.

Second, the most appropriate form of Government, which makes me ask myself whether there would be any governance at all. With a space ark being built in the United States, I am thinking access to it would be extraordinarily difficult, unless people had *paid* their way into it, which makes me ask those being paid to do that, "what do you want the money for?". Remember that scene in a 1997 blockbuster film[338] in which a wealthy man, Caledon "Cal" Hockley, paid his escape from a foundering ship to one of her officers, William McMaster "Bill" Murdoch, who curiously enough ended up committing suicide (though his living family claims otherwise)? My point exactly. Although said motion picture does not depict the end of the world, chances of survival in that specific situation are the poorest. You can either make use of that money or just die as if it had never been in your hands, hence the line, "your money can't save you more than it can save me". I mean, both the interviewees in the documentary and I are assuming the *boarding* alone of the space ark would have been peaceful, launching accordingly, without risking its very integrity. It does not take terrorists to make things go awry, every other person knows how to do that. People would have given anything to be aboard the Titanic, «the ship of dreams», one "God himself could not sink". However, when it came to leaving it, as it was not a synonym for a luxurious life anymore, things got ugly, bluntly put, and everyone just wanted to leave, apart from a few gentlemen who would not accept abandoning the ship before any other man. A desperate crowd fighting their way into the space ark, perhaps being shot and killed indiscriminately so as to make way for the really «important» people is a

---

[338] Vide note 75.

thought we must accept. Ironically enough, they would either get killed trying to save themselves or die from a cosmic chain of events, which could also happen to those aboard, should the space ark be on a collision route with a black hole, a star, an asteroid, a meteor, a comet, etc., unavoidable in time.

No matter how much faith we have in ourselves, and regardless of the kind of faith it is, we always rely on hope, either divine or not, it is irrelevant. We simply *hope* nothing bad is going to happen that could jeopardize our endeavors. The main endeavor here would be staying alive and avoiding the complete extinction of humans, hopefully looking to populate another planet gifted with Earth-like conditions and life sustainability, which is the assumption made regarding Kepler-452b. Right now, nobody knows, not even NASA, whether «Earth 2.0» can provide shelter for us or not. Should our knowledge of it be the same under escaping circumstances as it is now, it would be a complete and utter shot in the dark, just as much as believing survivors aboard the space ark would never, throughout the whole of the journey, endure something apparently as insignificant as a hull breach, which could put an end to the adventure in that precise moment. Either that, or the inability to keep producing water, food or oxygen. Without any of those, who is it that could possibly survive the trip and man the vessel on its landing? In an extremely farfetched hypothesis, I would say that, were that the case, and should the ship be big enough, an impact similar to the one featured in the Cretaceous-Paleogene extinction event could take place, we just do not know whether it would put an end to an era riddled with dinosaurs, depends on what creatures are living on Kepler-452b right now, if any at all. Just like an «Engineer» from the *Alien* saga sacrificed himself to spread the building blocks of life, those aboard the space ark, though long dead, could create the setup for the next stage of life on Kepler-452b to prosper.

I do not mean to presume any scientist would gain interest in reading this book (after all, I am a nobody), but should they do, and should they claim this is complete nonsense, just remember no one is calling Nick Bostrom or Elon Musk idiots for the simulation hypothesis, and neither is NASA being pointed fingers at for being incompetent at not knowing whether there is life on «Earth 2.0» or not. That is why it is called a hypothesis. Until you prove it wrong, it is perfectly valid. This is Literature, facts are handled together with fiction, so get over it.

Considering we would not traverse a transhumanist phase toward Posthumanism, remaining as we are now, every eighty years (*on average*, mind) a generation comes to an end, survived by the descendants of the deceased in question. In my opinion, I believe leaving a lineage is something that could keep people going, without the need to question their reason for survival, in detriment of others being wiped out as Earth was destroyed. It is the *purpose* of leaving said lineage that has to be questioned. Would you want to procreate and have offspring: for the sake of getting in touch with parenthood before you go? To help populate the new world they arrive to with your blood? To gain control of the space ark as a royal? For the sake of any of the previous, or all combined? It is a rather difficult answer, especially when it comes to either taking the altruistic or narcissistic side, if not both.

Wanting to help populate a new world that is, as far as we know, life-free, is a contribution to the prevention of Mankind's extinction. Taking the Bible for the absolute truth would make us think that, after the Great Flood, that was exactly Noah and his family's mission. God flooded the entire Earth with divine rain, sparing Noah, his family and a heterosexual[339] pair of each

---

[339] Every time words such as «sexual», «heterosexual», «homosexual», «bisexual», «transsexual», «transgender», «gay» or «lesbian» are used, people tend to take them out of context just so they can ignite a pseudo-discussion about an issue that does not even exist, apart from inside their own mind. I

animal species, so biodiversity could bloom once again, together with Humanity. The only problem to this is consanguinity and incest, which are against the Holy Scripture all by themselves, though thou shalt not question the Lord.

One of the problems that make the utopian concept next to impossible is being eager for freedom of choice, opinion, press, thought, etc., making the political system work *for* the people, *by* the people, *without* regard for what comes next, as it is highly likely that, amid all these cravings, those same people might want to be radical enough to take matters into their own hands, *forgetting* to instate the aforementioned and appropriate political system. It does not always happen this way, but if we were in a space ark headed some place far, far beyond, without having to recognize any authority on board, the dice would be cast so as to make chaos prevail.

La République Française may be a Democracy today, part of the heart of the European Union, but it was not so immediately after the Storming of the Bastille, on July 14th, 1789, when the French Revolution began. This event was an excuse to allow the face of it, Napoleon Bonaparte[340], to become Emperor, crowning himself as such without waiting for Pope Pius VII[341] to do it, on December 2nd, 1804. Some sources claim detractors of the new Emperor had people think it was an act of arrogance, placing himself on top of the Church and, consequently, God. Those defending him say it was previously arranged with the Pope, though

---

started off this book with a chapter titled «We Are One», claiming *differences* (condemning italic) like these are what keep bringing us apart as a species, but mostly, as a civilization. And it is precisely because of that first chapter, in which my vision of this kind of *diversity* (another condemning italic) is explained, that I store my faith in Humanity, hoping I have been making myself clear for over 360 pages, now. There has to be at least one sperm and one egg for reproduction to take place. Whether people (or even animals) were born heterosexual or not, is nobody else's business but their own.

[340] Vide note 49.

[341] Vide note 131.

I really cannot confirm this. The truth is Ludwig van Beethoven[342] also had faith in Napoleon, though he lost it after the latter was proclaimed Emperor, ripping the title page to his *Sinfonia Eroica*, in which there was a dedicatory to Bonaparte. How the Empire under Napoleon turned out is explained in the footnote I redirected you to after mentioning his name for the first time on this page.

The point in bringing back this issue has to do with the fact that people might be fighting (or claiming to fight) for freedom, equality and fraternity, but in the end, their sole interest is achieving absolute power, at the cost of a fictional revolution deposing a king and queen[343] by beheading, producing an emperor later. Like I said long before we reached this stage in the book, kingdoms and empires are *exactly* the same thing, apart from the title given to the monarch. Could a similar episode take place in a space ark run by and property of a country that no longer exists, heading to a lawless planet? Absolutely.

My understanding is guns would be stored in the ark, possibly to the worst of the escapees' knowledge, though it would not remain a secret forever. Also, with all the commotion generated because of both eminent and imminent destruction, gun control would be hard to engage. Processing people through a metal detector would take forever, let alone a full body scan and search. Plus, guns do not necessarily have to be made of said material to be able to fire[344]. So, either people are extraordinarily clean and

---

[342] 1770-1827. German composer setting the crossing between the Classical and Romantic periods in Western European music, bearing the most relevant name in this branch of the Arts immediately after Austrian composer Wolfgang Amadeus Mozart (1756-1791).

[343] Louis XVI of France (1754-1793) and Marie Antoinette (1755-1793).

[344] The fact there is a United States Undetectable Firearms Act of 1988 making it illegal to "manufacture, import, sell, ship, deliver, possess, transfer, or receive any firearm that is not as detectable by walk-through metal detection", does not obviously mean such events do not take place.

no criminal or terrorist is among those aboard (which is incredibly unlikely)[345], or there is at least one person capable of doing enough damage before they are stopped, and by whom? I am thinking military personnel, carrying standard-issue weapons, which makes governance militaristically authoritarian enough.

Either way, whoever is pointing the gun gets to decide what happens next. The fact a person is holding a gun, however, does not necessarily mean they will keep doing so indefinitely, and that is a time when the oldest means in the world to get something weighs in – sexual coercion. Survivors aboard the space ark, escape pod or arcology, as you prefer to name it, may not have use for money where they are going (unless the greed stays put and possibly the US Dollar takes over as the dominant currency, resembling the Euro in nineteen European Union Member-

---

[345] I would like to add a parenthesis here, in the light of what Europe has been experiencing since January 2015, when the offices of French weekly satirical newspaper *Charlie Hebdo*, in Paris, were invaded by a couple of terrorist brothers, Saïd and Chérif Kouachi, killing eleven people in the building, injuring eleven others and killing also a French National Police officer after that, on their way out. I would also like to add the European continent has not been the *only* victim of *Daesh*, though attacks on Democracy and freedom are always the most spoken of. Nationalist movement leaders (the same kind of movement inspiring Adolf Hitler to take on Politics, though current leaders would regard it as criminal to make such an accusation) take advantage of terror for their own gain, meaning their idea of nation is to break free from any international cooperation chains. The European Union has been dealing with the largest migratory crisis since World War II, ever since *Daesh* became a self-proclaimed independent State. An incredible number of Syrians has been constantly trying to flee their homeland because of the war in the Levant for nearly over two years. Europeans (*white* Europeans, come to that) under the influence of Nationalism claim terror in their continent is of the refugees' direct responsibility, adding terrorists arrive in Europe, off the Italian and Greek coasts, in the middle of said refugees. However, such statements cannot be considered to be truthful, for all of the terrorists identified up until now as the culprits of the European terrorist attacks were born and bred (or unborn, though bred since childhood) European. The refugees have nothing to do with this, and this is a situation I want to make perfectly clear as far as this stage of the essay is concerned, so as to discourage any inaccurate comparisons.

States[346]), but certain biological needs will not just go away. The mediatization of sexual activity on distasteful TV shows, television series, motion pictures and, of course, the pornographic industry, has since banalized an act of love-sharing in exchange for pragmatic achievements. Chances are one single sentence in this entire book may deem it family-unsafe, as children and teenagers nowadays are being secluded from the sad, pathetic truth, preventing them from growing responsibly, unknowing of what the outcome of sexual predation might be, resulting just as much in criminal activity from disrespect for somebody else's body through rape. All of this is *wrong*. Possibly, the italic is not enough to stress this, which is not just an opinion, it is reality. By prevention, authorities may be allowing the exact opposite to take place. No one has to be graphic about their explanation to the youth, though pinpointing the exact consequences of disrespect for others, regardless of their gender, is crucial to a healthy development as a human being.

I am talking the gender issue because there are a series of misinterpretations within the youth, such as boys being made champions for *scoring* (like a video game) multiple girls in a row, if not at the same time, and girls being made prostitutes for *messing* every other guy. Now, that is not right. It should not be either way. This kind of behavior usually (therefore, not always) takes place when young adults are inspired to believe in romanticism, that there is only one true love in our entire life (sometimes the very first), and because they are indeed so very young and inexperienced as far as the crudeness of life and reality is concerned, they experience some sort of a meltdown, engaging in and discarding people like the regular burner (or prepaid) phone. Once

---

[346] The Eurozone is made of the following: Austria, Belgium, Cyprus, Estonia, Finland, France, Germany, Greece, Ireland, Italy, Latvia, Lithuania, Luxembourg, Malta, Netherlands, Portugal, Slovakia, Slovenia and Spain.

they have had enough, they come to a halt, justifying their attitude with the need to harden against that aforementioned crudeness. Personally, I do not believe you have to be crude yourself to understand crudeness. You are much better off fighting it, rather than becoming a part of it. It does not have to work like a vaccine to be fruitful, especially because you are not injecting a weakened dosage of the bacteria in question, but rather taking your chances at a seemingly endless hangover, abusing of your liver. There is always somebody out there who deserves you. If in the meantime you get impatient, do not take it on other people, using them like some material asset. I hope you do not feel disappointed at me for making you read a self-help-toned excerpt of a Political Science book such as this (as the utopian concept is indeed Politics), but I thought of it as a piece of light-reading to help enlighten people looking for inspiration in their own life, instead of looking to mime others and become somewhat similar to a natural satellite of a planet (or superstar).

If privacy were to be kept aboard the space ark, there would obviously be no kind of surveillance at all within the survivors' quarters. Of course, there are always ways of concealing a CCTV[347] camera without having anyone else know about it – "Big Brother is watching you"[348]. Regardless, machismo could very well come alive through men sending women to those in charge, which would be majorly male, as it always happens in the Armed Forces, in order to distract them from something via a physical means of trade or to acquire an object of significant importance, changing the side the authority scale leans to.

This does not mean, however, the survivors would be the only ones interested in getting something for their own, personal gain.

---

[347] Closed-circuit television.
[348] Reference to ORWELL, George, 1949, *Nineteen Eighty-Four*, London: Secker & Warburg.

The military could have seen enough war in their lifetime to become fully trained and experienced so as to avoid being eluded that easily. Physical attraction is a weakness for all of us, but some can handle it better than others. If you are already holding the weapon, then why not make use of it? Not to kill, but as a visible form of threat. I am not tainting the image of the Armed Forces, whichever their nationality. That is how human nature works and, in a place guns are the only form of recognizable authority, it could well be possible.

Nobody else is making food or producing water (from which oxygen is synthesized, remember), apart from an automated farming process which can be ultimately overridden by *someone*. Having said *someone* barricade themselves in the farming control room by distracting whoever had been placed in charge of that area by whichever means necessary is nothing short of a likely possibility. This would implicate rationing all three basic elements keeping survivors alive on the space ark.

But a man or woman alone cannot rule an organized group of people without the aid of somebody else, placed in charge of security. All you have to do is be reminded of the natural course for civilizational development: there are too many people to feed, and a nomadic approach to natural resources is not practical. Better than exhausting them, you have them regrow (same as founding a business and making it work, instead of selling it straight away after both renovations and refurbishment have been made). Then, you store the results some place safe. You need a military body to do that for you, to guard your people's livelihood, registered by other instructed people who can write and read, so as to keep track of production. And how do you control all these people who, in the end, are working for you? You remember now – you become their ruler. And because you get to decide how much they eat, making money from their work, you become both an autocrat and a plutocrat. It is dystopia to its full extent. Where is my faith in Humanity heading to, after all?

If a survivor were to actually take control of the farming unit, eventually gaining sympathy from the people with the guns, they would be able to do whichever they pleased. People need to eat, drink and breathe. You take those away, what is there left? You have no other choice but to submit. Military-based dictatorships do not always require military personnel to be in charge. All they have to do is delegate power to someone holding political ambitions, even if they never dealt with Politics before. The Armed Forces will think they found a marionette they can pull the strings of, but it might just happen the tables are turned, having them oppose their new-born absolutist lackey, now in charge by their own hand. The path is then set to the return of nobility and feudalism. Even if a Valkyrie-like[349] attempt is made on the ruler's life, it cannot be turned into an explosion. The space ark is the only place in outer space capable of sustaining life. Explosions in space do not usually end well, so the solution is gunshot. How libertarians get access to a weapon comprises the same story I have been telling across the last few pages, in a seemingly endless cycle of events.

Still within authoritarian demands, the ruler would have their chance to choose the appropriate concubine among the crowd and procreate, making sure the lineage of power would continue, making it a reason why they would not have given up on surviving the destruction of Earth. It is not a question of being pessimistic. I prefer to call it «realistic». It is the worst case scenario, but remember our imagination is based primarily in both past and present, especially the latter, when projecting into the future.

Dystopian writers have the wisdom to translate into Literature the most common of human behaviors. I am not a dystopian, let alone a writer. I am an author. This is my fifth title, entirely

---

[349] Reference to the failed July 20th, 1944 plot by German officials to assassinate Hitler and gain back control of the nation via Operation Valkyrie.

signed by me (apart from the several quotes you have read, in the meantime, duly referenced), which makes me deal with authorship. Being a writer means you make a living from writing. I do not, so I know where I stand in the scheme of things. And though this book is about a *Utopian Ambition*, facing the music only means I am well aware of the obstacles preventing it from becoming real. I cannot change human nature all by myself.

If I were to be one of the survivors of that space ark and offered my assistance into shaping the basis to the rest of the journey as far as governance is concerned, I would have the opportunity myself to assume absolute control, one way or another. Would I want to do that? Absolutely not. But, how could I know? I can only *suppose* I would not. When the time came, and if the opportunity arose, would I prevent myself from absolutism? A tyranny based on claims that it lives momentarily to make things right and prevent abuse from the general population is the same as a sorry excuse to say, "I am in charge, I know what is best for the people, allow me to become a Leader, whichever language you might want to translate that to". Like they say, "*abusus non tollit usum*"[350]. This is why I want to become a University Professor, and this is why I am tremendously scary to some who already are. Being a University Professor is not about limiting your students' capabilities, but rather endorsing them to their full extent. Your seat will not become jeopardized for promoting talent, on the contrary, you will be held responsible for discovering people with extraordinary potential who can contribute both academically and scientifically to your own life as a human being. A chance is all everyone needs to prove it.

No one on the *Evacuate Earth* documentary referred themselves specifically to bringing wildlife aboard. Should it happen, and should the space ark from «Starship City» actually turn into

---

[350] Abuse does not justify use.

the modern-day Noah's Ark, keeping control of multiple animal species on the ship would have to result in an incredibly insurmountable zoo, and even in specialized places such as those (though some are not there exactly to help creatures stay alive, it is a fact), accidents happen. They are called wild animals because they have to live in the wild and cannot behave thoughtfully, as they do not have any rational spheres presiding over their judgment. Also, in the case there were any radical activists present, they would probably claim freedom for said creatures, being killed almost instantly by them the moment they opened the cage doors. As much as I believe animals have the right to live, those that cannot be domesticated should just be kept away from humans. Their relationship just does not work. Besides, you never know what to expect from them. Some can be trained, but they are used only to their trainers, not every other person. Perhaps surviving scientists could take a few samples with them and reproduce them once the ship reached its destination. We would just have to hope no one would do that while on board.

At last, and supposing it all went well, without any dystopian scenarios, regardless of having people reach Posthumanism and live indefinitely or counting on their descendants to live through the centuries, if not millennia, I imagine they would all have to get used to the idea of living on «Earth 2.0» with an entirely different continental layout, building civilization nearly from scratch. So, what of territorial distribution? Would they make a kind of law that says "finders, keepers", distributing the surviving nationalities across the land and handing over control of their own territory to themselves, so they could found a new, sovereign State, or would they *unite* into creating, for instance (you knew this was coming), the Atlantian Republic, made of World Citizens, cooperating with each other toward global sustainability, in their newly-founded second chance Earth? Everyone has been dreaming about a form of paradise up in the sky, either replenished of angels or seventy-two virgins. However, the sky we used to be familiar with is not there, anymore. The new planet could be an answer to the materialization of heaven.

Then, do these refugees take advantage of this new environment and reinstate countries like they used to be, with some minor changes made to the borders, according to Geography (which would probably generate a dispute based on arguments such as, "why is your country bigger than mine?"), or do they go utopian once and for all and generate a worldwide community without any wars between them?

We have to recall, once again, that God spared Noah and his family to repopulate an Earth that was supposed to be completely sin-free. There was also the image of a Messiah through which God made himself human, calling him his son, deliberately letting himself be killed, so as to redeem Mankind from their sins. This is where we are today.

If Earth's religions somehow did not survive the whole journey to Kepler-452b, another form of cult could find a way to spread and consume this new world[351]. Although a 2100 Atlantian Republic could take shape, the year would not be 2100, according to the Gregorian calendar. Then again, all other time divisions would become affected. Kepler-452b has twenty extra days around Kepler-452 than the Earth around the Sun. February would either get a few extra days, maybe up to thirty or thirty-one, permanently and possibly without any leap years, or a new calendar could be produced entirely. NASA has still not found out how long a day on Kepler-452b lasts. The idea of twenty-four hours (even if approximate, as it is on Earth) could have to be replaced by something either shorter or longer. A day on Mars

---

[351] You do remember what the Americas used to be called at the time of Christopher Columbus (1451-1506), together with the fact there was religious forcibility unto natives, right?

has been designated «Sol», so new naming could well occur, just as much. Also, just like Venus in the Solar System, if Kepler-452b were to spin clockwise, Kepler-452, the new Sun, would rise to the West, setting to the East.

I reenact my purpose of writing this book in the end, just as I so did in the beginning, and that is simply (though not elementary) Literature. Like I said not too long ago, I am not a writer, but those who are, as familiar as they are with Mankind, from either History, their experience dealing with humans, being humans just as much or all of those combined, either gifted with or condemned by human nature (whichever you think is best according to your own life), have the power to reach those who are interested in learning from reading, hopefully influencing them toward their own good, though it is important to make sure it is their decision entirely whether to accept things as they read them or to oppose them, it is their right. My only piece of advice directed to the latter option is to always listen and respect what others have to say to you, even when it is hard to endure their utter rudeness when speaking, often choosing to offend you for having no intelligent argument at all to use as a reply to your considerations. It is your purpose to defy other people's statements, should you believe they are wrong, by proving them wrong, and never by generating an endless argument based on personal aspects. Otherwise, you will not be proving any point whatsoever, rather you will turn out to be *exactly* like them.

I understand this may sound like cheap philosophy, perhaps even cheesy, like a lot of other things I may have written using the same tone across these pages, but from the moment you start writing something, you are turning it into a dogma. Even if you are producing an academic thesis, to which you presented a question-problem and then started providing hypothetical solutions, which may either work or not, and which are either based solely on the parroting of other people's thoughts or yours as well, you

Literatura", Moscow, 1952 *(in Russian)*.

32. Grenader A.B. — Impact of Cold Tempering and Winter Swimming on the Human Organism. 2nd Scientific and Methodological Conference on Cold Tempering and Winter Swimming. Minsk, 1967 *(in Russian)*.
33. Haich E. — Initiation. "Sfera", Moscow, 1998 *(in Russian)*.
34. Haig A. — Diet and Its Relation to Strength, Endurance, Training, and Athletics. Kiev, 1908 *(in Russian)*.
35. Harmony through Vegetarianism. "Society for Vedic Culture", Saint Petersburg, 1996 *(in Russian)*.
36. Hislop J.S. — Conversations with Bhagavan Sri Sathya Baba. "Society for Vedic Culture", Saint Petersburg, 1994 *(in Russian)*.
37. Hislop J.S. — My Baba and i. "Sri Sathya Sai Books and Publications Trust", Prasanthi Nilaym, 1985.
38. Keesling Barbara — Healing Sex. "Piter", Saint Petersburg, 1997 *(in Russian)*.
39. Khindhede M. — The Reform of Our Nutrition. "Novyi Chelovek", Saint Petersburg, 1914 *(in Russian)*.
40. Klyuchnikova M.Y. (compil.) — Living Ethics. "Respublika", Moscow, 1992 *(in Russian)*.
41. Lu Quan Yui — Taoist Yoga. Alchemy and Immortality. "Oris", Saint Petersburg, 1993 *(in Russian)*.
42. Perkins M., Hainsworth P. — The Baha'i Faith., Moscow, 1990 *(in Russian)*.
43. Platen M. — New Therapeutic Method. "Prosveschenie", Saint Petersburg, 1902 *(in Russian)*.
44. Radugin V.V. — Vegetarianism and the Reasons Why People Give It Up. Shuya, 1908 *(in Russian)*.
45. Sandweiss S. — Sathya Sai — The Holy Man and... the Psychiatrist. Saint Petersburg, 1991 *(in Russian)*.
46. Sathya Sai Baba — Sayings. "Center *Sathya*", Saint Petersburg, 1991 *(in Russian)*.
47. Sathya Sai Baba — Jnana Vahini. The Stream of Di-

vine Wisdom. "Society for Vedic Culture", Saint Petersburg, 1997 *(in Russian)*.

48. Sathya Sai Baba — Prashanthi Vahini. The Stream of the Highest Peace. "Sathya", Saint Petersburg, 1996 *(in Russian)*.

49. Sathya Sai Baba — Prasnottara Vahini. Answers to Spiritual Questions. "Society for Vedic Culture", Saint Petersburg, 1993 *(in Russian)*.

50. Sathya Sai Baba — Prema Vahini. The Stream of Divine Love. "Society for Vedic Culture", Saint Petersburg, 1993 *(in Russian)*.

51. Sathya Sai Baba — Sandeha Nivarini. Clearance of Spiritual Doubts. "Society for Vedic Culture", Saint Petersburg, 1993 *(in Russian)*.

52. Sathya Sai Baba — Sutra Vahini. "Sai Veda", Saint Petersburg, 1996 *(in Russian)*.

53. Sathya Sai Baba — The Art of Living. "Sai Veda", Saint Petersburg, 1999 *(in Russian)*.

54. Sathya Sai Baba — Yoga of Action. Significance of Selfless Service "Center of Sathya Sai Baba", Saint Petersburg, 1997 *(in Russian)*.

55. Shyam R. — I Am Harmony. A Book about Babaji. "Peace Through Culture" Association, Moscow, 1992 *(in Russian)*.

56. The Life of Saint Issa: Best of the Sons of Men, In: Around Jesus, "Society for Vedic Culture", Kiev, 1993 *(in Russian)*.

57. The Philokalia. "Molodaya Gvardia", Moscow, 1992 *(in Russian)*.

58. The Religion of Sikhs. God Is One and Only One. "Sikh's Missionary Center", 1997 *(in Russian)*.

59. The Way of a Pilgrim, Kazan, 1911.

60. Tolstoy L.N. — Critique of Theology. In: Beeryukov P.I. (ed.) — The Complete Set of Works of L.N.Tolstoy. "Izdatelskoye Tovarischestvo Sytina", 1913 *(in Russian)*.

61. Tolstoy L.N. — Cruelty-Free Diet or Vegetarianism.

Thoughts of Various Writers. "Posrednik", 1911 *(in Russian)*.

62. Uspensky P.D. — In Search of Miraculous. "Izdatelstvo Chernysheva", Moscow, 1966.

63. Yogananda — Autobiography of a Yogi. "The Philosophical Library", N.Y., 1946.

64. Zalmanov A.S. — Concealed Wisdom of the Human Organism. "Nauka", Moscow-Leningrad, 1966 *(in Russian)*.

65. Zhbankov R.G. — The Tasks and Prospects of Cold Tempering and Winter Swimming. 2nd Scientific and Methodological Conference on Cold Tempering and Winter Swimming. Minsk, 1967 *(in Russian)*.

Our video films:

1. *Immersion into Harmony of Nature. The Way to Paradise.* (Slideshow), 90 minutes (on CD or DVD).
2. *Spiritual Heart.* 70 minutes (on DVD).
3. *Sattva (Harmony, Purity).* 60 minutes (on DVD).
4. *Sattva of Mists.* 75 minutes (on DVD).
5. *Sattva of Spring.* 90 minutes (on DVD).
6. *Art of Being Happy.* 42 minutes (on DVD).
7. *Keys to the Secrets of Life. Achievement of Immortality.* 38 minutes (on DVD).
8. *Bhakti Yoga.* 47 minutes (on DVD).
9. *Kriya Yoga.* 40 minutes (on DVD).
10. *Practical Ecopsychology.* 60 minutes (on DVD).
11. *Psychical Self-Regulation.* 112 minutes (on DVD).
12. *Yoga of Krishna.* 80 minutes (on DVD).
13. *Yoga of Buddhism.* 135 minutes (on DVD).
14. *Taoist Yoga.* 91 minutes (on DVD).
15. *Ashtanga Yoga.* 60 minutes (on DVD).
16. *Agni Yoga.* 76 minutes (on DVD).
17. *Yoga of Sathya Sai Baba.* 100 minutes (on DVD).
18. *Yoga of Pythagoras.* 75 minutes (on DVD).

You may order our books and films at Lulu e-store: http://lulu.com/spotlight/spiritualheart
You can also download for free our video films, screensavers, printable calendars, etc. from the site: www.spiritual-art.info

See on the site www.swami-center.org our books, photo gallery, and other materials in different languages.

Design by
Ekaterina Smirnova

Scheme for Studying
the Structure of the Absolute

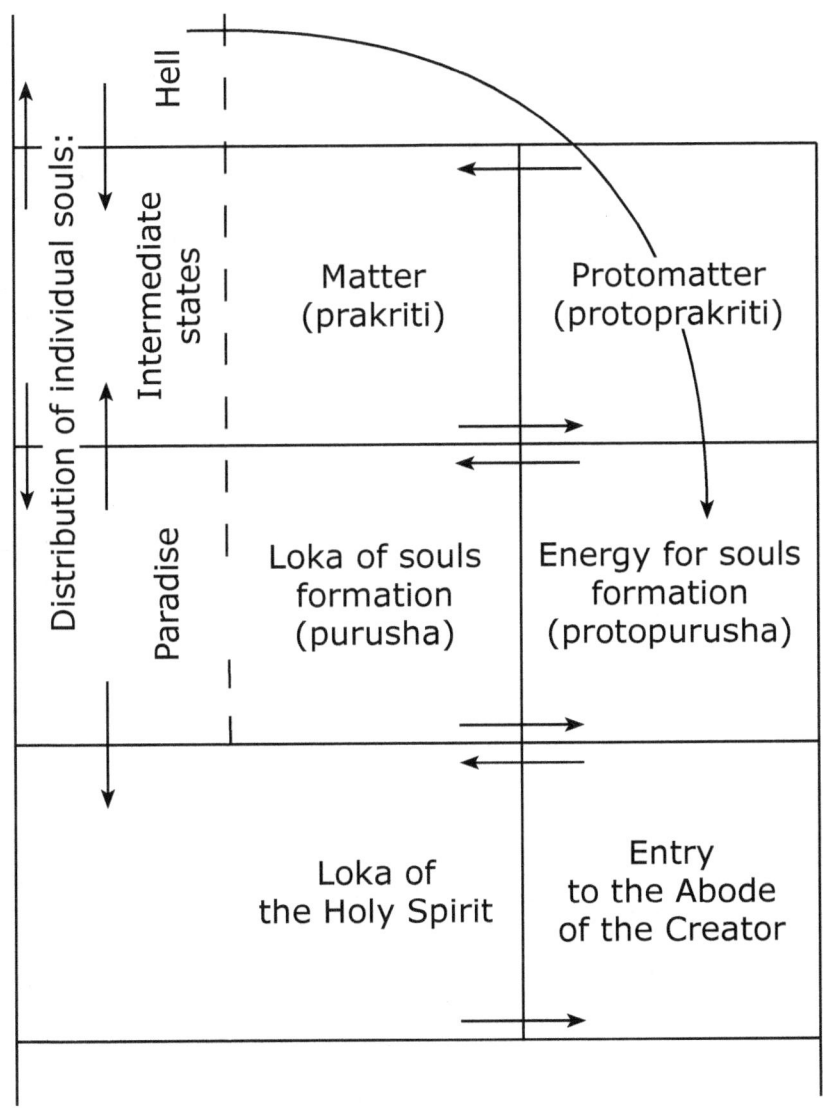

Comment: the arrows show the dynamics of processes within the Absolute.

www.ingramcontent.com/pod-product-compliance
Lightning Source LLC
Chambersburg PA
CBHW060612290526
45793CB00001B/6

CONTENTS

ACKNOWLEDGMENTS

Special Thanks

To my heroes: Dr. John L. Powell and Dr. Adnan Taj-Eldin for saving my life.

To my best friends: Mary Hughes and Laurel Schaefer for their prayers, cards, phone calls and encouragement.

To my brother: the Rev. Dr. William G. Waun for coming to my rescue whenever I needed him.

To all the nurses at the Zimmer Center and New Hanover Regional Medical Center who helped me through surgery and chemo treatments.

And to all my friends and family who prayed for me, emailed me, sent flowers and cards, and called to support me.

SURVIVOR'S GUIDE TO CHEMO 2.0

FORWARD

I have been treating women with ovarian cancer for over thirty years. Many changes have occurred in that time period in surgical techniques, new chemotherapy drugs, anti-emetics, and bone-marrow stimulating medicines. Throughout those years, I have always been amazed by and admired the courage, strength, determination to survive and endure, gratitude, and kindness of my patients. Deborah Waun's book will be a helpful guide with useful tips, and inspiration to other women facing the challenge of ovarian cancer.

The fortunate person, in my opinion, is he/she to whom the gods have granted the power either to do something which is worth recording or to write what is worth reading, and most fortunate of all is the person who can do both.

John L. Powell, M.D., FACOG, FACS
Director, Gynecologic Oncology
New Hanover Regional Medical Center
Southeastern Area Health Education Center
Professor Obstetrics and Gynecology
University of North Carolina School of Medicine

INTRODUCTION

I wrote this handbook in order to help those going through chemotherapy. I began taking notes during the time that I was undergoing chemo treatments so that I could pass along all of the information that I was learning through my own experience. I hope that these ideas and tips will help you get through your experience with as little pain and discomfort at possible.

In this book, I have included brand name products to have on hand and specific things that you can do to help relieve pain. This book is compiled in a way that is conducive to someone who does not feel well and just wants to go right to the information that they need. Often when one does not feel well, they may not feel like reading and searching through a book to find what will help them. This handbook is short and to-the-point, and easy to read. The purpose of this information is to empower you as you embark upon your own journey to wellness. Knowledge is power.

First, you should understand how urgent and life-threatening ovarian cancer is. According to Kunle Odunsi, M.D., Ph.D. (2018), "Ovarian cancer often progresses significantly before a patient is diagnosed. This is because the symptoms of ovarian cancer can be easily confused with less life-threatening digestive issues such as bloating, constipation, and gas. Roughly only 20 percent of ovarian cancers are detected before it spreads beyond the ovaries. The most prominent risk factor for this disease is a family history that includes breast or ovarian cancer. Women who test positive for the inherited mutations in the BRCA1 or BRCA2 genes are at significantly greater risk— 45% to 65% risk of developing breast cancer and

10% to 20% risk of developing ovarian cancer by age 70. Women at age 40 are at the highest risk" (para. 1).

Odunsi (2018) goes on to say that, "Globally, ovarian cancer is diagnosed in an estimated 300,000 women each year and causes roughly 180,000 deaths. In 2018, ovarian cancer was diagnosed in approximately 22,000 women and caused about 14,000 deaths in the United States, where it is the leading cause of death from gynecologic cancer. While significant advances have been made in surgical and chemo-based treatments for ovarian cancer, the survival rates have only modestly improved. The poor survival in advanced ovarian cancer is due both to late diagnosis as well as to the lack of effective second-line therapy for patients who relapse. Many women affected by advanced ovarian cancer respond to chemotherapy, but effects are not typically long-lasting. The clinical course of ovarian cancer patients is marked by periods of remission and relapse of sequentially shortening duration until chemotherapy resistance develops. More than 80% of ovarian cancer patients experience recurrent disease, and more than 50% of these patients die from the disease in less than five years post-diagnosis" (para. 3).

These facts are the reason why my doctor proclaimed that I am a miracle! I was sick for several months and had numerous symptoms many months prior to that, and I had a basketball-sized tumor. I beat the odds, but I attribute that to all of the prayers lifted up for me. God is certainly my shield and my protector! "The LORD is my rock, my fortress, and my savior; my God is my rock, in whom I find protection. He is my shield, the power that saves me, and my place of safety." Psalm 18:2.

MY STORY

When hearing the diagnosis of "you have cancer," everyone probably has the same reaction... "No, not me!" I was 48 and had been very healthy all of my life, so the idea of cancer seemed absurd!

I grew up in a small town in Indiana. My father was a minister, my mother was a social worker, and I was the baby and only girl in my family with two older brothers. After graduating from college and a brief marriage, I moved to Los Angeles and worked in the entertainment industry for 14 years. In 2000, I moved to Atlanta to help take care of my dad who had been diagnosed with a rare incurable illness. I helped my mom care for him for the last six months of his life. At the time, I believed that taking care of my dad and seeing him in pain would be the hardest thing I ever would do, but life is not always what we expect it to be.

I enjoyed living in California and especially loved my job in casting. It was fun being able to find the right actor for the television role. However, casting, as with any job, can be very stressful at times. The biggest take away from this book is that stress breaks down the immune system. So, if you have a lot of stress in your life, you need to find ways to relieve it.

I grew up in a Christian home with loving parents who did everything to enable me to have a good life. My parents sacrificed many things in order to provide for their children, so when my dad got sick, I knew it was time to make some changes in my life and help him. I quit my job in casting and moved to Atlanta to live with my parents and help care for my dad. This was a very difficult time because I watched my big strong father deteriorate and become weak and helpless.

My dad had dedicated his life to serving the

Lord and helping to lead others to Christ. My dad was a leader and a take-charge kind of man. He had a vision and worked hard to achieve it. But his illness got stronger and made him weaker and weaker. There were many times that he would fall and couldn't get up, which progressed to him not being able to get out of bed. It doesn't matter how old you are, when your dad can no longer be your protector, your security disappears.

On December 16, 2001, I was with him when he passed away. Even though I was in my 40's, I felt like a little girl when I lost him. It was during that time that I decided I wanted to help people who were going through rough times. While working full-time, I pursued my Masters' degree in Psychology and became a Licensed Professional Counselor.

For the next few years my mother and I lived together in Atlanta while I completed the required supervision for licensure. In the meantime, my brother and his family moved to North Carolina. I realized how difficult it was to take care of my dad and knew that I would probably need help caring for my mom as she got older, so I suggested that we move to be near my brother.

I cannot pinpoint the exact time that I started getting sick. Looking back on it now, I believe it was during the stressful time that I was caring for my dad. I did not take care of myself during that time. I worked full-time and then would come home and start taking care of my dad in order to relieve my mom. I would force myself to be positive and upbeat around my parents but at night when I would go to bed, I would cry myself to sleep. Also, my parents were old-school and believed that you don't pay for things that you can do yourself. So, I ended up being the lawncare service, house cleaner, shopper, etc. I realize now that I should have paid to have some of those things done but I was the dutiful daughter.

Deciding to move, added another layer of work to my list. My mother was 80 so I did most of the packing. I also contacted realtors, researched new homes in North Carolina, dealt with the financial advisor, screened moving companies, and continued packing. When the movers came, I helped them carry things to the moving van, I cleaned the house and helped with staging it for open houses. Once the house sold, I packed the car and drove 9 hours to our new home. Upon arrival, I helped the movers unload the van. I went through all of the boxes in the garage which was stacked full, I unpacked, moved furniture, moved heavy boxes to areas for unpacking, all in July with temperatures of 90 – 100 degrees. I never stopped going, until I collapsed!

While unpacking and organizing furniture, I was also filling out insurance paperwork for damaged property from the move, working on getting my counseling license in North Carolina, and looking for a job. My brother warned me to slow down and take a break, but that wasn't me. I guess they didn't realize that I was superwoman! I say this with tongue-in-cheek because nobody can be superwoman. Something has to give. All that stress was weakening my immune system.

I noticed that I was fatigued and would fall asleep while sitting in a chair in the early evening. That was unusual for me because I always need quiet and darkness in order to sleep. In mid-August, my stomach started hurting and I began to feel nauseated. I realized that I couldn't burp or pass gas. My stomach and abdomen began bloating and I had a fever. The fever started at 103 degrees for one night and then if ranged between 99 and 101. My stomach began cramping and I lost my appetite. I started feeling sick all of the time and it became painful to eat or even drink water.

As I reflect, I realize that I had other symptoms that I had chalked up to getting older. Five months prior to getting really sick, my abdomen started to bloat, and I had acid reflux when I went to bed. I was also on edge and irritable much of the time. And I had to urinate more frequently.

We had only been in North Carolina for a month, so I did not have a doctor yet. Since I did not have a doctor, I went to the Urgent Care where I was examined, and blood and urine tests were taken. The tests did not indicate any problem and my white blood cell count was not elevated so I believed that whatever the problem was, at least it couldn't be cancer because when you have cancer, your white blood cells elevate so they can fight off the infection. I was wrong! The Urgent Care doctor diagnosed me with gastroenteritis, suggested that I see a Gastroenterologist, prescribed an elixir (Belladonna®) to help with stomach cramps, and sent me on my way.

I immediately made an appointment with a Gastroenterologist, but his first opening was not until October 12th and this was mid-August. There are only two Gastroenterologists in the town where I lived, and they were both booked solid until Mid-October. I am usually a proactive person but when you are sick and new to an area, you feel helpless.

Things continued to get worse. My symptoms grew to include diarrhea. As previously mentioned, I had already lost my appetite and my

11

stomach hurt whenever I ate or drank. I felt sick all of the time and I began losing weight. Since I was getting worse, I went to the emergency room at the local hospital. I waited for six hours before I was seen by a doctor. He examined me, took more blood and urine, and an x-ray. All of the tests came back clean because they were not testing for cancer. I made the mistake of telling him the diagnosis that the urgent care doctor had given me. If you are ever in the situation where you are getting a second opinion, don't tell them what the first doctor said because it is too easy for the next doctor to just accept that diagnosis. And that is exactly what happened.

I went home to continue waiting for six long weeks for my appointment with the Gastroenterologist. I was so sick. It is hard to describe exactly how I felt. I had a fever, had constant stomach pain, was bloated and couldn't pass gas, was fatigued, had diarrhea, and was depressed. Since I was always in pain, I couldn't sleep. This continued to worsen in the next 45 days.

I was desperate to find out what was happening to me. I researched the internet searching to find out what I had. I thought that maybe I had a parasite since some of the symptoms were similar, so I went back to Urgent Care and asked them to test for that.

While I was at Urgent Care, the doctor told me that he could get me in with a local MD. I was able to get an appointment in the next few days and finally I was going to get a definitive answer. Dr. Eldin had a practice in the same neighborhood where I lived. He examined me and felt a tumor. In his words, he said he felt a "very large tumor!"

Two days later on September 25th I had a CT scan which revealed a huge tumor in my abdomen. This information was immediately given to Dr. Eldin who called me into his office right away. He explained to me that I had a "basketball sized" tumor which he believed was most likely ovarian cancer. He suggested that I see a cancer specialist at the Zimmer Cancer Center in Wilmington (1 ½ hours away). When giving referrals, most doctors hand the patient a card with the referral number on it and let them make the call. However, Dr. Eldin knew how urgent this was so he made the call himself.

When Dr. Eldin left the room to call the specialist, I prayed that God would help me, and that the specialist would be able to see me right away. After the call, Dr. Eldin came back in to tell me that the specialist would see me the next day at 9:00 a.m. What are the chances that a busy well-known cancer specialist, (Dr. John L. Powell) would be available to see me first thing the next day? As it turned out, Dr. Powell is not only well-known, but he is one of the nation's leading gynecological oncologists.

My brother (the Rev. Dr. William G. Waun) dropped everything on his busy schedule to drive my mother and me to Wilmington. Dr. Eldin had suggested that I take an overnight bag with me on the off-chance that they would admit me to the hospital. I also took the CT scan with me.

Dr. John Powell met with all three of us, looked at the CT scan and didn't pull any punches. He told me directly that I had ovarian cancer. He said that I needed surgery including a complete hysterectomy, and removal of other body parts such as my gall bladder, appendix, and lymph nodes. This was such a shock to me! I just couldn't believe that I had cancer! I questioned Dr. Powell and asked about the possibility that the tumor was benign. He replied that it most certainly was *not* benign.

My head was reeling, and I didn't even know what questions to ask. It is always a good idea to take someone with you in situations like this because your emotions make it difficult to concentrate and think clearly. My brother asked what my prognosis was, and Dr. Powell replied that he would not know until he opened me up in surgery. But he said one thing he could tell us is that this cancer was fast-growing and aggressive.

I was then ushered into another room where

15

I was examined, and several vials of blood were drawn. The realization of everything was setting in and a wave of fear and sorrow overwhelmed me. I was worried that I might not survive the surgery. One of the nurses (Nicole) came in to comfort me and reassure me. Even though I was scared, I desperately wanted to get the tumor out of me! I was concerned that I might have to wait for several days before Dr. Powell would have time to perform my surgery. As I sat there alone waiting for Dr. Powell to return, I started praying that God would work it out so that I could have the surgery right away. When Dr. Powell came in, he told me that he would be performing my surgery at noon the next day. I believe that this was another answer to prayer.

The next step was to be admitted to New Hanover Regional Medical Center which is adjacent to the Zimmer Center. My mother and brother accompanied me to my hospital room and helped me settle in for the night, and then they headed back home. That's when the fear really set in! As I sat

there all alone in the hospital room, the realization
of everything began to sink in. I called my friends
to say my good byes just in case.

As I was laying in the hospital bed, the
worst-case scenarios kept creeping into my head,
and I began to cry. I started praying and asking
God to help me. While I was praying the sweetest
nurse (Shirley) came in and asked me what she
could do to make me feel better. I asked her if she
would pray for me and she did not hesitate. She
hugged me and took my hand and began to pray.
Then she sat with me and reassured me that
everything would be okay. She was there when I
needed someone. Nurses give totally of themselves
and I was fortunate to have some of the best take
care of me.

The next morning before the surgery,
(thanks to Shirley), several nurses and a doctor
came into my room and formed a circle around me
along with my mother, brother, and sister-in-law,
and they all prayed for me. This kind of care and

concern is what makes a hospital stand out. Before I knew it, they were wheeling me down the hall for the surgery. As you are being wheeled on a stretcher to have major surgery, there is a real feeling of how alone you are. Your family can't be with you. It is just you and God.

My family was taken to a waiting room and I was taken to pre-op where I met the Assisting Doctor, the Anesthesiologist, and the Operating Room Nurse whose name was Ruth. Ruth was very kind and promised that she would watch over me during the surgery. The last thing that I remember is being offered a shot for pain. I don't even remember receiving the shot. And as if no time had passed, I woke up in my hospital room with a large tube down my throat which prevented me from speaking. And of course, nobody was in my room!

It wasn't long before a nurse came in and noticed that I was awake and shortly after that Dr. Powell came to see me. The surgery had included a complete hysterectomy and removal of some of my lymph nodes. Dr. Powell said that he usually removes certain organs during surgery because he knows where the cancer cells like to hide. He had planned to remove other organs but when he opened me up, he was surprised to see that the cancer was contained in the tumor! When you think about how long I had been sick, how large the tumor was, and the fact that ovarian cancer usually spreads throughout the body very quickly, it is a miracle that I am alive!

Dr. Powell said that I was in Stage One (the best stage) and he believed that he removed all of the cancer. He also said that all of my organs looked clean. I think that he was amazed that I was not filled with cancer. I later found out that I was in surgery much longer than what was anticipated because the extremely large tumor was wrapped around organs and muscles. I had to be given a transfusion because I lost so much blood. But God spared my life! Prayer still works!

Even though Dr. Powell believed he had

removed all of the cancer, he still suggested that I receive chemotherapy. He let me know that cancer cells can hide and there was still the possibility that some may be lurking inside of me. He said if I elected to get chemo, he wanted to wait for a month in order to give my body time to heal and build up some strength.

I will always consider Dr. Powell to be my hero because he saved my life. Webster's dictionary defines hero as, "One distinguished for action, a brave man, noble, conqueror, champion, man of great courage, a man among men." I submit that doctors who dedicate themselves to trying to save lives and go into battle daily against disease are heroes. This goes for nurses too. They have to face people everyday with bad news and sometimes watch them get worse while they do their best to fight their illnesses. I couldn't help myself, but my hero stepped in and saved me. I can't think of anyone who better fits the definition of hero than Dr. Powell.

I was fortunate to have a private room and wonderful nurses. Since visiting hours were over by the time that I awoke, my family had left, but I wasn't alone for long. I had caring nurses checking on me all night. I also had several phone calls from friends and family. Three things that I advise anyone to take if they are having an overnight stay at the hospital are earplugs, a neck pillow, and an eye mask. These three items will help you be able to sleep in a place that stays active at all hours.

I was in the hospital for seven days after the surgery and I was on a liquid diet most of that time. They switched me to solid food the morning that I was to be released with the condition that I had to eat solid food before I could leave. The problem was that food repulsed me. And they brought in bacon, eggs and a biscuit. This would not be what I would suggest for a first meal after not eating for a week. I wanted to go home so I nibbled on the biscuit, covered up the other food, and told them that I ate my breakfast. I guess nobody checked because they allowed me to leave!

On October 3rd I finally got to go home! I was very weak and still felt sick but there's no place like home! My brother and mother came to get me and helped me settle in to the backseat of his minivan for the 1 ½ hour ride home. My mom brought a blanket for me which was a good idea since it was a while before I could get my body temperature regulated and I was always cold.

Prior to leaving the hospital, I was told that I could eat anything that I wanted. It would have been nice if they would have given me a list of food that one should not eat when recovering from surgery because I chose one of the worst things to eat after I got home. I thought that eating a few bites of banana would be good but as I later found out, banana is very hard to digest. And I found out the hard way! It hit me around midnight and lasted for several hours. The pain was terrible! It felt like my stomach and intestines were on fire. All that I could do was stand and pace while holding my stomach and crying. I did not realize that it was the banana making me sick and I was worried that something serious was wrong.

The next day the pain had eased but I still felt sick, so I called the doctor's office and spoke to his nurse (Debbie) who told me that it was most likely the banana. She suggested that I take some Maalox to soothe my stomach and it really helped. She also asked the doctor to prescribe some medication (Aciphex®) which helps break down the acid in the stomach. In addition, she suggested that I try eating Jell-O, popsicles, or pudding along with drinking Special K water, Pedialyte, or Gatorade. These are all foods/fluids that are easy to digest along with helping to keep you hydrated and providing nutrients. I called Debbie several times with questions while I was recuperating, and she was always very kind and helpful.

In case you are not aware, you do not need to get your prescriptions fully filled. You can get them half-filled until you see if you need more. I spent a lot of money getting a pain medication (Oxycodone®) filled, only to find out that I didn't need it.

I experienced pain in my shoulders, upper back and sides which I believe was trapped gas. My mother suggested putting heat on the areas that hurt and much to my surprise the pain went away. Every time I had that type of pain, I heated up a little microwavable bean bag and held it to the area and the pain would dissipate.

On October 8th (5 days after being released from the hospital and 11 days after surgery) I had my staples removed. Since the tumor had been so large, I had to have an incision that was also very large, and that incision was held together by several very large staples! The doctor removed the staples with what looks like a very large staple remover. It was at this appointment that Dr. Powell gave me more information about getting chemo.

My sister-in-law (Cynthia) did some research for me so I would be better equipped to ask relevant questions regarding the chemotherapy. I asked what stage I was in and what my CA-125 count was. The CA-125 is a blood test that tells you if you have ovarian cancer. Dr. Powell told me that my CA-125 count was 126 but needed to go down to below 30. He also said that I was in stage 1C. He gave me a good prognosis and said that I had a 90% chance of a full recovery. My mom and I prayed and thanked God for the good news! Dr. Powell recommended the chemo to ensure that any hidden cancer cells would be destroyed. He said that he would schedule me for six hours of chemo once a month for six months beginning November 5th. While I was relieved and grateful for the good prognosis, I was also dreading the chemo!

My mother was caring for me at home while I recovered from the surgery, but she would leave to run short errands during the day. The next day after having my staples removed, I was standing in the kitchen when I felt water running down my leg. This was quite alarming! I rushed to the bathroom where I continued to release water. It felt as though I had no control over my bladder and the water was pink which made me think it contained blood. I was home alone, and I began to panic. I called the doctor's office but had to leave a message and wait for someone to return my call. I tried calling my mother on her cell phone, but it went straight to voicemail. I remembered that my brother (who lives right down the street) was home until noon that day, so I called him.

I didn't know what was happening and I was scared to be alone. My brother came right over and stayed with me until my mother got home. The nurse returned my call and explained that it was most likely that some of my internal stitches had dissolved which had been holding back some fluid. She also said that I could have a bladder infection which a urine test later confirmed. She asked the doctor to prescribe an antibiotic. After one day everything cleared up.

Having a hysterectomy is major surgery and it takes a long time to fully recover. Not to mention that I was malnourished and dehydrated due to not eating anything except bites of crackers for six weeks prior to the surgery. I was very weak and even had difficulty walking. I did not have an appetite, and nothing sounded appealing. Dr. Powell warned me that I needed protein to build up my white blood cell count, but I could not bring myself to eat meat.

It took a couple of months, but I slowly regained my appetite. My education has taught me that sometimes you have to start by retraining your brain, so I started watching the Food Network and my mother made me homemade soups and stews. I began by just eating the broth and then the gravy and worked my way up to eating vegetables. Finally, after a couple of months I was able to eat meat.

I don't know why I had to go through this experience, but I know that it has made me more sympathetic to people who are ill. At one point, I felt so sick and the pain was so bad that I actually understood how people with terminal illnesses would think about ending the pain. I want to use my experience to help others make it through their own journeys.

On November 5, 2007, I started my first chemo treatment at the Zimmer Center. It was an all-day process and I spent six hours in the chemo chair hooked up to an IV. While I write about certain things that happened to me in this book, it is not to say that those things will happen to you. Everyone is different. All in all, the chemo was not as bad as I had anticipated, and the chemo nurses took excellent care of me. I was never left alone, and they took a personal interest in my comfort every time that I received a treatment. The following chapters are filled with information based on my experience and what I learned during my fight for survival…

TIP ONE: TREATMENT PLAN & POSSIBLE SIDE EFFECTS

When your cancer is first diagnosed, your doctor will review a treatment plan with you. This may involve surgery, radiation therapy, chemotherapy, hormone therapy, and biologic immunotherapy or some combination of those treatments. All of these regimes kill cells. In the process of killing the cancer cells, some healthy cells are also destroyed. That is what causes the side effects of the cancer treatments. You may experience any or none of the following:

- Sore mouth or throat or dry mouth

- Sores or white patches on your lips, mouth or throat
- Loss of appetite
- A change in sense of taste or smell
- Weight loss or weight gain
- Lactose intolerance
- Diarrhea
- Vomiting and nausea
- Stomach pain
- Constipation
- Pain or burning when you urinate
- Frequent urination
- Not being able to urinate
- Reddish or bloody urine
- Dental problems
- Fatigue
- Depression
- Acing in the bones
- Muscle, bone, or joint pain
- Weak, sore or achy muscles
- Rectal bleeding
- Shaking or trembling

- Hearing loss
- Itching or hives
- Severe skin rash
- Darkened, yellow, brittle or cracked nails
- Warmth or redness in your face, neck, arms or upper chest
- Swelling in your face or hands
- Swelling or tingling in your mouth or throat
- Tingling/numbing/burning sensation in your hands, arms, legs or feet
- Chest tightness
- Fast, slow, or uneven heartbeat
- Light-headedness or fainting
- Trouble breathing
- Bloody or black, tarry stools
- Changes in vision
- Fever, chills, or cough
- Ringing in your ears or trouble hearing
- Unusual bleeding, bruising or weakness
- Hair loss
- Anemia
- Confusion or memory loss

- Loss of balance or clumsiness
- Walking problems
- Jaw pain
- Onset of menopause/hormonal changes which may include hot flashes
- Infertility
- Earaches
- Headaches
- Impotence (for men)

Please note that some people don't experience any side effects. Everyone is different and many things factor into whether or not you will have side effects. These factors include the type of cancer you have, the part of your body being treated, the type and length of treatment, the dose of treatment, your diet, your personal outlook or attitude, and the medications you are taking to prevent side effects.

There are lots of medications being prescribed that can prevent almost any side effect out there. I experienced loss of appetite, weight loss, some lactose intolerance, some constipation, some fatigue (although not as bad as most), one bout of rectal bleeding due to eating popcorn, a one-time experience of numbness and tingling in my hands, arms, legs and feet, a one-time experience of feeling nauseous, hair loss, and aching in my bones. The worst of the side effects for me was the aching. This may have been due partly to the chemo, but it is mostly attributed to a side effect of a shot (Neulasta®), that I had to take after each chemo treatment to increase my white blood cell count. This shot caused terrible aching in my back, legs and feet. The aching usually lasted around four days. Generally, side effects disappear after your treatments stop.

TIP TWO: CA-125

When working on a project, I like to keep a record of progress. I created an excel spreadsheet so that I could monitor my blood cell count as well as the score for the ovarian cancer test. The CA-125 is a blood test which is an indicator for cancer. The blood contains substances at certain levels that are called tumor markers. When the tumor markers rise above a specified range, it may indicate cancer. Please note that tumor markers are not an absolute when predicting cancer, but they are a great tool for doctors to use.

The tests usually used for breast cancer are the CA 15-3 or the CA 27-29. The test for ovarian cancer is generally the CA-125. There is also another blood test called OvaSure® which was developed by Yale University researchers that claims to detect early-stage ovarian cancer with 99% accuracy.

My first CA-125 score was 126. It is supposed to be below 30 (between 4.0 – 30.2). After the surgery it came down to 32.1. After my first chemo treatment my score was 9.4 and after my last chemo treatment my score was 4. The chemo nurses told me that they could not believe how low my score was. They said there are people who have never had cancer that have scores higher than mine. I had a lot of people praying for me and I also followed my doctor's orders.

Along with recording the various scores from my CBC, I also kept track of my blood count related to when I took antibiotics. I took antibiotics five separate times while I was sick and while taking chemo. I noticed that each time that I took antibiotics, my white blood count was lower than the times that I was not taking them.

TIP THREE: SIDE EFFECTS OF CHEMO

My first chemo treatment was the hardest one for me. Three days after my fist treatment, I was standing in the kitchen when I began to feel sick. I felt nauseated and also like I was going to have diarrhea. At the same time, my whole body started to severely tingle almost like I was being zapped by a stun gun. I broke out into a cold sweat and my ears went shut which caused dizziness. It was a terrible feeling! However, my doctor had prescribed a pill (Prochlorperazine®) that was for nausea, so I took it immediately. I was already taking other medications prescribed for nausea, but this pill turned off nausea responses in the brain while the other nausea medication worked in the stomach.

I felt terrible for about half an hour and then the pill must have kicked in because I started feeling better. I kept track on a calendar of when I felt bad so that I could see if there was a pattern. That way I could be prepared and possibly block the nausea before it started. I took the Prochlorperazine® on the third day after each chemo treatment prior to feeling sick and it worked! As Barney Fife would say, "Nip it, nip it, nip it!"

Chemotherapy can also cause anemia. Anemia is the result of the bone marrow's inability to produce red blood cells. Red blood cells carry oxygen to every area of your body. If there are not enough red blood cells, then your body will not get enough oxygen to operate efficiently. Anemia can cause several symptoms and problems in and of itself. You may feel fatigued, feel like your heart is pounding and beating too fast, have shortness of breath, or feel dizzy or faint. There is a shot to stimulate your bone marrow to increase the production of red blood cells just as there is a shot to increase white blood cells. My problem was insufficient white cells. Along with getting the shot, you should have well-balanced meals, get plenty of sleep, and don't attempt to do everything yourself. Rest and accept help from friends and family.

Along with the bone marrow's inability to produce white and red blood cells, chemo can also cause the bone marrow to stop or slow down the production of platelets. Platelets are the blood cells that help stop any bleeding by making blood clots. If you do not have enough platelets, you will bleed and bruise more easily. If your bone marrow is not producing enough platelets, you may have symptoms such as pinpoint red dots under your skin, bruising, nose bleeds, gums bleeding, vaginal bleeding, headaches, dark or bloody stool, pinkish colored urine, and blurred or changes in your vision. Blood work is always taken prior to administering chemotherapy and a complete blood count is included in that blood work. If your platelets are too low, your doctor may offer medicine to stimulate your bone marrow to produce more platelets or he may suggest a platelet transfusion.

TIP FOUR: DO NOT EAT POPCORN!

I gave this tip a page all to itself because of its importance. I had a bad experience which has been attributed to eating popcorn the day before getting one of my chemo treatments. I thought that eating popcorn would be a good source of roughage which would help with digestion. Boy, was I wrong! The popcorn seemed to gather in my intestines where it hardened. A few days later after being constipated, I finally went to the bathroom but because the popcorn had hardened into big clusters in my intestines, it was very painful! About an hour later I started bleeding from the rectum. That was extremely upsetting and scary.

Everything always seemed to happen to me on the weekends when I could not reach my doctor. I did not know why I was bleeding. The bleeding started on a Friday night and continued until Monday afternoon. I was bleeding what appeared to be approximately a teaspoon of blood every half hour and I felt an urge to go to the bathroom every time I would bleed. That feeling alone was terrible.

I had been given a magnet with a 24-hour nurse line called Vitaline. At the time, I did not remember that this line also had a physician on-call 24-7. I called on a Saturday morning to see what I should do. The nurse that I spoke with advised me to go to the ER. Before taking her advice, I had the presence of mind to ask her two important questions. 1. Was I losing a dangerous amount of blood? And 2. What would they do to me if I went to the ER? She told me I was not in any danger with that amount of blood loss and I could wait until Monday to contact my doctor unless the bleeding got worse. She also let me know that if I went to the ER, I would be examined and scoped. I did not like the sound of that, so I decided to wait until Monday.

In the meantime, the nurse suggested that the bleeding might be caused by hemorrhoids. I never had hemorrhoids before, but she told me that they could be caused by the chemo weakening the walls of my intestines. She suggested that I try Tucks which might have helped if the bleeding wasn't internal. It turned out that I made the right decision because the bleeding stopped by Monday afternoon. I found out later, after talking to my doctor, that popcorn can have that affect if eaten shortly before or after taking chemo. It was several months before I ate popcorn again!

TIP FIVE: FOOD

When I went in for my first chemo treatment, I was bombarded with information given to me by the nurses. One benefit that Zimmer Center offered was the consultation services of a dietician. A good dietician can provide you with important information about what type of diet is best for you and may be able to answer questions for you throughout the duration of your chemo treatments. A balanced diet can also help with side effects such as fatigue. It was suggested to me that I limit my caffeine intake and increase protein.

Chemo lowers your immune system and makes you more susceptible to foodborne illnesses.

There is a greater risk of contracting E-Coli when consuming fresh fruits and vegetables. I was tempted to eat salads, but I resisted the temptation because I did not want to take the chance of getting sick. You can substitute things for fresh fruit like eating applesauce instead of apples or canned pineapple, peaches, etc. You can eat fresh vegetables as long as you cook them. I love steamed broccoli and cauliflower and they even have cancer-fighting agents in them. Additionally, when thawing meat, you should place it in the refrigerator and not the kitchen counter. It is important to cook meat and eggs thoroughly and avoid raw shellfish. Also, you should only consume pasteurized or processed juices and ciders as well as only pasteurized milk and cheese.

For the same reason to not eat fresh fruits and vegetables, you should also not eat fast foods or at buffets when undergoing chemo. It is a good idea to stay away from fast food restaurants anyway. This should be a time when you start eating healthier if you have not been eating that way previously.

My doctor and a nutritionist at the Zimmer Center recommended higher calorie foods with lots of protein. Dairy products such as milk and cheese are great unless you are lactose intolerant. Forget the diet foods and sugar-free foods. This is the time to build up your body so you can withstand the effects of the cancer and of the treatments. You may not feel like eating a lot, so make a point to eat foods that are higher in calories. Some higher calorie food suggestions include: pancakes, cinnamon buns, doughnuts, cheeseburgers (but not from fast-food restaurants), grilled cheese sandwiches, milk-based soups, potato salad, biscuits, most meat, ice cream, milkshakes, cake, pie, and cookies.

While I am on the subject of food, I will include something that I learned from experience regarding what to eat around the time of each chemo treatment. I found that I felt much better if I only ate soft food or liquids like soup a few days prior to and a few days after each chemo treatment.

The chemo made everything I ate harden up during digestion. I would have a couple of days of constipation and that uncomfortable feeling that accompanies it around each chemo treatment. Although it was uncomfortable, I did not experience any rectal bleeding except for the popcorn incident. I just felt a lot better when I only ate soup or pudding or other soft foods during those few days. It took me a while to learn this, so I hope this tip will help you.

This leads right into the topic of using a stool softener. I recommend Senokot because it did not cause bloating or gas and it is a natural vegetable laxative. I did not need it every month but definitely used it after eating the popcorn! I suggest taking 2 pills once a day for however many days you feel you need it but be sure to follow the directions on the bottle. One of the chemo nurses said that some people take as many as four a day.

Chemo treatments can cause constipation in some people and some medications can also cause constipation. It is important to drink plenty of fluids to keep your stool soft. The usual recommendation is at least eight 8-ounce glasses per day. Increasing the fiber in your diet can also help but be sure to check with your doctor first because a high fiber diet is not recommended for certain types of cancer. Exercise can also help to keep you regulated.

Mouth sores, tender gums, and a sore throat or esophagus often result from radiation or chemotherapy. If this happens, you should consult with your doctor because it could be due to an unrelated dental problem and your doctor may be able to give you medicine that will help to control mouth and throat pain. Be aware that certain foods may irritate an already tender mouth or make chewing difficult.

As I stated earlier, I went on a soft food or liquid diet a few days prior to my chemo treatment and continued it for a few days after. I did not have any trouble with mouth or throat sores, but the soft diet helped with digestion. On the same note, you will want to avoid citrus fruits such as oranges, grapefruit, lemons, and spicy or salty foods.

Some foods you may want to include are:

- Instant mashed potatoes
- Milkshakes
- Applesauce or canned peaches
- Cottage cheese or yogurt
- Macaroni and cheese
- Custards, puddings and gelatin
- Ice cream
- Scrambled eggs
- Oatmeal

Additionally, you should stay away from sugar-free foods. Sorbitol, which is a sugar substitute that is used in many sugar-free foods, can cause diarrhea. I made the mistake of eating some sugar-free ice cream which caused cramping and diarrhea. Sugar-free gum can do the same thing. This isn't the time to be dieting so ditch the sugar-free foods.

Finally, it is important to drink a lot of water. Water keeps the body lubricated but it also plumps up your veins. When you receive chemo, it makes your veins shrink and hide making it difficult for the nurses to find a vein to draw blood or administer the chemo. Water helps fatten up the veins so drink a lot of water prior to any blood tests or chemo treatments. Drinking eight 8-ounce glasses of water a day is a good thing anyway. This is just another reason to drink a lot of water.

TIP SIX: LOSS OF APPETITE

Most people lose their appetite at some point during the duration of their chemo treatments. However, some people actually may gain weight. While most women do not like to think about gaining weight, it can be a good thing when you are taking chemo. You may lose your appetite due to the chemo treatments or even due to anxiety. Everyone reacts differently. I am a Licensed Professional Counselor and have seen people lose their appetite due to fear, anxiety, and depression. All of these emotions are normal when you are battling cancer. You may also experience a change in taste or smell which can influence your appetite.

I was sick for six weeks prior to having surgery to remove a large ovarian tumor. During that time, I lost my appetite because I was experiencing stomach pain and diarrhea. After surgery, I still did not have an appetite and my stomach was very sensitive. I explained some of this in the introduction of the book, so I won't go into detail again. My doctor prescribed two medications for me. One was supposed to help in the digestion process (Acipehx® in pill form) and the other one was to increase my appetite (Megestrol Acetate® in liquid form). I have to confess that I only took one dose of Megestrol Acetate® because I hated the taste. The way that I regained my appetite was by watching the Food Network and giving myself time to heal.

Even my favorite foods like bread and chocolate did not appeal to me and the thought of eating meat was disgusting! I knew that I needed to eat meat because I needed the protein to build up my white blood cells. I started by eating homemade chicken and beef soups. I only ate the broth at first and then I ate some vegetables. Next, I ate some beef stew. Once again, I only ate the gravy and vegetables. I kept watching food programs and pretty soon food started looking good.

One thing that may help is to try some of the food that you used to enjoy when you were a kid. I used to like Chef Boyardee Beef Ravioli. It has processed meat which isn't the healthiest thing to eat but it got me started eating meat again. As I continued watching the Food Network, I slowly regained my appetite. This process is an example of Cognitive Behavior Therapy. First you change your thinking (cognitive) and then your behavior will follow. Some other ideas that may help you with your appetite include:

- Have foods on hand that appealed to you when you were a child
- Keep snacks on hand. I began with Cheez-Its
- Remember that you can get protein from other sources such as peanut butter
- Liquid meals are an option such as Ensure

- Sometimes cold food is more appealing like pudding, yogurt, or popsicles
- Exercise stimulates the appetite

TIP SEVEN: NAUSEA

There are many different medications that
can help with nausea. My doctor prescribed three
different medications. Dexamethasone® which is a
steroid that helps prevent nausea and Ondansetron®
which works on both the peripheral and central
nerves. It reduces the activity of the vagus nerve,
which activates the vomiting center in the medulla
oblongata (the lower portion of the brain stem) and
serotonin receptors. These were given to me in an
IV prior to each chemo treatment and in a pill form.
I was told to take five tablets of Dexamethasone®
at 10:00 the night before taking chemo and five
more tablets at 6:00 the morning of my chemo

treatment. I was also prescribed to take one tablet of Ondansetron® at bedtime on the night of my chemo treatment and continue taking it twice a day for three days after my chemo treatment.

In addition, Prochlorperazine® was prescribed to be used as needed when I felt nauseated after chemo treatments. It acts by blocking dopamine receptors. Basically, the brain has neurotransmitters that send messages to your stomach which can cause the nauseated feeling. Prochlorperazine® blocked those messages and really worked for me.

I only felt nauseated once a few days after my first chemo treatment. It was a horrible feeling because it was combined with other side effects such as breaking out in a cold sweat, feeling dizzy, having severe tingling which felt like an electric shock in my whole body, and a lot of pressure in my ears. At the first sign of feeling sick, I took Prochlorperazine® and about half an hour later, I felt better. However, if your medications are not working for you, tell your doctor and try the same

things you would do it you had the stomach flu.
Try eating crackers, toast, ice chips, carbonated
drinks like ginger ale, yogurt, or rice. Sometimes
sucking on a mint candy can help. Other techniques
you may want to try, include breathing deeply and
slowly when you feel nauseated and using
relaxation therapy.

TIP EIGHT: HYGIENE

It will make you feel better if you take a lot of showers. This may sound like common sense, but I have included this tip because when you are taking chemo you lose your energy and it is easy to stay in your pajamas all day. Sometimes you have to push yourself to get moving or even to take a shower. But after you take a shower or a bath you always feel better. There is something refreshing about feeling clean and smelling good. It is also nice to feel the sensation of the warm water. In addition, taking a hot bath or shower can help you relax and sleep better.

Part of good hygiene is washing your hands,

but it is especially important to remember to wash your hands when you are taking chemo treatments because your immune system is compromised during that time and you are more susceptible to germs and illness. I was told that I should not clean or even be around any litter boxes, bird cages, or fish tanks. I was also told not to have close contact with other people such as shaking hands or hugging people in church. Most germs are passed by touching someone or something. That is why it is so important to wash your hands a lot.

Washing your hands all the time tends to make them dry. Buy a good moisturizer for your hands to keep the skin from cracking making you more vulnerable to germs. Buy an extra tube to keep in your purse or the car.

Chemo generally dries out the mucus membrane in your body such as the inside of your nose and mouth. I put Vaseline in my nostrils at night to keep them from drying and bleeding. I am prone to nosebleeds, but never had one during the six months that I was taking chemo. As long as I knew the possibility of what to expect or what could happen, I took precautions to prevent it.

When you are undergoing chemo treatments, you have little resistance to fight off the germs like you normally would. During that time, I had a parrot and a cat. While I was receiving treatments, my mother took over my chores of cleaning the bird cage and the litter box. I was very fortunate to have such a wonderful mother. I was very careful to do my best to follow the hygiene rules, so I did not complicate the situation.

I did not even go out of the house very much during the six months that I was taking chemo. I would sit in my secluded backyard a lot and enjoy the natural setting. I did go out a few times around Christmas, but I stayed away from people as much as possible. I did not go anywhere where I would be in an enclosed place with people for any period of time. I didn't go to church or to the theater. I didn't get in cars with anyone other than my mother and I asked that friends and family not come over if they were not feeling well. I felt bad enough with

what I was going through without making it worse
by getting a cold or the flu which could have turned
into something much worse due to having a low
resistance. I was fortunate that I did not catch
anything during that time, but I also remembered to
keep washing my hands.

When you are manicuring your finger and
toenails, flossing your teeth, and shaving, be careful
not to cut yourself. Also, do not pinch or squeeze
pimples. Don't scratch yourself too hard or rub
yourself too roughly when you are drying off after a
shower. And if you do accidently get cut, clean the
wound right away with soap and antiseptic. Also,
don't get any immunizations while taking chemo.
And stay away from standing water which can
breed germs such as bird baths, humidifiers, and
public bathroom sinks.

It is also important to remember to take care
of your teeth when you are undergoing chemo
treatments. There were days when I did not feel
like doing anything including brushing my teeth.
However, I did not want more problems than I

already had, so I flossed and brushed regularly. The one thing I skipped while on chemo was rinsing with a mouthwash. Most mouthwashes contain alcohol which can really burn your mouth if it is dry from the chemo. You may want to use a soft toothbrush and rinse your mouth with warm water if your gums are sore. You can also use a mouthwash with sodium bicarbonate (baking soda) which should not irritate your gums.

TIP NINE: HAIR

Chemo often causes your hair to fall out. I had long blond hair and hated to cut it, so I just let it fall out, which happened after the third round of chemo. This was a mistake because my hair was everywhere. I had to pick it off of my clothes constantly and it filled the vacuum when I would sweep. I was not that upset about losing my hair because I knew it would grow back. My focus was on getting well. I had been very sick and barely able to eat for six weeks before my diagnosis. Because I had been sick for so long, I just wanted to feel better so looks were not as important.

However, there was one instance when I

looked in the mirror and began to cry. My hair was falling out in clumps. It was Thanksgiving and my family was gathering at my brother's house just down the street from where we lived. I was going to attend but when I looked in the mirror, I suddenly felt very depressed and decided not to attend. I think I might not have felt so bad if I had gotten my hair cut before it fell out. It would have given me a little control over the situation.

I have always had a sensitive scalp, but it became extremely tender when I was going through chemo. It seemed to be especially tender when I was losing my hair. It hurt to even lay my head on a pillow. If this happens to you, buy a mild shampoo or even a baby shampoo and wash your scalp with it when you shower. It made my scalp feel better.

Speaking of losing your hair and a tender scalp, a lot of heat escapes through your head so if you don't have hair, it can make you quite cold. I started losing my hair in November and even though I live in the south, the temperatures were starting to drop. My scalp was very tender when I was in the process of losing my hair so at that time, I preferred to wear stocking caps around the house. They kept my head warm and were soft on my scalp.

I decided to look into getting a wig and ended up buying a moderately priced wig at a local shop. It looked pretty good but since it was not actual hair, it made my head hot and itchy. You can buy special wigs with gel on the inside that are much cooler to wear. You cannot always find them in wig shops, but most wig catalogs carry them. I bought one from a Paula Young catalog that was made with "Coolmax Fabric" which they advertise to provide "soothing, itch-free wear and maximum breathability." If you invest in this type of wig you will most likely feel more comfortable.

Since I had just moved to a new town, nobody knew me except for my family so most of the time I just wore a lot of different baseball caps when I went out. As I mentioned earlier, I did not have a job, so I did not need to dress up. It is also good to know that some health insurance policies cover the cost of a wig if your hair loss is due to chemo treatments. In addition, your wig is a tax-deductible expense.

TIP TEN: WHITE BLOOD CELLS

Having cancer may lower your white blood cell count. This does not happen to everyone, but it did happen to me. When you receive chemo treatments, your white blood cell count has to be at a certain level, or it is too dangerous to get the treatment. Therefore, prior to each chemo treatment, they will test your blood to make sure you have enough white blood cells. If your white blood cells are not high enough, you will be given a shot to increase them. Additionally, the chemo decreases your white blood cells.

I had to get a shot (Neulasta®) each month a day after receiving the chemo treatment to increase my white blood cell count. This is not uncommon. I was also told that taking antibiotics may decrease your white blood cell count although, I'm not sure if this is a fact or not. However, I had taken several rounds of antibiotics during this ordeal and my white blood cell count was below the normal range even before I started my chemo treatments.

Neulasata® has a side-affect that some people experience. One to two days after receiving the shot, the bones in my legs, feet, and back would ache. The ache was extreme, and nothing seemed to help. I tried soaking my feet in hot water and rubbing them, but nothing helped. Then one day while receiving my chemo, I overheard a nurse say that Duke University was doing a study on Claritin® and they were finding that it helped to relieve some of the aching caused by Neulasta®. I tried it and it worked!

I started taking Claritin® the evening of the day that I received the Neulasta® shot and continued to take one a day for the next several days until the aching stopped. In my experience, the aching usually started one to two days after I received the shot and it lasted three to four days.

Claritin® did not totally eliminate the aching but it really helped a lot!

Another thing that helps with the aching is to try to stay off of your feet as much as possible during the timeframe mentioned above. I made the mistake of taking a long walk a day after getting the shot since exercise was recommended. However, this made the aching worse. I found that I felt the best if I just laid in bed and took Claritin® for a few days. This is not to say that you should stay in bed all of the time. Do what feels best for you but it may be best to plan your exercise around the time when any side effects from Neulasta® have passed.

As I mentioned previously, I had a low white blood cell count even before my first chemo treatment. It had never been a problem before, but it is possible that having cancer made it low. I researched the internet and asked my doctor what I could do to increase my white blood cell count and the only answer besides getting a shot was to eat protein. A normal white blood cell count range is from 4.6 to 10.2. My count started at 4.7 and went as low as 2.2.

TIP ELEVEN: DEPRESSION

Crying is a way to release your emotions and it can be a good thing to do as long as you do not wallow in your sorrows. I had times when I really felt sorry for myself. I felt helpless and I questioned God. I couldn't understand why this was happening to me. I allowed myself some time to be sad, but I reminded myself that there were others who had it much worse than I. I started thinking of ways that I might be able to help others who were going through what I was. I also started counting my blessings. Every time I thought of something negative, I replaced it with a positive. When I thought about all the medical bills that were piling up and how I did not have a job, I thought about how nice it was not to have to worry about trying to take care of myself while having to work.

When you are told that you have cancer, the world stops spinning for a moment. Time just stands still as you are hit in the face with something you just cannot grasp. Cancer is something that happens to other people, not to me! I have been healthy all of my life. This cannot be true! But when the doctor looks you in the eye and tells you that it *is* true, you are slapped in the face by reality.

After denial, came a feeling of hopelessness. Since I have cancer, my life must be over. At the time that I was diagnosed, the doctor did not know my prognosis until he opened me up. He was basing his diagnosis on a CT scan and on the results of a blood test.

In my case, the CT scan revealed that I had a basketball sized tumor which was elongated throughout my abdomen. Dr. Powell is a full professor at UNC-Chapel Hill and one of the nation's leading gynecological oncologists, so he knew (based on his experience and expertise) that it was ovarian cancer.

The night in the hospital before my surgery was very scary. I did not know what to expect. I didn't know if the cancer had spread throughout my body or even if I would survive the surgery. All of those thoughts kept swirling around in my head. My mother and brother stayed with me in my hospital room as long as they were allowed but after they left, I was alone with those thoughts. That was the worst night of my life. I admit that I cried a lot that night. I cried out of fear and sorrow for myself. We all have our moments of weakness. It is part of being human.

Chemo zaps the body of energy and when you are fatigued, depression often follows. If you have been given a less than perfect prognosis, undergoing months of chemotherapy or radiation, feeling sick, hate the way you look because of hair loss or bloating, it is easy to become depressed. The most important thing to do is not to give up hope. Believe in a positive outcome and believe in yourself. Decide that you are going to do everything possible to beat the cancer.

It is also important to talk about your feelings. This may be the most fearful and anxiety ridden time of your life. It is great to have a friend or family member to talk to, but it is even better to be able to talk to a nurse, a therapist or another cancer patient. That is one reason why it is helpful to join a cancer/chemo support group. Eating a good diet, exercising, and getting enough rest are also important for good mental health. Try to stay away from stressful situations as much as possible. Stress is one of the worst things to have in your life, especially now. Think of little things that make you happy and surround yourself with as many of them as you can. Sometimes just having flowers in your room can change your mood.

Read positive and uplifting books and watch a lot of comedies. Think of ways you can help someone else. Listen to your favorite music. Don't focus on the negatives. Keep believing in miracles and keep praying. God is listening! If you do not understand something about your treatment or recovery, write down your questions and ask your doctor at your next appointment. Empower yourself with knowledge.

I'm a true believer that laughter is the best medicine. My brother and sister-in-law bought me a portable DVD player with headphones which I took with me each time that I went for a chemo treatment. It was a good distraction while I sat there for six hours. I watched funny movies and some old-time sitcoms which I bought ahead of time. One movie that I highly recommend is *Evan Almighty* starring Steve Carrell. It is not only funny but has a great message (i.e., have faith).

The sitcoms I bought were helpful because they were old ones from when I was a kid and they brought back good memories as I watched them. I was probably the only one in the chemo room who was laughing while I was receiving chemo. It really is good to take your mind off of your troubles and just try to relax. My friends and family bought me funny movies that I could watch at home while I was recuperating. It gave us something to do together and kept us laughing instead of focusing on my condition.

TIP TWELVE: KEEP A POSITIVE ATTITUDE

When we are sick it is easy to sink into depression. It is hard to be happy when you don't feel good. When you are given a cancer diagnosis and know that the road ahead will be a difficult one, it is easy to focus on the pain and anxiety of what lies ahead. Remember to take one step at a time. In the comedy movie, *"What About Bob?"* the psychiatrist wrote a book called 'Baby Steps.' It is a very funny movie, but it is also very true. Don't jump to conclusions and picture negative outcomes.

I had heard all kinds of horror stories about chemo which filled me with dread. You have to take one day at a time or "baby steps." I had many scary and upsetting things happen, but all in all, the chemo was not as bad as I had anticipated. Try to think positive thoughts and plan little things that make you happy. Plan to do something fun after your chemo treatments are finished so you have something to look forward to. Remember that there is new research going on all of the time and a new treatment for you may be just around the corner. Doctors and researchers have made so many advances over the past 40 years. My grandmother had colon cancer 40 years ago and she really suffered with her chemo treatments. Things are so much better today. Keep praying and believing in miracles. They still happen.

However, for those of you who have difficulty believing in miracles, let me give you something else to consider. When you are given a diagnosis of cancer, your emotions generally take over. You feel fragile because you are vulnerable. That fear may play a significant role in your susceptibility to disease and even to your recovery. But all is not lost. You have a choice in how you feel. You control the way you think and in turn control your emotions which can help or hinder your recovery.

The central nervous system and the immune system communicate with each other. Immune cells travel in your blood through your body and come in contact with all the other cells. If the immune cells recognize other cells, they leave them alone. But if they do not recognize certain cells, they attack them. Therefore, if the immune cell comes into contact with a cancer cell, it will attack it unless it misidentifies it. The field that studies the correlation between the immune system and the central nervous system is called psychoneuroimmunology.

Research has found that the chemical messengers that function broadly in the brain and immune system are the chemical messengers that are most dense in the neural regions that control emotion. They have actually identified a contact point where nerve cells release neurotransmitters which regulate immune cells. What all of this means is that your emotions directly relate to your immune system. Therefore, when you are extremely anxious or depressed, it can compromise your immune function to the point that it can speed the metastasis of cancer. That information should open your eyes to the reality that your mental attitude plays a part in your recovery.

TIP THIRTEEN: SUPPORT GROUPS

Some of your best support may come from being involved in a cancer support group. You will meet other men and women who are going through some of the same things that you are going through. They will have a lot of important information they can share with you and maybe you will be able to help one of them. Someone in that group may be able to answer some of your questions that even the doctors or nurses may not be able to answer due to firsthand experience. They might think to tell you something helpful that the doctors might have forgotten to mention such as "don't eat popcorn!" It is also good for your spirit to talk to people who are going through the same thing you are, so you do not feel so alone. And you may make a friend who will be there for you on a weekend when you may not be able to reach your doctor with a question.

I tend to want to be alone when I don't feel well. I want to stay in bed and isolate myself until I feel better. That may be okay when you have flu but when you have cancer, it is better to connect with a support group over the duration. Knowledge is power and support groups provide firsthand knowledge. Also, you can join a group just by talking on the phone if you don't feel like attending a meeting or distance is an issue. In addition, studies have shown that social isolation doubles the chances of sickness.

TIP FOURTEEN: 24-HOUR EMERGENCY HOTLINE

It was my luck that when something bad happened, it always happened on the weekend when I couldn't reach my doctor. If you are like me, it is scary when something strange happens to your body. When I was going through this time, I was inclined to become alarmed and worry that the situation was worse than it was. One time my port became infected and I had a fever of 102. This started on a Friday night. Another time I had rectal bleeding which also started on a Friday night. Those were just two examples.

Fortunately, New Hampshire Medical Center had provided me with a 24-hour nurse hotline called Vitaline which also provides contact with an on-call physician 24-7. Always be prepared for things to happen on the weekend. If you are starting to feel bad or starting to have a problem on a Thursday or Friday, don't put off making a phone call to your doctor. Things always seem to get worse on the weekend when you may not be able to reach your doctor. Just call to see if you need to do something before your situation worsens. And remember to ask if there is a 24-hour hotline that you can use.

TIP FIFTEEN: GETTING A PORT

Getting a port is a good option for a lot of people. However, for me, it was not a pleasant experience. A port is also known as a vascular access device. If you receive chemo intravenously, it makes your veins shrink and hide. This makes it difficult for the nurses to find a vein when they need to insert an IV.

I had been sick for six weeks prior to my diagnosis and during that time, my stomach felt like it was burning whenever I drank a sip of water. Therefore, I did not drink much water for six weeks. Because of that, I was severely dehydrated and finding my veins was next to impossible. I was not informed about ports before I started the chemo treatments. I had envisioned sitting in a chair with an IV inserted in my arm. That is not usually how it is done.

If you only need a couple of chemo treatments, they may not suggest a port, but most people need more than two treatments so in many cases a port is used. If you are given an IV without the use of a port, the nurse will try to find a vein near your wrist or in your hand. The nurses do not use the crook of your arm because they do not want the needle breaking off or coming out if you bend your arm.

My doctor ordered six chemo treatments of Paclitaxel® and Carboplatin® (one treatment a month for six months). My treatments were an all-day affair. I would go in around 8:30 in the morning and have blood drawn and have an IV inserted (for the times that I did not have the port). Then I would see my doctor for a quick exam and answer a few questions regarding how I was feeling and if I was having any side effects from the chemo. Also, during that time, I was attended to by one of Dr. Powell's nurses. All of his nurses are kind and empathetic. One nurse in particular (Melinda) was always upbeat and helpful. She continually let me know how much she cared by her kind words and encouragement.

After my exam with the doctor, I would go to the chemo room where I would wait until the results of my blood work came back from the lab. Once they had the results, they would hook me up to the IV and I would sit for approximately six hours before it was finished. The nurses had a very difficult time finding my veins. The first time I went in for chemo, the nurse searched my lower arms, wrists and back of my hands and stuck me several times before she hit the mark. This nurse was very kind and compassionate and did her best to make me comfortable, but my hands are very sensitive.

My first chemo treatment was given by IV inserted in a vein in my right hand. The chemo nurses were very kind and helpful. They suggested that I get a port because it would be a one-time procedure to insert the port which would eliminate the need to find a vein every time that I came in to get a treatment.

I must admit that the thought of having a port inserted under my skin really disgusted me. I had seen a lady with a port protruding out of her chest (near her neck) and it looked awful. It looked like something from a sci fi movie. However, everyone assured me that it was no big deal and I would be much happier after I had the port. I reluctantly agreed but something about it made me very anxious.

Getting a port did not seem like a simple procedure to me. The whole thing takes several hours. You have a choice of having it placed under your skin in your chest or your arm. The port is a catheter which is surgically inserted into a tube that is pulled from a vein in your arm or chest through to a larger vein in your chest which leads to your heart. The larger the vein that is used, the less chance that it will be destroyed by the chemo. Also, the larger veins carry the blood faster. The port is approximately the size of a half dollar. The middle of the port is rubbery and can be punctured with a needle that is specially designed to connect with the IV tubing. The port can then be used for blood tests, IVs and even medications so you don't have to be continually stuck with needles.

You are prepped for the surgical procedure and an IV is inserted for the anesthesia. Some of my anxiety was due to the fact that my veins were hiding and once again it was difficult for the nurse to find a vein to insert the IV. I admit that I am a big baby when it comes to needles so keep in mind that you will probably have a much better experience if you keep a positive attitude.

The anesthesia puts you into a twilight feeling and you are not completely put out, but you don't feel any pain. A local anesthetic is used. The procedure is usually performed in radiology where they can use a type of x-ray machine to see what they are doing when they insert and thread the tube. The actual procedure takes about half an hour. I remember the radiologist talking to me while he did the procedure, but I kept my eyes shut because I didn't want to see what was happening.

My problem began shortly after the procedure. When they had finished the procedure, the nurse applied a type of glue that helps hold the skin together. The problem was that the nurse did not wait for the glue to dry before he put the bandages on. The bandage adhered to my skin so after several days when I was supposed to take off the bandage, part of it would not come off. I called the radiologist and asked what I should do about the bandage and I was told to leave it on and eventually it would fall off. That is what I did, however, I think this is when the area became infected.

The bandage eventually fell off, but a day later the area on my arm around the port became red and began to hurt. Once again, this happened on a weekend when it would have been difficult to reach my doctor. I developed a fever and I was warned not to mess around if the wound became infected since the port led to my heart. I was also under the impression that they may not be able to give me the rest of the chemo treatments if I did not use a port. So, I was very upset and concerned when it became infected.

It was a Saturday, so I went to the local ER. The doctor in the ER had never worked with ports so he did not know what to do. This was at my local hospital (not at New Hanover). The ER doctor ended up calling another doctor who said I should be put on antibiotics. However, he scared me because he said I might have to have the port removed due to the infection. This news was upsetting because at that time I thought that there weren't any options for getting the chemo and I would not be able to receive the rest of my treatments. But that was not the case. When you first get the port, they put you on antibiotics for a week while you heal. Three days after I finished taking the first round of antibiotics, my port became infected. Four days after taking the second round of antibiotics, I started feeling better and my arm started to look better. But there was a small area in my arm that would not heal.

There was a small hole in my arm where the port was inserted that just would not close. Two weeks after receiving the port, I went back to the radiologist so he could look at my arm to see why it was not healing. He said it looked pretty good and to just give it more time to heal.

When I first got the port, I was told to not get the area wet and not to let the area rub against anything. The port was inserted on the inside of my upper left arm. That meant that I had to hold my arm out away from my body all of the time. I was supposed to let the air get to it so I did not have it bandaged. I had to sleep in one position with my arm on a pillow and try not to move it all night long. I had to take sponge baths instead of showers, so I did not get it wet. And it was winter, and I could not wear a sleeve on that arm. This went on for two and a half months!

My back ached from having to hold my arm out away from my body and I was cold all of the time because I could not wear anything on that arm. I got to use the port twice before it became infected again and I had to have it removed. After they removed the port, I had to return to the hospital four times to have the area cleaned and bandaged due to the infection.

I was able to receive my last three chemo treatments in a vein in my hand. I went through all of that pain and aggravation for two and a half months only to be able to use the port twice! Some people opt to get another port inserted if the first one becomes infected. I was given that option but did not want to take the chance that the second port might become infected.

Maybe if I had complained more to my doctor, things might have been different, but I did not want to be a complainer and did not think that there might be another option. Sometimes we need to be our own advocate and speak up. Doctors cannot read our minds and may not realize what we are experiencing unless we tell them.

TIP SIXTEEN: ANTIBIOTICS

Some antibiotics can cause allergic reactions and if severe, can cause a fever. When my port became infected for the second time, my local doctor prescribed Septra DS® which is a strong antibiotic. It turns out that I am allergic to it but at the time I did not know it. I had been taking it for eight days when I woke up one morning covered in a red rash and my face was bright red. I was aching and I had a fever of 102. I called a nurse at the Zimmer Center and she said that I needed to come in right away. Before I went in, I called my local doctor who suggested that I might be having an allergic reaction to the antibiotic. He told me to stop taking it which I did. I still went to the Zimmer Center to see the nurse and she ordered some blood work. She said she did not believe it was an allergic reaction since I had a fever. As it turned out, it was a severe allergic reaction to the antibiotic. In some cases, a severe allergic reaction can cause a fever. A day after I quit taking it, I was fine.

TIP SEVENTEEN: ACCEPT HELP

I always hate asking for help. I try to be self-sufficient. However, sometimes you need to ask for help. I was fortunate to have my mother who nursed me back to health. However, she was 80 years old at that time and she needed support too. My mother and I had just moved to North Carolina, so we did not have a big support group. Fortunately, we moved to be near my brother and his family, and he provided a lot of help. My brother (the Rev. Dr. William G. Waun) took me to my first couple of chemo treatments which were an hour and a half away. He did this until I was well enough to drive myself. He also came to my rescue on more than one occasion. My sister-in-law (Cynthia) researched my condition on the internet and provided me with information and questions that I could ask my doctor. My friends sent flowers, cards, and letters.

My mother did the most for me. She went to every chemo treatment with me. She made me homemade soups and stews when I didn't want to eat. She ran to the grocery store and bought me whatever I needed or wanted. She sat with me, laughed with me, cried with me, and prayed with me. I don't know what I would have done without her. Accept the help and love that others offer. You can pay it back or pay it forward when you feel better.

TIP EIGHTEEN:
FINANCIAL ASSISTANCE

I had an unusual situation because my job had ended along with my insurance coverage when I moved to North Carolina. I have never gone without health insurance even though I have been very healthy all of my life. I was paying for my own health insurance and thank God that I hadn't let it lapse! However, the one thing that I did change was that I decided to make my annual deduction higher and also selected a plan where the percentage I paid was higher so my monthly payments would be lower.

I had only been in North Carolina for a few days when I started to get sick. When I first became ill, I was covered under the policy that I had purchased in another state prior to moving for the first month. Then it switched to my North Carolina policy. The problem was that I had to meet the other state deductible in November and then meet the North Carolina deductible in December. Then I had to pay another North Carolina deductible in January because it was a new year! Besides all of the deductibles, I had to pay 30% of my medical expenses. Thirty percent may not sound like that much but when you are dealing with hospital stays and shots that cost $7,000 each, it really adds up! On top of that, I was unemployed, so I did not have an income.

One day while I was sitting in the chemo chair, I heard one of the chemo nurses telling another patient about how to get financial help. When she came over to check on me, I asked her about it, and she told me about a program that the hospital has. She even went and got me the paperwork to apply. After I applied, I waited for a few weeks but was fortunate to receive a letter stating that I had been approved through March. That was wonderful news since March 24th was my final chemo treatment.

This particular financial assistance program did not pay for everything associated with the hospital. I still had to pay for each doctor visit and for anything associated with radiology such as getting the port. But my insurance paid for 70% of those things so at least I was not responsible for as much. It was a huge relief to receive this financial help form the hospital since I was not eligible for any government help. So, if you are in need of financial help, it can't hurt to ask if your hospital has a financial assistance program.

CORRESPONDING THERAPIES

There are many other types of therapy you can receive while taking chemotherapy which can help you through this difficult time. They can help with the healing of your mind and body while reducing stress and easing side-effects. As a licensed professional counselor, I highly recommend counseling therapy. Counseling can include many other therapies such as journaling, art therapy, imagery, rhythmic breathing, and visualization. I also suggest the following:

<u>Massage Therapy</u>: The Zimmer Center where I received my chemo treatments offered massage therapy during my treatment. Massage therapy uses different styles of touch, stroking and manipulation of the muscles to help you relax and release tension.

Pet Therapy: The Zimmer Center also offered pet therapy. During chemo treatments a pet therapist would come for a visit with a dog. This is an animal that has been trained to work with sick or injured people. The pet therapist would walk the dog around the chemo room and ask patients if they would like to pet or talk to the dog. Animals are generally accepting of anyone. They do not judge us by our looks or loss of hair. It is comforting to touch a dog or cat and have them relate to you. It has even been proven that stroking a cat or dog can decrease your blood pressure.

Biofeedback: Biofeedback teaches you how to control different body functions such as blood pressure, heart rate, breathing, and muscle tension that used to be considered involuntary. This is usually done with the use of a machine where you can learn by watching monitoring instruments attached to your body that record changes in your physiology. Then, eventually, you will have a better self-regulation without the aid of those devices. There are also other means of reading biofeedback such as a chemically coated card which detects rises and falls in your skin temperature or hormonal changes. Biofeedback is a good tool to help you when you are tense and anxious and need to learn how to relax.

Progressive relaxation: This is a method where you sit in a comfortable chair or lay down in a quiet atmosphere. You slowly take a deep breath and concentrate on the muscles in your feet. Contract and relax those muscles and then exhale. You continue to breath while contracting and relaxing muscles in your legs and on up in your body finishing with the muscles in your face. Each time that you exhale and release your muscles, you release tension and relax that part of your body.

Visualization: I mentioned visualization earlier but want to touch on it again because many people use it to fight cancerous tumors. By using visualization, you can picture the tumor in your mind and think of the chemotherapy as soldiers or bombs crashing into the tumor to destroy it. You can create whatever picture you want to use and imagine it often throughout the day as you think about eliminating the cancer.

Reframing and Thought Stopping:
Reframing is changing the way you talk to yourself. It is a conscious change of an automatic thought from something negative or unrealistic to something positive, neutral, or objective. Thought stopping is interrupting your thoughts by ordering them to stop. When you feel anxious or upset, this is a sign that your thoughts are making you feel that way. If you have a belief about something such as, "I know I will get sick whenever I have a chemo treatment," this is jumping to a conclusion. You may not get sick every time that you have a chemo treatment and in fact, you may not get sick at all. But when you have those kinds of thoughts, they add to your anxiety and stress. The way to change those thoughts and consequential feelings is to use thought stopping. You can combine your thought stopping with reframing to improve the way that you feel. In other words, when you are anxious or worried about something, your body will usually

cue you by making your heart beat faster or you will get sweaty palms. When you have these types of cues, think about what is going on in your head. If you are having negative or unrealistic thoughts or jumping to conclusions, then tell yourself to stop. Realize what you are doing to yourself. Then use reframing to replace that negative thought with one this is more realistic or objective.

Hypnosis: The use of hypnosis can help to reduce pain and anxiety. Hypnosis places you in a deep relaxed state of mind. A qualified hypnotist may be able to help you with many side effects.

Prayer and Meditation: For me, having ongoing communication with God is something I do throughout the day every day. The first thing that I did when I received my diagnosis was to pray. I know God is in control of my life and I cried out to Him for His help. Every time I was scared or uncertain, I prayed. When I felt alone, I prayed. I continue to pray and listen for His answers. I am fortunate in that I have many Christian friends and family members who prayed with me and for me during my crisis. My brother who is a priest anointed me with oil and prayed for my healing. Don't underestimate the power of prayer. Along with prayer there is meditation. Meditation is a form of relaxing and being quiet or listening. By being quiet and focusing on something specific such as killing the cancer cells or listening for an answer from God, you are freeing your mind from distractions and releasing stress from your body.

My prayer for you is that you will use this time in your life to stop any negative behavior and replace it with a renewed spirit. I hope that you will read this book and use it as you go through your own journey and that it will help you along the way. I believe that God wanted me to stop and pay attention to Him. I usually have to learn things the hard way in life, but once I learn a lesson, I remember it! God has opened my eyes to the pain and hardships of others. Now it is my turn to do what I can for other people who are going through difficult times and while easing their pain, help them to see that God is there for them too.

OVARIAN CANCER INFO

The following information was taken from The American Cancer Society (2018) website and the cancer-info-guide.com website:

Ovarian cancer is one of the most common types of cancers in women. According to research studies, ovarian cancer ranks fifth in cancer deaths among women. The chances of surviving ovarian cancer are better if the cancer is found early. But because the disease is difficult to detect in its early stage, only about 20% of ovarian cancers are found before tumor growth has spread into adjacent tissues and organs beyond the ovaries.

Stages:

Stage 1: The cancer is still contained within the ovary (or ovaries).

Stage 1A: Cancer has developed in one

ovary and the tumor is contained to the inside of the ovary. There is no cancer on the outer surface of the ovary. Laboratory examination of washings from the abdomen and pelvis did not find any cancer cells.

Stage 1B: Cancer has developed within both ovaries without any tumor on their outer surfaces. Laboratory examination of washings from the abdomen and pelvis did not find any cancer cells.

Stage 1C: The cancer is present in one or both ovaries and one or more of the following are present:

- Cancer on the outer surface of at least one of the ovaries.
- In the case of cystic tumors (fluid-filled tumors), the capsule (outer wall of the tumor) has ruptured.
- Laboratory examination found cancer cells in fluid or washings from the abdomen.

Stage 2: The cancer is in one or both

ovaries and has involved other organs (such as the uterus, fallopian tubes, bladder, the sigmoid colon, or the rectum) within the pelvis.

Stage 2A: The cancer has spread to or has actually invaded the uterus or the fallopian tubes, or both. Laboratory examination of washings from the abdomen did not find any cancer cells.

Stage 2B: The cancer has spread to other nearby pelvic organs such as the bladder, the sigmoid colon, or the rectum. Laboratory examination of washings from the abdomen did not find any cancer cells.

Stage 2C: The cancer has spread to pelvic organs as in stages 2A or 2B and laboratory examination of washings from the abdomen found evidence of cancer cells.

Stage 3: The cancer involves one or both ovaries, and one or both of the following are present: (1) cancer has spread beyond the pelvis to the lining of the abdomen; (2) cancer has spread to lymph nodes.

Stage 3A: During the staging operation, the

surgeon can see cancer involving the ovary or ovaries, but no cancer is grossly visible (can be seen without using a microscope) in the abdomen and the cancer has not spread to lymph nodes. However, when biopsies are checked under a microscope, tiny deposits of cancer are found in the lining of the upper abdomen.

Stage 3B: There is cancer in one or both ovaries, and deposits of cancer large enough for the surgeon to see, but smaller than 2 cm across, are present in the abdomen. Cancer has not spread to the lymph nodes.

Stage 3C: The cancer is in one or both ovaries, and one or both of the following are present:

- Cancer has spread to lymph nodes.
- Deposits of cancer larger than 2 cm across are seen in the abdomen.

Stage 4: This is the most advanced stage of ovarian cancer. The cancer is in one or both ovaries. Distant metastasis (spread of the cancer to the inside of the liver, the lungs, or other organs located outside of the peritoneal cavity) has occurred. Finding ovarian cancer cells in pleural fluid (from the cavity that surrounds the lungs) is also evidence of stage 4 disease ("Ovarian Cancer Stages," 2018).

SYMPTOMS

Ovarian cancer symptoms are nonspecific and mimic those of many other more common conditions, including digestive and bladder disorders. It isn't unusual for a woman with ovarian cancer to be diagnosed with another condition before finally learning she has cancer. The key seems to be persistent or worsening signs and symptoms. With most digestive disorders, symptoms tend to come and go, or they occur in certain situations or after eating certain foods. With ovarian cancer, there's typically little fluctuation where the symptoms are constant and gradually worsen. The most common symptoms are pain and swelling in the belly and gas. Other symptoms are diarrhea or constipation, or an upset stomach. Symptoms may include:

- Pressure or pain in the abdomen, pelvis, back or legs
- A swollen or bloated abdomen
- Nausea, indigestion, gas, constipation, or diarrhea
- Feeling very tired all of the time
- Shortness of breath
- Feeling the need to urinate often
- Unusual vaginal bleeding (heavy periods, or bleeding after menopause) ("Symptoms and Types," 2019).

NEW RESEARCH

New options are constantly being discovered
as researchers use genetic testing and genomic
sequencing to gain a better understanding of the
characteristics of ovarian cancer and how it can be
targeted with drugs. According to an article written
by Brielle Urciuoli (2018), some of the
advancements were reviewed by Ursula Matulonis,
M.D., chief of the Division of Gynecologic
Oncology at the Dana-Farber Cancer Institute in
Boston, on July 14th at the 2018 Ovarian Cancer
National Conference, in Washington D.C. In her
presentation which was sponsored by the Ovarian
Cancer Research Fund Alliance, Matulonis said,
"We know that ovarian cancer is not one cancer, but
trials in the past have really viewed it that way, so
advancements have been slow" (para. 1).

According to the American Cancer Society (2018), "research has led to better ways to detect high-risk genes and assess a woman's ovarian cancer risk. Studies suggest that many primary peritoneal cancers and some ovarian cancers (such as high-grade serous carcinomas) actually start in the fallopian tubes. According to this theory, the early changes of these cancers can start in the fallopian tubes. Cells from these very early fallopian tube cancers can become detached and then stick to the surface of the peritoneum or the ovaries. For reasons that are still not understood, these cancer cells may grow more rapidly in their new locations" (para. 4).

Detecting ovarian cancer early could have a great bearing on the cure rate. New ways of testing to screen women for ovarian cancer are being developed. "One method being tested is looking at the pattern of proteins in the blood (called proteomics) to find ovarian cancer early. For women who have an ovarian tumor, a test called OVA1 can measure the levels of 5 proteins in the blood. The levels of these proteins, when looked at together, are used to determine whether a woman's tumor should be considered low risk or high risk. If the tumor is labeled "low risk" based on this test, the woman is not likely to have cancer. If the tumor is considered "high risk," the woman is more likely to have a cancer and should see a specialist (a gynecologic oncologist). This test is NOT a screening test and it is NOT a test to decide if you should have surgery or not– it is meant for women who have an ovarian tumor where surgery has been decided but have not yet been referred to a gynecologic oncologist" (American Cancer Society, 2018, para. 9).

According to Cancer.net (2017), other targeted therapies include:

- "Immunotherapy. Immunotherapy is usually designed to boost the body's natural defenses to fight a cancer. It uses materials made either by the body or in a laboratory to bolster, target, or restore immune system function. Researchers are examining whether drugs called checkpoint inhibitors may boost the immune system's ability to destroy cancer cells. Drugs in this category target PD-1, PD-L1, and CTLA4. They have been shown to shrink tumors in other types of cancer, such as melanoma and some lung cancers, and have had some effectiveness in patients with ovarian/fallopian tube cancer.

• Cancer vaccines are another type of immunotherapy that researchers are testing for use against ovarian/fallopian tube cancer. Some approaches, called 'adoptive cell therapy,' use killer T cells from the immune system in an individual patient. Researchers take these cells and grow them in the laboratory, training them to attack certain targets, such as MUC 16 (CA-125), that are found on ovarian/fallopian tube cancer cells. Doctors then put the T cells back into the patient via an IV. This approach has been

tried with some early success in patients
with blood cancers.

- Hormone therapy. For treatment of
  recurrent or later-stage ovarian/fallopian
  tube cancer, tamoxifen, aromatase
  inhibitors, and enzalutamide (Xtandi), a
  blocker of the androgen receptor, are being
  studied.

- Gene therapy. A new area of research is
  discovering how damaged genes in
  ovarian/fallopian tube cancer cells can be
  corrected or replaced. Researchers are
  studying the use of specially designed
  viruses that carry normal genes into the core
  of cancer cells and then replace the defective
  genes with functional ones.

- Palliative care. Clinical trials are underway
  to find better ways of reducing symptoms
  and side effects of standard cancer
  treatments to improve a patient's comfort
  and quality of life" (para. 5).

AUTHORS NOTE

No financial gain was received by the author
from the Zimmer Center, New Hampshire Regional
Medical Center or any other company associated
with any brand name mentioned. This publication
is designed to provide accurate and authoritative
information in regard to the subject matter covered.
It is sold with the understanding that the author is
not engaged in rendering psychological, financial,
legal, or other professional services. If expert
assistance or counseling is needed, the services of a
competent professional should be sought.

REFERENCES

Ellis, A. (2019). Ovarian cancer research alliance FDA approved drugs for ovarian cancer. Retrieved from https://ocrahope.org/wp-content/uploads/2019/04/2019-SGO-report-final.pdf

Odunsi, K. (2018). How is immunotherapy changing the outlook for patients with ovarian cancer? Retrieved from https://www.cancerresearch.org/immunotherapy/cancer-types/ovarian-cancer

Ovarian cancer guide: Symptoms and types. (2019). Retrieved from https://www.webmd.com/ovarian-cancer/guide/ovarian-cancer-symptoms-types

Ovarian cancer stages. (2018). Retrieved from
https://www.cancer.org/cancer/ovarian-
cancer/detection-diagnosis-
staging/staging.html?sitearea-cri&r=&bc=

Ovarian, fallopian tube, and peritoneal cancer:
Latest research. (2017). Retrieved from
https://www.cancer.net/cancer-
types/ovarian-fallopian-tube-and-peritoneal-
cancer/latest-research

Urciuoli, B. (2018). Exciting advancements
underway in ovarian cancer. Retrieved from
https://www.curetoday.com/conferences/ocn
c-2018/exciting-advancements-underway-in-
ovarian-cancer-

What's new in ovarian cancer research? (2018).
Retrieved from
https://www.cancer.org/cancer/ovarian-
cancer/about/new-research.html

ABOUT THE AUTHOR

Deborah Waun is a Licensed Professional Counselor, public speaker, and published author with a Doctorate in Leadership and a Masters' Degree in Psychology. She is an advocate for women's rights and for helping women of all ages to reach their greatest potential. Deborah became ill in July and was diagnosed with ovarian cancer in August of 2007. She spent close to a year recovering from surgery and chemotherapy and was considered in remission in July of 2008. During her recovery, she wrote this book as a form of therapy for herself and to help others going through similar situations. She has been cancer-free since her recovery.